The Voiced
Connections of
James Dickey

The Voiced Connections of James Dickey
Interviews and Conversations

Edited by
Ronald Baughman

University of South Carolina Press

Copyright © University of South Carolina 1989

Published in Columbia, South Carolina, by the
University of South Carolina Press

Manufactured in the United States of America

Library of Congress Cataloging-in-Publication Data

Dickey, James.
   The voiced connections of James Dickey : interviews and
conversations / edited by Ronald Baughman.
     p. cm.
   ISBN 0-87249-670-8
   1. Dickey, James—Interviews. 2. Authors, American—20th century-
-Interviews. I. Baughman, Ronald, 1940– . II. Title.
PS3554.I32Z476   1989
811'.54—dc20   89-22413
                                                                                 CIP

—to Deborah
my rare unswerving company
—JLD

Contents

Preface by James Dickey	xi
Acknowledgments	xiii
Introduction	1
Chronology	5
Primary Bibliography	9

1. An Interview with James Dickey
   Eclipse 1965 — 12
2. Things Happen: An Interview with James Dickey
   Wisconsin Review 1966 — 28
3. Poet with Power: James Dickey
   Nancy Malone 1967 — 37
4. James Dickey: An Interview
   Francis Roberts 1968 — 41
5. James Dickey Describes His Life and Works as He "Moves Toward Hercules"
   John Logue 1971 — 50
6. An Interview with James Dickey
   David L. Arnett 1972 — 71
7. Interview: James Dickey
   Unmuzzled Ox 1972 — 84
8. James Dickey: The Archer's Author
   Glenn Helgeland 1973 — 94
9. James Dickey at Drury College
   Wayne Holmes,
   Joseph Costello,
   Mark Greenberg,
   Randy McConnell 1973 — 101
10. *Playboy* Interview
    Geoffrey Norman 1973 — 109

11. "That Plain-Speaking Guy": A Conversation with
    James Dickey on Robert Frost
    Donald J. Greiner   1974   133

12. Interview with James Dickey
    L. L. Simms   c. 1976   143

13. Dickey
    Jim Townsend   1977   147

14. James Dickey on Yeats: An Interview
    W. C. Barnwell   1977   154

15. Interview: James Dickey
    Phil Patton   1977   161

16. An Interview with . . . James Dickey
    Earl Turner   1978   166

17. A Conversation with James Dickey
    Peggy Friedmann,
    Betty Bedell   1979   169

18. An Interview with James Dickey
    Ron McFarland   1979   173

19. James Dickey Rides Again
    L. Elisabeth Beattie   1982   187

20. An Interview with James Dickey
    *Dictionary of Literary Biography
    Yearbook: 1982*   1983   193

21. An Interview with James Dickey
    William W. Starr   1983   201

22. Recovering the Cosmos: James Dickey at 60
    Leslie Bates   1983   207

23. Interview with James Dickey
    Bettye Givens   1984   214

24. River City Interview with James Dickey
    William Page   1984   224

25. James Dickey: Limitations and Infinities
    Hank Nuwer   1985   235

26. **Living Beyond Recall: An Interview with James Dickey**	
Gordon Van Ness 1987	**247**
27. ***Alnilam*: James Dickey's Novel Explores Father and Son Relationships**	
William W. Starr 1987	**258**
28. **James Dickey Talks About Story Behind *Alnilam***	
Bob Gingher 1987	**263**
Notes	**269**
Index	**274**

PREFACE

In the course of these interviews I became increasingly aware of the fact that one will say things that one would hesitate to write, or would not write at all. The interview "form," if such it may be called, not only makes possible but in a sense creates another self, and in my opinion this self should be allowed its say. The unconsidered and spontaneous nature of the spoken answer to a question may have a kind of value which a more pondered, covering-all-bases formulation, such as one inevitably adopts in writing, is not likely to have. Norman Mailer once said to me that the interview bid fair to become the truest form of communication that our age—the age of the tape recorder—can boast. Be that as it may, it is true that I had almost invariably rather read a transcription of an interview than a full-scale essay on the same subject, though one must—unless the interviewee is Oscar Wilde—count out stylistics and the rhetorical devices available under more leisurely circumstances. If the subject feels strongly enough about the material, however, he will be almost certain to write about it, and if one wishes that version of his thought it will soon be available, if it is not already. Meanwhile the unpremeditated word is almost always interesting, as extreme and even as oddball as it may sound in the coming forth. The quick answer seems more fully human than the considered statement; one feels closer to the person, and involved with what he is saying, and this seems to me a fortunate condition.

Looking over my own answers to various questions—and sometimes to the same questions—I can't help noting that some of the material in this book deals with events, historical and other, that are no longer of much or any interest, but which seemed to the interviewers at the time to be worth bringing up. I have let some of these conversations stand as they are, such as those in which I express my attitude toward propaganda poetry, brought out in the late 1960s by the Vietnam War. My position on this use of poetry, or what passes for it, has not changed, and should—I believe—be recorded.

As for the rest, I hope that readers will find here something helpful in their own conditions, and in the processes of thought that will be part of their lives.

—James Dickey

ACKNOWLEDGMENTS

I wish to thank Dean Harry E. Varney and the College of Applied Professional Sciences, University of South Carolina, for the sabbatical leave that made this book possible. I also thank Judith S. Baughman and Elizabeth Smith Baughman for their lovingly critical counsel and advice. I am deeply grateful to all those interviewers who have so richly documented James Dickey's career. Most of all, I wish to thank James Dickey, whose life and work is the center of this creative wheel.

—**Ronald Baughman**

The Voiced
Connections of
James Dickey

INTRODUCTION

Among contemporary writers, James Dickey is an especially compelling conversationalist and a highly sought-after subject for interviews. The affable, inquisitive Dickey seems to enjoy such discussions, perhaps because the dynamics of these exchanges approximate his own artistic method. In his poetry and fiction, Dickey dramatizes his invented Self's encounter with the Other, that perspective of anyone or anything outside himself—another human, or animal (a deer, an owl), or inanimate object (a pinetree, a mountain cliff). During an interview, Dickey literally addresses the point of view of the Other; he responds to the questions posed to him by another mind whose angle of vision serves as a catalyst for his own comments. What emerges from a collection of such discussions is a profile of one of America's best literary minds.

In *Night Hurdling,* his collection of mainly prose pieces, Dickey reprinted nine interviews, including those conducted by William F. Buckley, Jr., for *Firing Line;* Paul Christensen for *Lone Star Review;* William Heyen and Peter Marchant for *Southern Review;* Bruce Joel Hillman for *Writer's Yearbook, 1981;* Carolyn Kizer and James Boatwright for *Shenandoah Review;* Bill Moyers for *Bill Moyers' Journal;* William Packard for *New York Quarterly;* Terry Roberts for *Arts Journal;* and an unidentified editor for *Mademoiselle.* Still other significant Dickey interviews have been collected in widely accessible volumes: Franklin B. Ashley's *Paris Review* interview in *Writers at Work;* Matthew J. Bruccoli's in *Conversations with Writers: Volume I;* and John Graham's in *The Writer's Voice: Conversations with Contemporary Writers.* Dickey's own *Self-Interviews* is yet another extremely important source for information about the writer's life and creative processes.

In part, *The Voiced Connections of James Dickey* is intended to ease the Dickey scholar's research task. Rather than duplicate those interviews available in the volumes noted, this collection assembles important and, for the most part, previously uncollected interviews. Some Dickey interviews, especially early in

1

his career, appeared in small-circulation, often university-based journals, many of which are now defunct. As his career gained momentum, he appeared increasingly in respected academic journals, popular trade magazines, and large-audience newspapers. Yet, early or late, Dickey's discussions have proved evocative and enlightening, no matter who the interviewer or what the publication.

Predictably, interviewers tend to ask Dickey the same questions again and again—about his relationship to nature, about his perceptions of the South and of Southern writers, about his war experiences, for example. In some cases, such repeated material has been cut, except when Dickey has provided interesting variations on previous responses or when the logic of the discussion would be unduly disrupted. These few eliminated passages are marked by ellipses. The first names of writers perhaps unfamiliar to most readers have been added, and misspellings and typographical errors have been silently emended. Works by Dickey mentioned but unidentified in the text have been footnoted. With these few exceptions, the texts of the interviews are presented in their original forms.

The chronological organization of this volume allows the reader to discern the evolution of Dickey's career and ideas. Each interview was selected because it addresses one or more elements of the writer's experience: his major themes and subjects; his career's key stages; his assessment of his own works or his evaluation of other major writers; his nonliterary interests and activities. Since many interviews range over the entire expanse of these topics, a chronological rather than a thematic organization avoids forcing the discussions into rigid classifications that are counter to the original intention and tone of the conversations.

Like many other writers of his own and previous generations—for example, Norman Mailer, Philip Roth, Robert Lowell, Ernest Hemingway, F. Scott Fitzgerald, Robert Frost—who have achieved both critical and popular acclaim, Dickey has sometimes found his work overshadowed by the extraordinary elements of his life: his combat experiences in two wars; his love for and participation in athletics; his years as an advertising executive; his pursuits of hunting, archery, canoeing, guitar playing; his penchant for living close to the edge. Although all these experiences and avocations help define him as an artist and man, they also sometimes obscure other more subtle but equally important dimensions. For

Introduction

example, Dickey has a deep, inclusive knowledge of literature from many historical periods and in many languages, and quotes with ease from what he has read. He has been a college professor—though certainly his own iconoclastic brand of professor—for over a quarter of a century. He has an extensive background in philosophy and astronomy and a working knowledge of the mathematics that connects these two fields. Though sometimes referred to as an anti-intellectual writer, Dickey's intellectual strengths are formidable. Yet he blends the mental with the physical, moving beyond reason into the uncertain vicissitudes of human emotion. He is in this sense a more complete intellectual than the term usually connotes. He is a writer who feels as well as thinks deeply. Interviewing James Dickey is a richly rewarding experience. Collected here are some of the results.

—Ronald Baughman

CHRONOLOGY

1923 2 February, James Lafayette Dickey, the second son of lawyer Eugene Dickey and of Maibelle Swift Dickey, is born in the Atlanta suburb of Buckhead.

1942 Graduates from Atlanta's North Fulton High School, and enrolls at Clemson A & M College, where he plays in the backfield on the freshman football team. Leaves school before the end of the first term to enlist in the Army Air Corps.

1943–45 Logs approximately 500 combat flying hours as a member of the 418th Night Fighters in the South Pacific.

1946 Leaves service and enrolls at Vanderbilt University, where he majors in English and philosophy and minors in astronomy. Between 1947–1949 publishes four poems in *The Gadfly*, Vanderbilt's literary magazine.

1948 4 November, marries Maxine Syerson.

1949 Receives B.A. in English, magna cum laude, from Vanderbilt.

1950 Receives M.A. in English from Vanderbilt University.

1950 September–December, teaches at Rice Institute, Houston, Texas, until he is recalled to the Air Force for service in Korea.

1951 Son, Christopher, is born.

1952–54 Resumes teaching position at Rice Institute. Receives *Sewanee Review* fellowship funded by the Rockefeller Foundation and leaves Rice in summer of 1954 to write in Europe.

1955–56 Teaches at University of Florida, but resigns appointment in spring of 1956 over a dispute concerning his reading of his poem "The Father's Body."

CHRONOLOGY

1956	April, begins successful career as an advertising copywriter and executive for McCann-Erickson agency in New York, and, later, for different agencies in Atlanta. Leaves advertising 1961.
1958	Son, Kevin, is born. Receives Union League Civic and Arts Foundation Prize from Union League Club of Chicago for a poem or group of poems published in *Poetry: A Magazine of Verse*.
1959	Wins Longview Foundation Award and Vachel Lindsay Prize.
1960	Publication of *Into the Stone and Other Poems* in *Poets of Today VII*. Wins a Guggenheim Fellowship allowing him to spend 1961–1962 writing in Positano, Italy.
1962	Publication of *Drowning With Others*.
1963–64	Poet-in-Residence, Reed College.
1964	Poet-in-Residence, San Fernando Valley State College, Northridge, California, through 1965.
	Publication of *Helmets, The Suspect in Poetry*, and *Two Poems of the Air*.
1965	Publication of *Buckdancer's Choice*.
1966	Receives National Book Award for *Buckdancer's Choice*, the Poetry Society of America's Melville Cane Award, and an award from the National Institute of Arts and Letters.
1966	Poet-in-Residence, University of Wisconsin at Madison. Appointed Consultant in Poetry for the Library of Congress, serving through 1968.
1967	Publication of *Poems 1957–1967* and *Spinning the Crystal Ball*.
1968	Publication of *Babel to Byzantium: Poets and Poetry Now* and *Metaphor as Pure Adventure*.
1969	Named Poet-in-Residence and First Carolina Professor of English, University of South Carolina.

Chronology

1970	Publication of *Deliverance; The Eye-Beaters, Blood, Victory, Madness, Buckhead and Mercy;* and *Self-Interviews.*
1971	Publication of *Sorties* and *Exchanges*. Receives France's Prix Medicis for *Deliverance* and *New York Quarterly* Poetry Day Award.
1972	Becomes scriptwriter and consultant for the movie version of *Deliverance,* in which he plays the role of Sheriff Bullard. 18 May, is inducted into the National Institute of Arts and Letters.
1974	Publication of *Jericho: The South Beheld.*
1976	Writes script for the television production of Jack London's *Call of the Wild.* Publication of *The Zodiac.* Wife, Maxine, dies. Marries Deborah Dodson.
1977	Reads "The Strength of Fields" during President Jimmy Carter's inaugural celebration at the Kennedy center. Publication of *The Owl King* and *God's Images.*
1978	Publication of *Tucky the Hunter, Veteran Birth, In Pursuit of the Grey Soul, The Enemy from Eden,* and *Head-Deep in Strange Sounds.*
1979	Publication of *The Strength of Fields.* 26 April, delivers Ezra Pound lecture, *The Water-Bug's Mittens: What We Can Use,* University of Idaho.
1980	Publication of *Scion.*
1981	Daughter, Bronwen, is born. Publication of *The Starry Place Between the Antlers: Why I Live in South Carolina.* Receives the Levinson Prize for five poems from *Puella* published in *Poetry: A Magazine of Verse.*
1982	Publication of *Puella, Deliverance* screenplay, and *Värmland.*
1983	Publication of *Night Hurdling: Poems, Essays, Conversations, Commencements, and Afterwords* and *False Youth: Four Seasons.*
1986	Publication of *Bronwen, the Traw, and the Shape-Shifter.*

1987   Publication of *Alnilam*.

1988   18 May, inducted into the 50-member American Academy and Institute of Arts and Letters. Assigned Chair #15, previously occupied by scholar Wilbur Cross, painter Raphael Soyer, and novelist John Steinbeck. Publication of *Wayfarer: A Voice from the Southern Mountains*.

PRIMARY BIBLIOGRAPHY

(INCLUDES LIMITED EDITIONS)

Into the Stone and Other Poems, in *Poets of Today VII,* ed. John Hall Wheelock. New York: Scribners, 1960. (Fifteen of the 24 poems are reprinted in *Poems 1957–1967.)* Poems.

Drowning With Others. Middletown, Conn.: Wesleyan University Press, 1962. (Twenty-five of the 36 poems are reprinted in *Poems 1957–1967.*) Poems.

Helmets. Middletown, Conn.: Wesleyan University Press, 1964; London: Longmans, 1964. (Twenty-two of the 27 poems are reprinted in *Poems 1957–1967.*) Poems.

The Suspect in Poetry. Madison, Minn.: Sixties Press, 1964. Essays.

Two Poems of the Air. Portland, Oreg.: Centicore Press, 1964. Poems.

Buckdancer's Choice. Middletown, Conn.: Wesleyan University Press, 1965. (All 22 poems are reprinted in *Poems 1957–1967.*) Poems.

Poems 1957–1967. Middletown, Conn.: Wesleyan University Press, 1967; London: Rapp & Carroll, 1967. ("May Day Sermon" & the poems of the *Falling* section were previously uncollected by Dickey.) Poems.

Spinning the Crystal Ball. Washington, D.C.: Library of Congress, 1967. Essay.

Babel to Byzantium: Poets and Poetry Now. New York: Farrar, Straus & Giroux, 1968. Reprinted with a new Afterword, New York: Ecco Press, 1981. Essays.

Metaphor as Pure Adventure. Washington, D.C.: Library of Congress, 1968. Essay.

Deliverance. Boston: Houghton Mifflin, 1970; London: Hamish Hamilton, 1970. Novel.

The Eye-Beaters, Blood, Victory, Madness, Buckhead and Mercy. Garden City, N.Y.: Doubleday, 1970; London: Hamish Hamilton, 1971. Poems.

Self-Interviews, recorded and edited by Barbara & James Reiss. Garden City, N.Y.: Doubleday, 1970. Essays.

Stolen Apples, by Yevgeny Yevtushenko. Garden City, N.Y.: Doubleday, 1971. (Includes 12 poems adapted by Dickey.)

Exchanges. Bloomfield Hills, Mich.: Bruccoli Clark, 1971. Poem.

Sorties. Garden City, N.Y.: Doubleday, 1971. Journal & essays.

Jericho: The South Beheld, text by Dickey & paintings by Hubert Shuptrine. Birmingham, Ala.: Oxmoor House, 1974. Prose.

Call of the Wild. Produced by Charles Fries, 1976. Screenplay.

The Zodiac. Garden City, N.Y.: Doubleday, 1976. Limited edition of 61 numbered and signed copies, each of which contains one page of the revised working draft of the poem, Bloomfield Hills, Mich. & Columbia, S.C.: Bruccoli Clark, 1976. Poem.

The Strength of Fields. Bloomfield Hills, Mich. and Columbia, S.C.: Bruccoli Clark, 1977. Inaugural Poem.

The Owl King. New York: Red Angel Press, 1977. Poem.

God's Images, text by Dickey & etchings by Marvin Hayes. Birmingham, Ala.: Oxmoor House, 1977. Prose.

The Enemy from Eden. Northridge, Calif.: Lord John Press, 1978. Essay.

Tucky the Hunter, text by Dickey & illustrations by Marie Angel. New York: Crown, 1978; London: Macmillan, 1979. Children's poem.

Veteran Birth: The Gadfly Poems 1947–1949. Winston-Salem, N.C.: Palaemon Press, 1978. Poems.

In Pursuit of the Grey Soul. Bloomfield Hills, Mich. & Columbia, S.C.: Bruccoli Clark, 1978. Essay.

Head-Deep in Strange Sounds. Winston-Salem, N.C.: Palaemon Press, 1978. Poems.

The Water-Bug's Mittens: Ezra Pound: What We Can Use. Moscow: University of Idaho, 1979; Bloomfield Hills, Mich. & Columbia, S.C.: Bruccoli Clark, 1980. Essay.

The Strength of Fields. Garden City, N.Y.: Doubleday, 1979. Poems.

Scion. Deerfield, Mass. & Dublin, Ireland: The Deerfield Press/The Gallery Press, 1980. Poems.

The Starry Place Between the Antlers: Why I Live in South Carolina. Bloomfield Hills, Mich. & Columbia, S.C.: Bruccoli Clark, 1981. Essay.

Deliverance. Produced by Warner Brothers, 1972. Carbondale & Edwardsville: Southern Illinois University Press, 1982. Screenplay.

Puella. Garden City, N.Y.: Doubleday, 1982. Poems.

Värmland. Winston-Salem, N.C.: Palaemon Press, 1982. Poems.

False Youth: Four Seasons. Dallas, Tex.: Pressworks, 1983. Poems.

Night Hurdling: Poems, Essays, Conversations, Commencements, and Afterwords. Bloomfields Hills, Mich. & Columbia, S.C.: Bruccoli Clark, 1983.

Bronwen, the Traw, and the Shape-Shifter, text by Dickey & illustrations by Richard Jesse Watson. San Diego, New York, & London: Bruccoli Clark/Harcourt Brace Jovanovich, 1986. Children's poem.

Alnilam. Garden City, N.Y.: Doubleday, 1987. Novel.

Wayfarer: A Voice from the Southern Mountains, text by Dickey & photographs by William A. Bake. Birmingham, Ala.: Oxmoor House, 1988. Prose.

1

AN INTERVIEW WITH JAMES DICKEY

ECLIPSE / 1965

ECLIPSE: When did you begin to write poetry?

DICKEY: Well, I began, the nearest I can remember, in writing long letters. The early 40s were great times to write letters to girls from the people in the service, and I wrote long, romantic letters to girls and out of those, somehow, developed a kind of rudimentary poetry.

ECLIPSE: You've told me, I believe, that you have had about 500 hours of combat flying or approximately that.

DICKEY: A good many. I really don't know how many.

ECLIPSE: Yet the war doesn't really appear directly in an awful lot of your poems. There are a few in which it does. How, generally, do you feel it influenced your writing?

DICKEY: A lot, a lot. I was a member of the war generation. I remember almost every day that I was in the war, and I think almost everything that I've done is influenced, at least to some degree, either directly or indirectly, most probably directly, by the fact that I was in the war. I write mainly from the standpoint of a survivor.

ECLIPSE: I believe you mentioned once that you began majoring in astrophysics when you entered college.

DICKEY: No, actually I minored in that.

Reprinted with permission from *Eclipse* [San Fernando Valley State College/California State University at Northridge], No. 5 (1965–1966), 5–20. Interview conducted in October 1965.

An Interview

ECLIPSE: Do you feel that this scientific background has influenced the direction or the content of your poetry?

DICKEY: I've never really found a way to use it in poetry. I've never really found a way to get it into verse, but there must surely be a way. I can claim but a very modest scientific background, but this I think is really a kind of enlargement of view which any poet would like to have more of. That's about all I can say; I really don't base a poetic on it.

ECLIPSE: You're one of the few, one of the very few poets writing in America today who uses the long narrative form as in "The Fiend" or "Slave Quarters." Do you find yourself particularly at home with the form, and how does it serve your particular poetic purposes?

DICKEY: Well, I like to get the reader more or less involved in the poem. I know that there is a school, such as Robert Bly and Jim Wright belong to, and they're from the school of the drop-their-nugget-in-your-hand-and-run type of poem. I don't feel that way. I feel that what I really want the poem to do is to devour the reader. I want it to engulf him. I want him to become entangled with it inextricably, and, in order to do that, you can't use just a line or two, you have to draw him in and then throw your lassos.

ECLIPSE: Do you have any particular concept or aesthetic of poetry?

DICKEY: I guess in a way I do, a tacit one, but if you do as much reading in the English poetic tradition as I do, you see how much lip service is given to a kind of sterile convention in various eras. You know, the sterile convention of the Elizabethan blank verse line or the sterile convention of the eighteenth-century couplet. Now they're not *necessarily* sterile. They were practiced as external forms by people who were in that particular period, and who practiced the form because everybody else did it. My feeling is that the first allegiance that one owes to the reader is to deliver to him something which is of viable coin as the communication between human beings, something you can believe in as a statement of how somebody *feels,* not as he feels out of a predetermined poetic convention.

ECLIPSE: In a script for the Voice of America about your poetry,[1] you talked about meters and rhythms, and you said that, for you, the anapest more satisfied your needs than the usual iambic line of English poetry. Why, and is this still true for you?

DICKEY: No, it isn't still true, but for one period of time that I was writing or developing or whatever you might want to say, it had a very powerful attraction for me. I used to read a lot of Poe, and the *carrying* power of the metric seemed to me to be very powerful, although what was being said was not especially interesting. It seemed to me that despite everything that I'd heard to the contrary, that the anapest or the dactyl, I guess, or whatever you call it depending on where you start counting, really is capable, if you vary it strategically, of a new kind of sound, or a kind of sound which is unusual because one thinks of it mainly as something connected with either Poe or "The Shooting of Dan McGrew"; but this doesn't exhaust the possibilities of the anapest, and I began to experiment with it to see what could be said this way which would give this great, powerful, surging rhythm. It seemed to me that the thing would be solved if you could say something which was poetically viable in this way; then the sound, and the fact that it was real poetry and not fustian like Robert Service, would create a kind of new aesthetic effect. That's all. This is what I was trying to get at.

ECLIPSE: Part of the reason I asked that question is because the form in *Helmets* was different from that in *Drowning With Others*. It changed again in your most recent book, *Buckdancer's Choice,* and you told me that it underwent still another change in your next book, *Falling,* which isn't yet published.[2] Where is this leading you? What are the changes basically?

DICKEY: I don't know where it is leading, but I have one firmly rooted conviction about poetry and about the role of the poet; he must always be exploring and he must always try to get out beyond the frontiers where he has previously been. This is a great lesson of Picasso; you know, in an analogous art. I remember one time that in *Paris Soir,* or in one of the other French newspapers, they interviewed Jean Cocteau, and they asked him what his advice to poets was, and he said, "Find out what you can do best, and then don't do it."

ECLIPSE: In the same article you talked about the "split line." How do you use it?

DICKEY: What I'd like to think one can use it for is to present a wide variety of states of mind which are continuous with each other, but which are also sort of coterminous. It's a kind of an impressionistic technique which as nearly as I can tell approximates as close as I myself can get to the way the mind really associates. It doesn't really associate in sentences so much as it does in word clusters. I tried this, in the few poems that I've written using this technique, if such it may be called, this kind of technique for writing in word bursts. If words occur to you in your mind, they only occur one, two, three at a time, but sometimes those are startling in their conjunctions as they do turn up, and in the effect of one word to another running together to form a complete subject. This is the feeling that I have been trying to get with the split line, but I don't know, I don't think the possibilities of it have been touched in anything I've done.

ECLIPSE: In other words, you separate the bursts, one from the other?

DICKEY: Right, just with space. It might be as easy as that.

ECLIPSE: Robert Bly once described you as a "bull moose" in *The Sixties* magazine in one of the reviews he did of your work. What was he getting at, and what was your reaction?

DICKEY: Fine, it's all right with me. I think that the type of criticism Robert Bly does when he compares John Logan to a one-legged crane or me to a bull moose is fun and games, but it doesn't have anything to do with any real description of what we're doing, either Logan or myself and probably Bly either, as he likens himself, I think, to a whooping crane. I think that— well, I don't know; if you want to play that game it's a lot of fun. I'd like to be as big and powerful as that, but I don't think such analogies can be pursued without a certain danger of misrepresenting everybody concerned.

ECLIPSE: In your own criticism, in the book review section of the *New York Times*,[3] you've dealt rather shortly and sharply with Allen Ginsberg and other poets of his ilk. Do you feel that Ginsberg and the movement he represents have no redeeming features?

DICKEY: No one said they did not have any redeeming features. It's just that it seems that when one writes this much—as much as Ginsberg and Gregory Corso do, and as much as Robert Duncan does, and other people like Robert Creeley—they have no block against writing. They write an enormous amount. There was a fellow in San Francisco who's always writing about dope addiction; he's another one of them. But you see right then that something that has to do with the selectivity of the linguistic instrument has been left out—they maybe have bypassed this. The first thing one thinks is: Hallelujah, here is somebody who has bypassed the difficulty of writing, and they're just pouring it out. If it were all gold, if it were all wonderful, then the whole problem of writing would be solved. But then one looks at it, and one sees *no,* the problem of writing is not solved, because they have a congenital inability to turn a memorable phrase. They're writing like the monkey in the hunt-and-peck system. You know, like the battery of monkeys postulated by Thomas Henry Huxley which, because of the laws of permutation and combination, would eventually produce, just by random hitting of the typewriter keys, all the works of Shakespeare and the Bible—the whole canon of English literature. They just keep pouring it out, hoping that something wonderful is going to happen, but it almost never does, and when it does it's buried so deeply in the mass of claptrap that it would take a truly dedicated person to dig it out. Even then, I doubt very much if it's worth it. All the work of Ginsberg and Corso and all those people is not worth one really well-said thing, one well-said thing by John Berryman, one well-said thing by William Stafford, Louis Simpson, Jim Wright, or any of these people who are real poets. I was at Yaddo last summer, and I sat at the breakfast table next to a composer, and wishing to be knowledgeable, I said to him, "What do you think of John Cage and all these experimental composers?" He turned to me curtly and said, "I like *real* music, not joke music," and I feel the same way about poetry—I like *real* poetry, not joke poetry.

ECLIPSE: In *Helmets* you have a long poem called "A Folk

Singer of the Thirties." Now your latest book, *Buckdancer's Choice,* is titled after a folk song or folk tune—

DICKEY: Yes, right.

ECLIPSE: What do you feel your connection is? How are you influenced by this rather loose genre we call folk music?

DICKEY: I don't have any real connection. I'm really sort of a latecomer to the game although I was raised among a sort of folk music, but I don't claim any tapping in on the real thing any more than anybody else has. *Buckdancer's Choice* was just a song that I learned on the guitar which reminded me of a song I used to hear my mother whistle at home. I'm not sure it isn't the same, although I'm not sure that it is. "A Folk Singer of the Thirties" came from reading Woody Guthrie's autobiography, and reading Burl Ives's ghosted autobiography, *The Wayfaring Stranger,*[4] and wondering what those guys must have had despite the deprivation and the poverty, in the Thirties, when they rode the rods and sang their songs for their meals in the little depression-ridden towns all over the country—what the difference between that would be and what they have now in the great affluent society when they live in those uptown apartments and purvey their folksy humor on quiz shows and become actors and that sort of thing. There seemed to be a very great cleavage there. Something definitely has been lost. The music really has been lost. Burl Ives can sing "Jimmy Crack Corn" all he likes in night clubs, but it won't be the same as when he was poor. It's not better that he should be poor, merely that it's closer to the true folk thing that he should wander and sing for his supper.

ECLIPSE: Your poems tend to be more descriptive than instructive or moralistic. For example, "The Fiend" is an almost lyric description of what the newspapers would call a sex pervert or a maniac, but there is nothing really judgmental about the poem. Do you feel that moralizing or judgmental tones do not belong in poetry?

DICKEY: No! Or I think they do, but it depends simply on where you feel the judgment lies. Myself, I wrote "The Fiend" so long ago that, unlike most of my things, I can't remember exactly when I wrote it; it seemed like I worked over it a long time. But I feel a very strong sympathy for "The Fiend." I like

"The Fiend." I think women, who are explained endlessly to us, have that air of mystery and beatification and pedestal-dwelling for us, and can have it only in this kind of inaccessible state, such as you would behold them in if you looked in the window of an apartment when they were undressing. They have a marvelous, absolutely untouchable, transcendent quality there, and it seems to me that to say something about this would say something very real, not only about American life, but about the man-and-woman situation generally. One doesn't want a woman to be too accessible, one wants her to be beyond—beyond and yet visible.

ECLIPSE: You do feel that moralizing—in other words, judgmental tones—do come into poetry?

DICKEY: Oh yes, they do. Poetry cannot avoid that. I mean the judgment that you pass on a subject that you're writing about is either absolutely overt or is implied. You might leave it up to the reader to decide what is meant by what you've said, but you know, as the writer, what you feel about it yourself. You know whether you detest it or whether you like it, whether you have mixed feelings about it or whatever it happens to be. But you know you've taken a definite stand, and the poem necessitates that. You can't write a poem without a definite stand. You can't always straddle a fence. Robert Frost was a very good fence straddler, but he really didn't straddle it that much. He has an implied opinion in almost everything he says, although he, above all other poets, seems to give with one hand and take away with the other.

ECLIPSE: There seems to be a tremendous apathy towards poetry in America today, especially among the younger people of high school age. Do you see any way of overcoming it? I mean ways poetry might be taught in high school?

DICKEY: I don't know. I myself was a victim, a product of that apathy. But now it seems to me like the pendulum is swinging the other way. I've never seen so much interest—in fact, the interest frightens me. If you predicated an apathy to begin with, and asked what I would think would be some kind of remedy, I would simply say stop teaching bad poems in high school! Stop teaching "Bob-o-link, bob-o-link, spink-spank-spink," and teach something of Randall Jarrell's, John Berryman's, or William Stafford's, or something that will have some connection with the life that the student might be presumed to know something about. Teach Karl Shapiro's poem about the drugstore where "they sprawl in the booths like rags, not even drunk." That's them you're talking about. It might arouse their indignation, but at least they would know what you were talking about. Teach poems which have a connection with something that they themselves are prepared to judge and have an opinion about.

ECLIPSE: Speaking of Randall Jarrell, in your critical article on him in *The Suspect in Poetry* you seem very split in your opinion. In the end it seems that you come out favoring the views of both favorable critic "A" and unfavorable critic "B."

. . .

DICKEY: I'm "A."

ECLIPSE: The one "conjured up out of the wind"?

DICKEY: Right. I'm "A." I just wrote an article in the *American Scholar*[5] which I hope resolves this. It haunts me, and will haunt me until my dying day, as to whether Randall Jarrell, when he committed suicide last week,[6] ever saw this. Because this is something I intended to get before the public. I do think that he is a valuable man. I do think that because of his very caustic tongue he made an enormous number of enemies, and, despite the powerful friends he had—like Robert Lowell, Delmore Schwartz, Allen Tate, and John Crowe Ransom—the fact that he had such an overwhelming number of enemies that he himself had made finally weighed on him too much and he snapped.

ECLIPSE: It's difficult to go through your poetry and really conclude that you are, say, addicted to one theme more than another. Do you feel that there are any basic themes which underpin most of your poems?

DICKEY: I don't know. I think that most poets are not looking mainly for themes, but they are looking for occasions. They're looking for things that will make good poems in the kind of style that they themselves have developed. My own work, I'd say—well, I don't know. I remember Theodore Roethke, who was one of the unhappiest men I ever knew, saying that he strove all his life to proclaim a condition of joy. My work, despite all the emphasis on death and the sadness of so much of it, is essentially affirmative. As I said earlier, I write from the standpoint of a survivor, and everything I do seems, when I stop to reflect on it, or, better still, when I don't stop to reflect on it, very largely miraculous. It's miraculous to sit here and talk; to have a beer, to play a guitar, to make love, or any of these things is wonderful to me. That's gravy. That's something I probably don't deserve to have, but who does?

ECLIPSE: Who do you think might have influenced your writing, other writers that is, or did any?

DICKEY: I have no notion at all. I've never read anybody that had exactly the sound that I have or that I wanted to emulate. I emulated a lot like any young writer. George Barker was a person that I technically imitated very early, but, luckily, none of those poems have ever been preserved. Dylan Thomas was somebody that fascinated me, and I liked him a lot. Also, Gerard Manley Hopkins, but I didn't have the right feeling or the right rhythm for them. T. S. Eliot: he's somebody I acknowledged as an *eminence grise,* but he never meant anything to me really from the standpoint of what I was trying to do. Theodore Roethke later on I liked, but, again, his rhythm was so different from mine. I guess the poets that I feel closest to—and this may be one of those kinds of dim, magical things that's a result of the fact that you don't really know the language yourself well, and you impute to the foreign-language poets that you read haltingly in their language some qualities they don't actually possess—but the poets that have influenced me in my fashion from the time I really started publishing books were foreign-language poets, mainly the French: Jules Supervielle, Pierre Reverdy, André Frénaud, René Guy Cadou, and other writers of the contemporary French scene. Now these are not names that are known much by people here, but they were wonderful to me. I discovered them when I used to sit in cafes in France in 1954, and, you know, in those days you could walk into a French book store with five dollars and walk out with as many poetry books—or any kind of books—as you could carry. I just took them to a cafe and sat down and tried to puzzle out what these guys, who might have been from the planet Mars, were saying. What I got was very exciting to me, and, I suspect, that influenced me more than anything in the English tradition because I was struck by it. I knew the English traditions. I knew the old "Intimations of Immortality" and I knew "To His Coy Mistress" and I knew *Hamlet* and I knew "Il Penseroso." I knew all that; I mean, I was tired to death of that. This was something new for me, and the excitement of it carried into the work I was trying to do at that time, which in turn was the work that was fundamental to what I did later on and what I'm doing now. So it was very much a matter of chance.

ECLIPSE: No one, then, really sort of played Mr. Pound to your Mr. Eliot?

DICKEY: No. No.

ECLIPSE: How do you feel what you're working on or what you write relates, say, particularly to the contemporary world or to the modern United States? You seem to deal mostly with things that bring in the imagery of nature, but your imagery does not come a great deal in contact with urban life.

DICKEY: I guess not. I've written some things about cities, about the apprehension of a city by somebody who is not himself a city person. To him, I would like to think that the city has the quality of a vision. It's strange; I have one poem about going up to the top of a hotel or motel in New York and looking out over the city as the sun comes up. That I have done, but it's really not my kind of thing. My feeling is this: there are lots of poets who very effectively deal with the colored theme, civil rights crisis, and with the Vietnam situation—with the public occasions of that sort. I, myself, have no compulsion to do that. As I get older, I feel I have only one mission as a writer, and that is to try to render what life has felt like to one person who just happened, incidentally, to be myself. That's all.

ECLIPSE: You mentioned not being primarily a city person. You're a country person, someone from Georgia, and Southern writers have always been sort of distinct from the rest of the country. The Southern poets form a very individual group. Do you consider yourself among that group to any degree?

DICKEY: I would like to, although I don't think my work really has a strongly regional flavor. Some of the things couldn't have been written if I hadn't been a Southerner, but most of them probably could have—although I may be fooling myself there. I am not a deliberate regionalist like Donald Davidson or the early Robert Penn Warren was. I don't really insist on that. I only sort of relate it or record it as something that is indigenous to my particular life, that's all. But as a panacea or a code of action or a way of looking at existence as a Southerner, I don't really hold with it. I've been gone too long, although, again, as I say, I may be fooling myself. The best things I have ever done may very likely proceed from the fact that I'm a Southerner. I don't know, I think that in any person's life, as he gets up into his 20s and 30s—and, as I am now, in my 40s—he realizes the implacability of one thing, and that is there is only one past, and that can't change.

ECLIPSE: How has teaching at a California state college struck you? Has it been a favorable experience? Have you enjoyed it?

DICKEY: Yes, I have enjoyed it enormously. I can say something scandalous here.

ECLIPSE: You can say whatever you please.

DICKEY: I'll tell you: one of the nicest things about Valley State is that it's confirmed me in my lifelong propensity as a fanny watcher. There are some very nice things going on at the campus every time classes change. As to writing students, I've had some very good ones. It's a sad thing to me that I only get them for six months or a year. I can't know what's going to happen to them after that, and this puts an enormous burden on the teacher. You've got to give them everything you can give them in one semester. You've got to fix them. You don't want them to imitate you as a writer. You don't want them to do *your* thing—you want them to do *their* thing. But, discovering what their thing is, or helping them to discover it, is one of the most difficult things there is, and since you're bound by the peculiar limitations of mortality yourself and judgments subject thereto, you're never sure that you're right in what you tell them to do. But, if I were to mount my seat on my Parnassus, which I have not really achieved or earned, and looked down on the people at Valley State, I would pick out ten students who I think, if assisted enough and if they go through the agony and the ecstasy of it enough, will make a place for themselves on the American Parnassus. That is, I've got ten, and surely five, that I would lay my cold coin on.

ECLIPSE: How did it compare with your experience at Reed College?

DICKEY: I probably shouldn't make a comparison like this. The Reed people are, head for head, more brilliant, more knowledgeable, better read, more dedicated. There are three or four excellent people I had at Reed that were really unbelievably good—good students, promising writers. But what Reed doesn't have and what Valley State—or a huge, amorphous kind of school like this—does have, is innocence. Innocence; and out of that it very well may be that all good things can flow. They have no preconceptions; they're willing to swing with themselves as they find themselves. Knowledge is a fine thing, but it can also be crippling. Too much book-learning can interrupt the flow.

ECLIPSE: You mentioned something about *Falling,* something new you were trying in form.

DICKEY: Too early to talk about it. I think I've got a new kind of sound again, another beat, a halting, hesitant, stuttering kind of sound. I haven't really made it go yet, but occasionally I can hear a halting voice saying amazing things, and I would not permit myself to say anything more than that right now.

ECLIPSE: Are you going back to a shorter line?

DICKEY: No, no. I want to mix them up. I think what I really want is a sense such as if you stumbled on to the village idiot, and he began to mutter amazing things to you, and, like in "The Ancient Mariner," you could not help but hear—you know? That is the sound. That's what I want to try to get down, but, God knows, no telling what's going to happen.

ECLIPSE: Other than poetry and criticism, you're working on a novel—

DICKEY: I'm less sure there.

ECLIPSE: What else?

DICKEY: That's all; just poetry, criticism and a novel and some reviews. I just tried my hand at reviewing some children's books for the *New York Times*.[7] I don't really know what to say about children's books, but I found something to say. George

Santayana or somebody, may it was Friedrich Nietzsche, said, "The poet is he who, not having anything to do, finds something to do." That's what I did; I found fourteen children's books to review, and I wrote on those with, if maybe not a great deal of erudition, at least enthusiasm based on my own innate childishness and the more authentic childishness of my own children.

ECLIPSE: Both your earlier books were dedicated to your family. Is *Buckdancer's Choice* also dedicated to them? Your family plays a great part in your life and your poetry, don't they?

DICKEY: Right. All of them in one way or another. I believe in the continuity of the blood lines. I believe in the possibility of some kind of miraculous birth occurring. The oddest thing about it is that when the birth of any child, any human child, occurs it's as miraculous as anything could conceivably be. My great love of my middle years is my children. I just regret so much that I didn't have whole lot more of them. I would like to have had eight or ten children, but what I hope is that my boys will be more productive than I am or I have been, because what I really hope to be is a patriarch. I'd like to have hundreds and hundreds of them running around. Population explosion be damned! Let those others be sacrificed; my brood will be indispensable.

ECLIPSE: James Dickey, the patriarch, one of your many different facets.

DICKEY: Right, right. I remember saying in an article that was published in the *New York Times Book Section*,[8] about a man going around giving poetry readings, who didn't know how to act before an audience, and he says to himself, "Well, it will be all right, just be yourself," and then, in the next breath, he thinks, "Ah; but which self?" The same with any writer, because every man has in himself such a plethora of different personalities. Everybody has in himself a saint, a murderer, a pervert, a monster, a good husband, a scoutmaster, a provider, a businessman, a shrewd horse trader, a hopeless aesthete. Everybody has all these and more in one proportion or another, as it's determined by his personality. There are all kinds of contradictory selves. Essentially, the most exciting thing for a writer, especially a young writer, is to get as many of these energized as he can, to let the monster speak as well as let the prospective husband speak. You know, you shouldn't limit it all to one thing, and if these selves are contradictory, say with Walt Whitman, "Do I contradict myself? / Very well then I contradict myself, / (I am large, I contain multitudes.)" Which you do, which everybody does. I think the great thing for the young writer is to let as many possibilities swing as he can confront, and to get these out.... There are so many different people in the self and each one of them has a voice, and it is listening to these different voices in the self that makes it so enormously exciting. America is famous for writers beginning well and then petering out or repeating themselves and not being able to develop; but these are people who had early success and who fastened on to the one voice that produced their early success as their voice, as the only voice. Stephen Crane did this, for example. If I could just get people to see that they're not limited, that if somebody is crazy about their first book that's no sanction to do nothing else but the same manner or the same style as the first book for the rest of their lives. That way lies sterility and madness. Let the first book speak for itself and its voice; but then go on and ask that diametric opposite in the soul, all right, buddy, the good guy had his say, what are *you* going to say? Then let him write the next book or the next poem.

ECLIPSE: And that's what you've done?

DICKEY: That's what I've tried to do.

ECLIPSE: You've let all the various aspects of yourself speak; the archer, the sportsman, the guitarist, the husband—

DICKEY: The fiend had to have a say. The best fan letter I ever got was from a police lieutenant who read "The Fiend" in the *Partisan Review*,[9] and he wrote to me and said, "I've always had a sneaking sympathy with you guys. Please don't answer. I'm not going to sign this, and I won't give you any return address, but I'm a member of the New York City Police Department." That's the most rewarding letter I've ever gotten in twenty years as a writer, not twenty, but surely twelve or fifteen years as a writer. In that one I was convinced that I'd said something that mattered to somebody, and, while maybe it shouldn't have mattered to him specifically, the fact that it did pleases me very much. "I've always had a sneaking sympathy with you guys." I think every male in America, and probably the world, is gorgeous material for a peeping tom anyway, don't you?

ECLIPSE: Definitely.

DICKEY: If he had the right situation.

ECLIPSE: Having had it when I was a boy—

DICKEY: You never forget it.

ECLIPSE: One last question. Where do you think poetry in America today is going, and what is its promise? What are the poets going to be doing, because, you know, poetry today is so amorphous; if it isn't the Beats, then what is it?

DICKEY: It's not the Beats, and it's not the Academics; it's the mavericks like Stafford and the—

ECLIPSE: But the mavericks aren't getting that much published.

DICKEY: No, God knows. It's a question of what you think is going to happen on the one hand, and what you hope happens on the other hand.

ECLIPSE: What are both?

DICKEY: What I think is going to happen, and, maybe what I hope is going to happen, are not too far apart. I think there is going to be more of an introspective kind of poetry and a personal kind of poetry. You think of Salvador Dali, the painter, as being a sort of primary exemplar of the surrealist movement; but surrealism in writing is probably going to have more far-reaching effects than surrealism in painting ever had: people like Wright and John Knoepfle in Chicago, and Robert Bly and Bill Knott. And there are others who are essentially late blooming products of the surrealist movement of the 20s in France. I think that the surrealists—Paul Eluard, Tristan Tzara, André Breton, Robert Desnos, Maurice Blanchot, and all those people of the 30s—broke down a linguistic barrier that these people like Bly and Wright are just sort of timidly going through. Not surrealism itself and the odd images like the "white haired revolver" and that sort of thing—that's not the fruit that is going to be born; but the general sense of the breaking down of linguistic and psychological barriers that the surrealists began is going to result in a kind of an odd new poetry that nobody has ever yet written or heard of or envisioned. The whole business of what the New York literati like to call "the deep image" has not really been explored at all. The timid little forays into the unconscious that have been taken by Bly and Wright and these people are almost nothing to what possibly might come later. If I were to cast now a literary horoscope for the poetry of the future, I would say that it would be a kind of a responsible free association as opposed to irresponsible free association. Now, the joker in the deck is what constitutes responsibility? What I would posit would be some guy who had a strong personal sense and a strong personal control—which amounts to a creative sense—over an extremely powerful and sensuous subconscious. Now, out of that the new poetry will come. I'm looking for it.

2
THINGS HAPPEN: AN INTERVIEW WITH JAMES DICKEY

WISCONSIN REVIEW / 1966

EDITOR: Mr. Dickey, you have traveled around the country a great deal and taught in many different areas. Could you give us something of an overall view of the American student? Tell us what kinds of literature he reads and the kinds of things he writes.

DICKEY: Yes, he reads of his own volition, for some reason or other, preponderantly literature of writers who are not awfully good, but who for some reason or other he feels a kinship with, writers of the so-called Beat movement. Everybody always asks me what I think of Ginsberg and Lawrence Ferlinghetti and these incompetent people. I don't quite understand that. It seems to be an indication of a certain insensitivity, or certain exhibitionism, in the young which could be put to some good uses but not those uses. But they also read a great deal of continental literature, especially of the theater, and, surprisingly, large amounts of philosophy, which I think is a good idea. Of course, I'm conditioned in these opinions by the fact that I taught at Reed College in Portland where people are so voracious about reading that it seems incredible.

The students in other schools are not like they are at Reed. I somehow have fallen into the notion that Reed is typical and actually the students there are profoundly atypical. But most of the American students that I have met, which are really only a very small fragment in any given school, have expressed a very vital interest in the current literary scene. It is just too bad that they believe that the current literary scene is comprised entirely of Jack Kerouac and Allen Ginsberg and those

Things Happen 29

people, when they are really the fast-fading, fragmentary part of it. There was a mild, and maybe legitimate, excitement about them, especially Kerouac, whom I rather like as a writer and like very much personally. But they don't have any staying power. The sensationalistic part of it has worn off now; it's hard to be sensationalistic anymore, what with the general relaxation of censorship. Without sensationalism, it seems that they have almost nothing to say.

EDITOR: What kinds of things are you apt to read, and what kinds of things would you recommend to the student to read?

DICKEY: Well, I don't know. I'm not really competent in any field except my own, and I'm not sure about my competence in that. If a person is interested in poetry, I would like to see him throw a fairly wide net, read different kinds of things, as well as translations. He can read his beloved Beatniks if he wants to, but let's not exclude everybody else. If one reads a broad spectrum of poetry, one comes to realize very quickly the kinds of things that are possible. It's a good idea, I think, to get as many angles of vision as you can through the poems of as many people as you can read.

EDITOR: Since Dylan Thomas there has been something of a movement back to writing poetry for the listening audience. Some poets, however, still write for the printed page. Does this distinction affect your poetry?

DICKEY: I'm never really conscious of it. I just try to make a good poem. I'm conscious of the sound patterns, and I try to make them interesting so that, if read aloud, the poem will gain rather than be diminished by the way the sound patterns run. But I don't consciously think of the poem as being read aloud or on the page. I would like it to be equally good either way. Thomas's influence on poetry for the so-called spoken word is, in my opinion, absolutely disastrous. I think he is one of the worst readers that I have ever heard, because he brings in that awful theatricality which is the last thing in the world one would want in a poetry reading—some kind of a performance by an actor. I don't doubt that Dylan Thomas was sincere about his work; he just made it sound insincere, and this bothers me very much. And it bothers me also that so many people like it, because it makes me think that what people really want out of a poet is a sincere phoniness. That's wrong. You should get an absolutely convincing kind of sincerity.

EDITOR: Robert Lowell has said that public reading affected his style. After reading to an audience he has become more aware of his use of language and has embodied somewhat of a change in style more suitable to public reading. Has public reading done anything to affect your style?

DICKEY: Not consciously, no. I can almost categorically say that I would write exactly the same way whether I had never read anything in public or not. What Lowell said may be true for him, and may be true to a lesser extent for other people. But it surely isn't true for me, except perhaps to a very small extent. I am not at all conscious of my poems as being public performance pieces. Again, it is just something between me and the piece of paper that I am trying to get said.

EDITOR: Recently there appears to have been a shift in your style. You seem to be using longer lines and setting phrases apart by double spacing rather than punctuation. To what do you attribute this?

DICKEY: Well, it's a search for another way to make the line work. It seems to me that the mind normally (or abnormally) associates in jumps rather than in a smooth, continuous flow. One tends to think in image clusters. I do anyway, and I thought that if I split the line with this kind of gap device it would be more of an approximation of that way of thinking. We thereby have a greater degree of psychological verisimilitude, or at least the illusion of such. I don't know that this is true, but I thought it at least worth trying.

EDITOR: Critics have said that much of your earlier poetry was influenced by Roethke, not only in content but also in style. Do you feel that this shift in style is getting away from his influence? Would you comment on your latest collection, *Buckdancer's Choice,* and do you feel this collection to be much different from some of your earlier works?

DICKEY: I was not consciously influenced by Roethke, although I admire him enormously. That is mainly a spurious comparison, I think. I would be the first to own that he would be somebody I would like to be influenced by because I think he is the best poet we have ever had in this country. But if any such influence exists, it is more of a temperamental affinity rather than anything stylistic. *Buckdancer's Choice* is different from any of the other books, and the new manuscript is different from it. I don't want to be bogged down in any one aspect of my own style. This is a fatal thing that has happened to so many American poets. Dick Wilbur, for example, doesn't seem to be able to do anything else. Neither did Roethke. At the end of his life he was pretty much up against the same thing. Lowell to some extent has avoided this. He changed from his first style, which made him famous, into another style which was akin to it but not like it very much. You could tell the same man wrote the two different kinds of poems. But he has now become sort of bogged down in the new style.

I think the poet must keep moving on. It's the poet's business to try out new things, to push out the frontiers of consciousness in some way, to experiment continuously instead of just consolidating his own position. Risking failure, that's what you must do.

EDITOR: In that light, what importance would you place on form and tradition in poetry, and how much do you think the prospective young poet should adhere to form and tradition?

DICKEY: Like everybody else in the generation, I've been very conscious of the crippling clutch on poetry of tradition under the influence of Eliot. Eliot's notion of this is that the tradition is larger than any one poet, and that the poet would do well to take from the tradition what he can and make his own work a modification of what has already been done. I look at it in exactly the opposite way. My viewpoint is that tradition is waiting, always waiting, for some new writer to bring to it what no one else could bring, to modify it and make it a different thing. We are conscious of the English verse tradition, for example, in Dylan Thomas. But what we are mainly conscious of in Thomas is what only he does and what only he can do. That is the thing that ought to be stressed: the individual contribution, and not the huge weight of the tradition against which he struggles.

EDITOR: Recently you commented in *Sports Illustrated*[10] that if you hadn't been a poet, you would have liked to have been a high school track coach. Is there any connection between that comment and feelings expressed in "Buckdancer's Choice" or in any of your other poems?

DICKEY: In some ways I suppose so. I hadn't thought of it that way. I am indebted to you for pointing that out. I'll give it some thought. I have thought of myself as not really an intellectual poet, but mainly a poet of the bodily processes, and the viscera and the muscles and actions. For this reason I want to get sports things into poetry. I don't think it has ever been done at all, not even by Pindar. Sports are among the most beautiful things on this earth to me. They represent the nearest thing that we can get to some kind of bodily perfection, especially in those "use" situations which are also aesthetically pleasing. I haven't quite found a way to do it yet, but I think it can be done, and I think it will be very exciting to try. I haven't done more than hint at it in two or three poems, but they are late poems. One was published in June's *Harper's* and is called "The Bee." In this a middle-aged man calls on his athletic experience, which has been dead for twenty years, to save his little boy from running out on the highway and getting run over. This is only a beginning though. I am trying to write a long poem now about a sprinter who has diabetes, as I do. It has a lot to do with blood sugar levels and that sort of thing. I haven't quite found a way to do it yet, but again it's this bodily thing. He tries to get this balance between sugar and insulin which will enable him to function at absolutely top efficiency for a hundred yards.

EDITOR: Recently Robert Bly organized a program of oral poetry readings, "The American Writers Against the War in Vietnam." It was presented here in Milwaukee and at Wisconsin State University at Oshkosh, as well as in other parts of the country. I am told that Mr. Bly and yourself are friends. Is there any reason why you weren't included in that program?

DICKEY: Mr. Bly and I are old friends and acquaintances, and I like him personally very much indeed. He is one of my former publishers, as a matter of fact. But I disapprove thoroughly of that kind of use of poetry. I don't share Bob's views on Vietnam either, and I wouldn't have participated if he had asked me. But mainly I think that poetry is very badly served by being used as a medium for propaganda. I don't know whether it is wrong for those poets to do it, I only know that it would be wrong for me to do it. That is the thing that concerns me when I am asked, or not asked, to participate in these things.

I signed a petition for the release of those two Russian writers.[11] I did that because I wanted to do anything I could to get them released. I think that they were unfairly imprisoned, from what little I know, and I was happy to sign the petition for the *Partisan Review*.

My ability to prognosticate on international politics is very, very limited, and I do not, and would not, set myself up as a moral force knowing the right thing to do when the President and the Secretary of State presumably, as far as I'm concerned, do not know. This seems to contain a rather large element of hubris, of which Mr. Bly sadly is not lacking. Bob is a person whom I respect and like very much, but I cannot, in all honesty, say that I approve of his participation in things of this sort. He writes poems telling about what a contemptible man Dean Rusk is, for example, as though he knew this to be a fact. The fact is that Dean Rusk is a man of enormous integrity as far as I can tell. That is, I don't have any secret insights to say that he isn't. Bly apparently assumes that he isn't, but speaks as though he knows it to be the case. This seems to me to be immoral. He obviously does not know.

EDITOR: The program in Oshkosh was prefaced by the statement that these poets were not attempting to give the last word on what should be done in Vietnam. They were commenting on a human condition, war, that they very much disapproved of. They were trying to give the first word on the basic approach that should be taken to this enormous problem.

DICKEY: What is the basic approach?

EDITOR: More of a humanitarian approach than a strictly political approach.

DICKEY: I don't know that you can separate those things. Obviously men of good will are going to use politics to further humanitarian aims, but so too are men of bad will going to use politics and military aggression to further their aims. I am really not competent to go into the whole Vietnam question. I don't know that much about it. I am not a statesman; I am not an international economist, nor a militarist, nor a political observer. I don't like to see people get murdered by napalm. I don't like to see mass bombings. I don't like to see people killed on the other side of the world or near home. But I have seen the results of appeasement, and I know how many lives were lost when Hitler was not stopped at Munich. This is the lesson that I think of. There may not be any parallels here; again there may be. I am in some senses rather naive politically. But I do not assume that I know all the answers so that I can get up on a platform and blithely give people the word. I do not presume that I have the competence.

If we could abolish war and have a world where everybody loves each other, that would be fine. If we could do that by getting up on platforms and reading mediocre poems, as Bly does, then that also would be fine; that would serve a very great purpose if it really would abolish war. However, in the world as it actually exists, freedom and human rights that men have fought for, for hundreds and thousands of years, under certain circumstances have got to be protected by force. What would Hitler have done? What would Hitler not have been able to do if we had taken a pacifistic attitude toward him? We'd say, "Gee, it's awfully inhuman of you to put those people in those furnaces; you shouldn't do it!" You have to recognize the fact that there are certain people who are not at all amenable to any kind of moral appeal. When they threaten you, you have no choice but to meet them with force.

EDITOR: In the spring issue of *The Sixties* there was a parody of your poetry. It is called "James Dickey in Orbit." Are you familiar with it?

DICKEY: Yes, I am, and I know the boy who wrote it. He is a very good friend of mine. I saw him in Washington last month and I told him the best parody of my work was in his own book, which is published by the Louisiana State University Press, and is supposedly serious poetry.[12] I think his first book is very good, and he is going to be a very good writer, but that parody, and the parody he did of "Nimera," are not very funny. That's the trouble with *The Sixties* anyway. They are so heavy-handed, so obvious. I got a few chuckles out of a few of the Awards of the Blue Toad, but the accusations that Bob makes are so wild, so obviously untrue, in most cases, that the satire is pretty much lost.

EDITOR: Robert Lowell commented that he would rather not

Things Happen 35

publish his poetry in the *New Yorker* because of the things they do with the presentations, such as putting the poem on the same page as a cartoon. Have you any comment on this?

DICKEY: No, I don't object to that at all. In fact, I have been trying to get them to put me on with a better class of joke. Why should I object? Does it always have to be nothing but the sacrosanct presence of the Lowell poem on the page? I used to get a little perturbed with *Harper's Bazaar* when I was between the girdles and the brassieres. Sometimes in those magazines, the glossy women's magazines, I do think that poetry is a throwaway item. But not in the *New Yorker*. They make a conscientious effort to get the best they can get. Elizabeth Bishop, who is a good friend of Lowell's, a very much overrated writer, is always in the *New Yorker*. Roethke, by far the best poet we have ever had in this country, a hundred thousand times better than Lowell himself in my opinion, was in there a good deal.

They publish a lot of things that are supposed to be only momentarily amusing. They are making an anthology of poems that have appeared in the *New Yorker*[13] which will be out, I guess, next year. I challenge any other magazine to put out a comparable one. The *Kenyon Review,* the *Sewanee Review,* I challenge any of them. Really, that is the test, I think.

EDITOR: Getting back to the students in America, and your travels to universities around this country, what do you have to say about the general quality of literary magazines that are published by students?

DICKEY: I don't know. I don't think they are very good usually. I've seen some good ones. Poems—of course those are the first things I read—seem to be more or less of the "fuck you" type, you know, the Ginsberg type. People can't realize how profoundly unshocking that is, and how really uninteresting. It's like that same kind of lingo in the army. They use that particular Anglo-Saxonism. It has become so much of a cliché of military lingo that it has nothing whatever to do with what it purports to talk about, sex. It's only something you say, a stock response, like saying "red is a rose." It is only dirty rather than picturesque. Poetry is the unique verbal formulation, rather than the stock, or cliché. And the clichés of the Beatniks are among the most dreary that I can conceivably think of. This is the kind of thing that you find mostly in college magazines. They seem to think that in order to say something memorable, one has only to say something which in the 1920s was thought shocking or daring. That is not so. It is difficult to make a good phrase. Let them try *that* for a while.

3
POET WITH POWER: JAMES DICKEY

NANCY MALONE / 1967

When I first entered Mr. Dickey's office,[14] he was going through a stack of mail and handed me a letter. A college wanted him to read poetry and play the guitar—a program he enjoys giving whenever time permits. Also on his desk was a letter from sixth graders in California. They had studied his poem, "The Shark's Parlor," and had some questions. "Why," one boy asked, "is the poem so long?" Mr. Dickey laughed at that one as though he'd heard it before—especially from young people.

After he had finished his mail, we began talking, and I asked how a high school football star had turned out to be a poet. He smiled broadly and leaned back in his chair. "I'll have to confess," he said in his mellow Georgia accent, "that when I grew up in Atlanta, poetry was the last thing on my mind. I had time for nothing but sports.

"You'd have to say I backed into poetry. I had a very good freshman year at Clemson and dreamed of being a big football star. But World War II was on, and I left to join the Air Force. I ended up flying night missions in the Pacific. This meant that I spent all day in foxholes beside airstrips. I either had to read or write or stare at my feet.

"I read—everything I could get my hands on. I was fascinated by William Faulkner and Thomas Wolfe. I felt these authors were somehow trying to use words for higher things. And I thought that if they were reaching for something higher, that was the direction to go. So then I began reading anthologies of poetry."

When the war was over, James Dickey sacrificed football at

Reprinted from *Read*, 17 (15 November 1967), 10–12. Permission granted by *Current Science*, published by Field Publications. Copyright© 1967 by Field Publications.

Clemson for poetry at Vanderbilt University. As a transfer student, he could not play varsity football, but he was still active enough in sports to become the Tennessee state champion in the 120-yard high hurdles.

He was graduated with highest honors in 1949, took his master's degree in 1950, and began teaching freshman English at Rice University in Houston. When the Korean War broke out, he went back into the Air Force as a training officer. Later he became a well-paid advertising man in New York City. During all this time he worked seriously at poetry. In 1961 he quit his advertising job and devoted full time to writing.

What kind of poetry comes from a man who has been a football player, a track star, a night fighter, and a successful ad man? Powerful poetry.

All of these roles required enthusiasm and dedication. As James Dickey talked, I could see that his energy now poured into his poetry. He wanted to savor life, to understand it, to put it into words.

Read had arranged his poem, "The Shark's Parlor," as a choral reading. It is a powerful work, and I wanted to know how it had come about. "Usually my poems are triggered by something that actually happened," Mr. Dickey explained. "But I just made up 'The Shark's Parlor.' The poem was supposed to be in two parts. The first would describe a skin diver swimming in the sea—the shark's parlor. Then the shark would come into the man's parlor. But the first part didn't work out.

"The poem is really a tale of pure adventure that takes place off the coast of Georgia. It's a poem about being young and having to face more than you're prepared for. The speaker is a middle-aged man who is remembering when he was a boy and suddenly had to fight the full force of nature as represented by the shark.

"If there's symbolism in the poem, that's it. The speaker has hooked on to more than he can handle, and the world explodes in his face.

"The boys in the poem know the rudiments of shark fishing. You put some bait on a hook, tie a buoy to it, and wait until a shark takes the line and pulls the buoy under. But the boys get something big, something they didn't bargain for—an eight- or nine-foot hammerhead.

"It would be the same as boys hunting for rabbits and flushing a bear. There are plenty of small fish in the sea, even small sharks. Who'd ever expect anything like this?

"When the speaker recalls this scene as a man, he remembers not the panic but the results—the blood that's still on the wall. That blood is his evidence. It proves that a tremendous natural force once came right into his parlor.

"The incident has a special place in the man's memory. It speaks to him in his middle age. It reminds him how close he was to the world of wild nature. Other people might remember a hurricane, a mountain-climbing trip—anything that tested them against the force of nature.

"The man tries to see into the depths of this incident. At the end of the poem he is just beginning to get its importance. He places his head against the blood spot on the wall to communicate with this essence of raw nature. He feels an exhilaration—'something like three-dimensional dancing.' You know, like moving in the water.

"He feels himself in many opposite worlds—the world of the shark and the world of man, the world of death and the world of life, the world of youth and the world of age, the world of the actual and the world of the symbolic. He begins to understand that his encounter with the shark was an important event in his life."

Mr. Dickey paused, then continued. "I really believe that. But you know most people don't take the time or don't dare to think about the significance of encounters. Everybody is so busy being cool, acting like John Wayne. I'll tell you," Mr. Dickey said, his voice rising, "those John Wayne roles are responsible for a great deal of America's misconceptions of life. John Wayne projects an ideal of manhood that leaves out eighty percent of the personality. He's cool. He doesn't dare be tender or let anything touch him.

"Well, I do. I think my poems are a success when I can combine daring *and tenderness*. When you eliminate feeling, what's left? Kids should let themselves feel. The universe is a very great thing. Young people are seeing it fresh and they should savor it— take time to look at an ant crawling up a tree. They should get into themselves and relish their experiences, think about them, compare them to other things.

"That's not childish," Mr. Dickey said, his voice now quiet and serious, "that's mature. Maturity is realizing that the world is much more mysterious than you thought it was. Any incident in your life is more significant than you think it is at the time. It keeps growing and enlarging—just as you grow as a person. Each encounter has more implications than you could have expected. That's what 'The Shark's Parlor' is about."

Then with a smile he added, "I hope your readers enjoy my poem."

4

JAMES DICKEY: AN INTERVIEW
FRANCIS ROBERTS / 1968

ROBERTS: Jim, what is the merit, if any, in a poet's winning a prize like the N.B.A.?

DICKEY: I think it has some merit on the logistical side. It helps call attention to poetry and poets and helps to get them read. But if anyone enters into the writing of poetry for the purpose of awards, he's putting himself on and he's trying to put his readers on, too. That isn't what poetry's all about. That isn't what poetry must necessarily aspire to be.

ROBERTS: After all your other lives, in two wars, in the advertising business, what brought you finally to the life of the poet?

DICKEY: I'd been writing poetry all along. I was nineteen when I first went into the service and I had plenty of time between flying missions to read. My mother sent me some books, some of them with poems in them. I've never seen anybody do anything I didn't believe I could do better, and I started in writing poetry and, somehow, I got hooked on it and I've been at it ever since. I didn't mind the business world while I was in it. I liked business people, and I liked the horse trading I had to do. I was a damn good horse trader, too. I drove a damn hard bargain. If I had seven or eight lives, I'd like to spend one as a football or track coach, and I'd like to spend one as a deep sea diver or professional hunter, but I have only one life, so I choose the thing that is most indispensable in my life and swing with it.

ROBERTS: Have you drawn heavily on your war experiences in your writing?

Reprinted from *Per/Se* [Stanford, Calif.], 3 (Spring 1968), 8–12.

DICKEY: My first book had a section about war. My second book had a couple of poems about war, and my third book had a long one called "Drinking from a Helmet." In this new one, *Buckdancer's Choice,* I have a very long poem called "The Firebombing," which was first published in *Poetry,*[15] but I think that's about all the writing about war I'm going to do.

ROBERTS: The Vietnam War hasn't restimulated you?

DICKEY: No, because I've only experienced it vicariously.

ROBERTS: Is that one of your tenets as a writer: that you write always from direct experience?

DICKEY: No, not always. Sometimes I do write about things that happen to me, or I could write about something I've only heard about, or, very frequently, I'll write about something I've wanted to happen to me. It can be that I'll write a poem because I'm bothered by a single word or an image or a rhythm I can't get out of my head that seems to demand expression.

ROBERTS: Do you think these lyrical, arialike passages you write are attuned to a basic rhythm that underlies your whole life experience?

DICKEY: That's almost impossible to say. If anybody were to ask me which my work owed the most to—the English prosodic and syntactical tradition or the folk guitar, I wouldn't know how to answer. I do play the guitar—at least I play *at* it—and I have an idea that the consistent listening to chord changes and the way the rhythms go and the pulse of the music have a great deal to do with the way I write. I'm sort of afraid to examine exactly how it works. If you examine something like that too much, you become too rational about it, and you lose the natural reflex of it.

ROBERTS: Who are some of the writers you like or borrow from?

DICKEY: I have no conscious feeling of ever borrowing from anybody. My first reaction when I read somebody I like is to say, "Dickey, go thou and do otherwise." I don't want his thing. I want my thing. I generally admire writers whose work doesn't have any direct affinity with my own. I think Theodore Roethke is the greatest poet we've ever had. I like Whitman very much and Emily Dickinson, although read in bulk she

An Interview 43

tends to be less rewarding. This is never true of Whitman. He has a great cumulative effect. In the English language I like— oh, Lord, there's so many—I think Yeats is a very great poet and Ezra Pound. Pound rid poetry of all the decor and poeticisms and nineteenth-century trappings, the age-of-Tennyson things that sounded pretty but didn't mean anything.

ROBERTS: What about Dylan Thomas?

DICKEY: He's magical some of the time, but a little bit too rhetorical for me.

ROBERTS: How about Eliot?

DICKEY: Eliot is someone I like and admire without loving. Edwin Muir is a wonderful poet, and not many people know him over here, but I think he's almost the equal of Yeats and maybe even his superior. Among the younger fellows, I think Ted Hughes is very good and Geoffrey Hill and Jon Silkin.

ROBERTS: Why can't you love Mr. Eliot?

DICKEY: He seems to be fending off experience with one hand and clinically noting down clever things to say about it with the other. I like someone who is more involved, a little less Olympian in his judgments. I think a very great poet in French is Jules Supervielle. I don't think he's even been translated here. Eluard is another French poet I like. In Italy: Montale. I think Montale is the greatest living poet and he hasn't even been translated over here. I mean, when they give the Nobel Prize to Salvatore Quasimodo and they ignore Eugenio Montale and Giuseppe Ungaretti, there's something rotten in Denmark, or wherever it is they give all that money away.

ROBERTS: Don't many of these Nobel Prize winners, like George Seferis and Alexis Leger [Saint John Perse] have that scholarly, eclectic tone of voice in their poetry that Eliot has?

DICKEY: Seferis has a Mediterranean warmth and responsiveness Eliot doesn't have, although he has translated some of Eliot's things.

ROBERTS: Isn't Hemingway one writer you both admire and love?

DICKEY: What I love is his ability to say so much in so little space—his ability to use silences and understatement. He doesn't talk a subject to death. In a sense, the reader becomes a creative writer by following his hints and filling out the story he leaves blank. It reminds me of a story I heard once—perhaps apocryphal—about Mozart. Someone asked him what kind of music he liked best and he said, "No music." By which he meant that the expressive part of music is contained in the rests between the notes. The sounds are put there just to make the silences more pregnant. There's a very real sense of silences in Hemingway. He once said that he wrote on the principle of the iceberg. The part that wrecks your ship is the greatest part, and that's under water.

ROBERTS: In your poems I notice you use a contemporary American idiom and your settings and characters are contemporary.

DICKEY: I'm not really conscious of that. I have no Apollinairian sense of striving after the necessity of being absolutely modern.

ROBERTS: Although I know you've studied philosophy in college, you strike me as being anti-intellectual.

DICKEY: I've been called that before. I read a good deal and ponder, but you're right: I don't consider myself to be an intellectual at all. I suppose what I really want is to find a way to experience and to write without too much intervention of thought, without the ratiocination people like Proust do so well. I want to be able to love somebody without endlessly analyzing my motives.

ROBERTS: You sub-majored in astrophysics, didn't you? What is it you get out of subjects like astrophysics and philosophy?

DICKEY: I don't study them actively to get images for poems. I guess I just enjoy knowing things. I like to work my mind, such as it is, to see what I can get out of it and put into it. As John Livingston Lowes revealed in that wonderful book on Coleridge, *The Road to Xanadu*,[16] if these things are in your mind, Lord knows what amalgams you can get out of it.

ROBERTS: You don't believe, then, that "Euclid alone / Has looked on Beauty bare"?

DICKEY: Lord, no! I think Euclid had a relatively bleak view of things. Pythagoras is much more exciting to me because of the connection with music, the music of the spheres, the admixture of geometry and music as being concommitants of the same entity. I like the pre-Socratic philosophers a lot. Heraclitus of Ephesus and Anaximander are great people to me.

ROBERTS: Am I to assume, then, that all your poetry is an evocation of a human situation you're aware of or have been involved in?

DICKEY: I suppose, though I wouldn't be capable of saying anything definitive about it. So much of it's a matter of feeling. What I really do want in living, as well as in writing, is a kind of an animal-like response. The best line of poetry I know is by a little-known French poet named René Ménard: "Beasts, before you my body is a lost grace." I was watching birds today perching on telephone wires, and I never saw one remotely missing what he was trying to do, no matter how hard or which way the wind was blowing. They were always perfectly and instinctively masters of their situation. That kind of thing is what I aspire to do in writing—to make the thing seem so natural that the earth itself might have said it, and that's mighty hard to get. I firmly believe if it could really be understood and somehow maybe miraculously gotten into language, the whole concept of what poetry is and what it can do would be immediately changed. I read the so-called great poems in the English language—Donne, Yeats, Hopkins—and it seems to me the surface hasn't even been scratched yet. It seems to me that a poetry can be written that is so far beyond any of these pleasant little tinkling, proper, sonnetlike forms that somebody's just got to do it.

ROBERTS: Do you think this proceeds from a kind of a Swedenborgian or Jungian stream—?

DICKEY: God, I don't know.

ROBERTS: Is it oracular? Is it Delphic?

DICKEY: Yes, I guess ultimately it is, but, again, I can only catch a glimpse of it, but I can't sustain it. I can sometimes keep it going for a line or two, sometimes, maybe, for part of a stanza, but the form hasn't yet been found. I don't know that it can be found or that this kind of writing can exist, but I'm going on the assumption that it could exist.

ROBERTS: Is writing difficult for you? Is it something you enjoy?

DICKEY: Both, both. I work on things an awful long time. This poem on slavery, "Slave Quarters," that was first published in the *New Yorker*,[17] has been in my notebook in one form or another for seven or eight years. Somebody called me facile once. It made me mad as hell. I don't usually take exception to any adverse reviews, but that really bugs me. It's so irresponsible. They have no idea of the work that goes into this stuff for me. A good many things of mine are coming out now because they've matured now, though I've been working on them some five, maybe even ten years. People think I just dash the stuff off. Well, nothing could be further from the truth. However, the first part of writing is always the most exciting, when you first get an inkling and you get a few scrappy lines down that seem to connect with each other and seem to have some imminent connection with what you suspect the poem might ultimately be about. The completed poem never is, nor could be, as good as you think it's going to be at that first flush of excitement over it. Listen, I've just started a poem today. It's about cave men, and I call it "Cave Master." I don't know anything at all about cave men, and I'm not going to do very much research; but it's about this primitive thing I was telling you about and about animism. You know there are all those marvelous prehistoric bison and caribou that were painted on the walls of the caves at Altamira in Northern Spain. They were ritual objects, and the paintings themselves are slashed and stuck as if they were used as the surrogate for the real animal. It seemed to me that this kind of magical interpretation in this kind of stony, bleak place could be a kind of a paradigm for the artisitic endeavor anyway. Whoever controls the cave controls the world. I think that's going to be the idea. I'm not sure.

ROBERTS: While you were talking, I thought of Whitman's poem about the learned astronomer.

DICKEY: Yes, the astronomer could tell you a lot of facts about the stars, but only someone like Whitman could appreciate their natural, marvelous, magical power. What did he say in the poem? "I wandered off by myself, / In the mystical moist night-air, and from time to time, / Look'd up in perfect silence at the stars." I'm reminded of when Juan Ramón Jiménez, a poet I greatly admire, won the Nobel Prize and there was a flurry of journalistic excitement; they tried to get him to make some profound statement about poetry. They asked him who was his favorite poet and he said, "God." That's the only interview they ever got out of Jiménez.

ROBERTS: I get a very strong feeling from reading your poems that you're a moralist.

DICKEY: I guess in some ways I am. I'm not an excessively moral man, but I know what morality is, and I aspire to it. I write about family things because it seems to me to be so miraculous. To have a child, to give somebody else a chance to be! I mean, what could be more miraculous than that? They'll never explain that to me in terms of—what is this new thing? DNA? But to bring a little creature into existence, who can in the end stand up and tell you to go to hell, that's wonderful. My children do all the time. Their favorite word for me is "decadent." Doubtless, they're right.

ROBERTS: I don't sense in your work any of the feeling of alienation that is found in so much modern writing.

DICKEY: Life to me is an incredible joy. You were in the Korean War, Frank. You survived somehow. So did I. . . . That's largely my orientation. Just to drive down the street, or to sit around and play the guitar, and to have a couple of beers with the next fellow—that's wonderful to me. Do you remember the scene where Odysseus goes down to the shades and sees Achilles again and Achilles tells him that he'd rather be the lowliest pot boy among the living than king of all the dead?

ROBERTS: After your first book, which was all in rhyme, you've gotten more and more away from it. Why is that?

DICKEY: Because of the element of artifice in rhyme. I like rhyme less and less and, even in great poems, I dislike it. No matter how well it's handled rhyme as artifice sets me at just that much more of a remove from the situation depicted. Rhythm? Fine. Meter? Fine. But the English language is rhyme-poor and you have to go through such contortions to get your poem to work out. I don't want to have to concentrate too much energy on that particular problem of poetry. I think the poem should sound as natural as if told to the reader in confidence. I distrust anyone whose heart breaks in faultless hexameters.

ROBERTS: Who is this reader you want to be confidential with? What is he like?

DICKEY: He's one person, carefully selected, a person called "Humanity." No, he's not. He could be, or you'd like him to be. He's the person who might conceivably be able to take something useful to him from the poem. He's that person and, believe or not, I get mail from him. You know you get some strange mail when you write poems. One fellow wrote to me who was out on a lion hunt in Africa. Another one wrote from Australia. You don't know, when you beam out your poem into space, who's going to hear it and be moved by it. It's a very strange kind of—almost metaphysical kind of—communication. What fascinates me is that you not only don't know who's going to read it, but you don't know how they're going to accept it or how they've come to encounter it in the first place.

ROBERTS: Do you believe, as Frost did, that a poem is a momentary stay against confusion or mortality?

DICKEY: If you knew, as they say in reviews, that your poems "will be read as long as the English language is spoken," that would be an added increment, earned or even unearned. I'm conscious of working in a tradition with great poets, but I don't write for that reason. I don't write to become immortal. I only want to articulate as accurately as I can something that has caught my interest as potential material for a poem because it moved me as a man.

ROBERTS: Jim, you've been teaching for several years and you travel around the country a lot reading, appearing on panels and so on. Does this add to or take away from your writing?

DICKEY: Teaching is a welcome respite for me from writing. I'm a compulsive writer. I have to find ways to get away from it. It's a disease and has, I guess, been fatal in more than one instance.

ROBERTS: To ask you a final question: What is your advice to a beginning writer?

DICKEY: I'd say to him, "Don't fool yourself." The worst thing a young writer can do is to say, "I wrote this thing and it's good because I wrote it." That's very self-defensive. You've got to be able to do two things. First, you've got to be able to cut loose and get it down spontaneously and let the thing flow of its own nature. Second, you've got to have another part of your personality that stands back and looks at it to see if the direction is right, to see if this or that detail needs changing. You've got to be both spontaneous and critical at the same time, and this may seem contradictory, but it really isn't. When the stuff is really flowing, the critic in you folds his arms and sits back and says, "Yes, Dickey, you're on it. Keep it going." But he also, when the élan and the spontaneity have run out—which it sometimes does after only a few words—must be able to say, "Now look, Jim, I like it when you say this, but you're wrong when you say that." So the best thing for a young writer is to develop his spontaneity and also his critical faculty, which is as unvarying as the metrical measures of distance—as Hemingway suggested somewhere. It's got to be absolutely inflexible, and the poet has to make himself stick to it. A poet trains himself to stand out in a storm and be struck by lightning. If he is lucky enough to be struck six times, he becomes immortal. Randall Jarrell said it, and he's right.

5
JAMES DICKEY DESCRIBES HIS LIFE AND WORKS AS HE "MOVES TOWARD HERCULES"

JOHN LOGUE / 1971

LOGUE: Just let us pick it up on the status of *Deliverance* at this point.

DICKEY: Well, as far as the sales are concerned—the last bestseller list I saw was yesterday, and it has been on the bestseller list for seven months now and I think it is about sixth or seventh at the end of seven months. I don't have any idea how long it will stay on there. It should be a good long time—about 100,000 copies sold.

LOGUE: When you finished it, did you anticipate a great public success?

DICKEY: I had no idea, because I didn't have any precedent—that is, I had never published a novel before and I didn't really know how it would be received or how it would be reviewed. There are an awful lot of novels that are published, but as soon as there was such an enormous advance sale on it, I began to take a very lively interest in that aspect. It was a whole new ball game, I'll tell you, as far as money and publicity are concerned. It was quite a different ball game from publishing poetry in the *Kenyon Review* at 50 cents a line.

LOGUE: I think I started this thing backward, since you are first a poet and not only a novelist, but has this—the publication of a novel and certainly becoming such a public person—

Reprinted with permission from *Southern Living*, No. 6 (February 1971), 44–49, 60, 65.

has it made your work any more difficult or any more pressurized?

DICKEY: No, that doesn't seem to figure into it because I've been a public person in some way or another for ten years, going around lecturing and giving readings in colleges, and it really is no different to me to speak at a book-and-author luncheon than it is to speak to a group of people who come to hear a poetry reading. It is not any cataclysmic change for me. It was a little bit intensified when I was trying to give readings and do all these publicity things for the novel too, but I solved all that simply by not taking on any more readings.

LOGUE: I was thinking also of now and forever more being under the gun, in the sense that your first time out of the chute you were such a success with this book and, of course, you have been quite successful as a poet, winning the National Book Award for *Buckdancer's Choice*.

DICKEY: I don't feel any commitment at all to the novelistic hit parade, as someone else like Philip Roth or Bill Styron or Norman Mailer might do; to feel that I have to have a bestseller every four years or something. I don't feel any such compulsion at all. I do want to write one more novel, or maybe two, but they are a long way away. I've got to think them out. I don't really care for the money and all the rest of it, if what I write does not satisfy me. If you let go the standards by which you work, which should be as high as you can set them within the realm of reasonability, if you let those standards go, then you are really not worth anything to yourself as a writer or as an artist. The writer himself should be the hardest to please of anybody.

LOGUE: You have been functioning against your own standard of perfection?

DICKEY: That's right. Yes, that is really all I have.

LOGUE: Then success is not going to increase that?

DICKEY: No. Not a bit. It stays the same.

LOGUE: You, I believe, told me earlier that you had worked on *Deliverance* off and on for about six or seven years.

DICKEY; Yes, but that is kind of misleading in a way, because that might cause people to suppose that I did nothing but sit down and work on that one book four hours a day for all those years. That's not true. I wrote five other books during that time and *Deliverance* was really not the high priority item at all. It was just something I enjoyed messing around with, changing the elements of it around and seeing if I could get the characters distinct from each other, working out the problems of prose fiction that I hadn't very much acquaintance with. I enjoyed it, but I never thought I would finish the book until Houghton Mifflin sent a man out to Portland, Oregon, where I was then living, with a contract for it. They agreed to publish it on the strength of a very skimpy ninety-page draft. Then I figured, well, goodness, I've accepted the money from these people and I really have some kind of moral obligation to finish it one of these days, but the emphasis was really on "one of these days." I kept plugging away at it, though, and changing it around and I finally got the style I wanted, which was the hardest thing of all.

LOGUE: Was this because you did not want to repeat yourself as a poet?

DICKEY: Well, I didn't want to write so-called (and I'll put this in quotations) "poetic prose"—most of that is awfully dull, makes very bad reading. The center of this novel is the action line—the narrative thrust of it—and if you impede that, or sidetrack it with a lot of fancy descriptive stuff, you are bleeding out the most effective element of the story. So, I had to have something, a kind of style that was unobtrusive and that would be convincing as something spoken by the narrator, given his life situation. For example, Ed Gentry is above average in intelligence—maybe a little bit more than that—but he's not a literary man; he's no John Updike going down the river. His perceptions are good and clean, but I tried not to put them in language that would call attention to itself. The story is the main thing, and not the language in which the story is told—that is secondary.

LOGUE: We are just going to assume that everybody has read *Deliverance,* and if they haven't, they should. We are not going to give any massive examination of the novel here, because it's become so celebrated that I don't think it's necessary. Now last

Dickey Describes His Life and Works 53

night, I read your screenplay for a movie on *Deliverance*. I was not aware that you had done this.

DICKEY: My agent in New York, when he negotiated the contract with Warner Brothers for the novel, got one of the stipulations to be that I would do the screenplay. Doubtless there are a lot more experienced people in Hollywood who might conceivably do it, but there is not anybody in the world since time began who knows *that* story as well as I do. After all, I made it up!

LOGUE: I was struck by your awareness of the mechanical or the technical problems in making a movie. Did you research this?

DICKEY: No, I wrote a couple of movies—documentaries—when I lived in Hollywood.

LOGUE: What were they about?

DICKEY: One of them was financed by Grumman Aircraft and was about aircraft carriers.[18] I didn't really much like what I did. Rather, I liked what I did well enough, but what *they* did with what I did, I didn't like. The only screen credit that I have got that I have any sense of accomplishment in is a film that I did for USIA[19]—it was loosely based on John F. Kennedy's *A Nation of Immigrants*. A very creative young fellow named Bill Hale and I did that and it ran, I think about twenty-five minutes. I did the voice-over narration and the continuity and Ben Gazzara did the voice for us, and it came out very well.

LOGUE: Have you picked a director for the movie?

DICKEY: I want John Boorman, who did *Point-Blank* and *Hell in the Pacific*. My business was to turn the script in, which I have done, and so I've fulfilled my part of the contract. Now it depends on what John Calley and the other people at Warner Brothers do; they have all their commitments and their deals and their know-how.

LOGUE: What was their reaction to your screenplay?

DICKEY: They liked it very much.

LOGUE: But you wrote the screenplay after they bought the novel?

DICKEY: Yes; they bought the novel and then they bought the screenplay. The script was a whole separate contract. They give you a certain amount of money on turning in the script and then if they don't want to do it, you just keep the money—it is their property since you accepted their money for it, and they just go ahead and do with it whatever they want to do. But this time they're going to do it my way. If there is some revision to be done, then they ask you to do that and there's a new contract and some money for doing it.

LOGUE: You mentioned John Boorman.

DICKEY: Yes; he's a brilliant director.

LOGUE: Let me ask you this. Do you have any personal preferences for who is going to have the lead roles in the film?

DICKEY: John and I have talked about it.

LOGUE: What has been the reaction of the acting world?

DICKEY: Apparently it has stirred up more response among directors and actors than anything that has been out there in a long time. It is one of the two major wide-screen productions that Warners is going to take on this year.

LOGUE: When are they going to start?

DICKEY: In April. What I would like is to do a good deal of the filming around the time the paperback comes out, which'll be in the spring. That is when books really get read. To make a profit, say, comparable to what we have made on *Deliverance* in hardbacks so far (that is, to this particular day as we sit here now, on about a little over 100,000 copies), Paperback Dell Books, who is going to do it, would have to sell a million copies. There is just a different order of production and so on. But that is where the book really gets read: when it comes out in paper. I would like to coordinate the release of the movie with the height of the paperback readership, if I could.

LOGUE: Without getting into any of your personal financial life, this book has really changed your picture totally. I mean, as a very successful poet, one who has won most of the awards in this country. I don't know how books of poetry sell—yours have been popular—

Dickey Describes His Life and Works

DICKEY: Well, they have been popular, but only compared to other poetry. They sell very well, though. My most recent book that came out in February has sold about 15,000 copies, which is remarkable for a book of poems, unless you are Rod McKuen or some other pseudo-poet.

LOGUE: Is that *The Eye-Beaters?*

DICKEY: Yes.

LOGUE: It's the best cover I've ever seen.

DICKEY: I suggested the cover—I used to be an agency creative director. You liked that sort of psychedelic, garish stuff?

LOGUE: I don't know anything about art, but this thing just leaps across the room.

DICKEY: It stands out very well in the bookstore. Alex Gotfryd is one of the art directors at Doubleday, and he and I got together on it. I asked him what his idea was and he wanted to do kind of a serene blue sky thing, and I said, "No, no, Alex. I want something with abstract properties that give the effect of chaos, turbulence, violence." And so what he did was to take some indissoluble dyes and put them in a solution (I forget what it was) and swirled them around and photographed the whole whirling mass of different colors.

LOGUE: What I was thinking just now was that your poetry, as opposed to other poetry, has been popular, but the advent of this novel and the motion picture contract has changed your financial structure as far as your working base, and it makes you more independent.

DICKEY: Yes. And I am very grateful for that. I am not a frugal person. I spend most of my money on other people. You know, I just have a few things of my own that are expensive. I like to collect guitars and archery equipment and books and records, but outside of that I don't have anything to spend money on except my family. And it *is* nice to be able to travel. Money really buys life; it buys experience. If you have it and if you want to go for a while to Europe, you can do it. Most people long for things like that all their life and they are not able ever to do them. I like to have the feeling of mobility that money gives you. I believe this business of penny-pinching and economizing and so on is spiritually degrading to people, don't you?

LOGUE: I tell you what: I think that poverty is not a noble thing.

DICKEY: No, I don't think it has anything noble about it at all.

LOGUE: Somehow some people seem to think it is—I would say it is even a philosophy of a breed of modern persons.

DICKEY: That's a terrible mistake. There is a point beyond which money is not desirable. I mean, when it bleeds off into frivolity and spending money to keep yourself amused. But there are different kinds of people with money. I am not positing myself as someone who is all that rich. I am only rich compared to what I was before.

LOGUE: I believe you told me that maybe your screenplay might be published.

DICKEY: I may publish parts of it in magazines, I think, and then maybe bring it out in a book if people are interested enough in it.

LOGUE: I think they will be. Have any actors contacted you?

DICKEY: Yes, a good many. And I've talked to a few of them on other occasions. I was on the Jim Conway Show in New York with Charlton Heston about two months ago, for example. He is an awfully nice fellow. I said, "How would you like to play Lewis?" And he said, "I'd give anything to play Lewis." Of the actors I've talked to, that's the part they all want to play. They don't want to play the narrator; they want to play Lewis. Lancaster, for example. He'd be awfully good, too.

LOGUE: Why is this, since Lewis disappears for so long during the heat of the book?

DICKEY: I don't know. It's the kind of person he is, I guess.

LOGUE: Did that surprise you?

DICKEY: Yes, it did. The big part is the part of the narrator, of course.

LOGUE: Well, since we have put the cart before the horse, let's go back just a minute. When I first knew you passingly in Atlanta, I don't think you were practicing poetry at the time.

Dickey Describes His Life and Works

DICKEY: Well, I was. I don't know how long ago that was—in the mid-50s?

LOGUE: Middle 50s—1957.

DICKEY: Yes, I was publishing in magazines. My first book came out when I was thirty-seven, ten years ago. It was called *Into the Stone* and it was published by Scribners in their large economy-size package of three first-poetry books. They had a series called "Poets of Today," in which eight volumes were published. They had three first books of three writers every year, and they packaged them in a very handsome format and published the three together. I was in the seventh of the eight volumes.

LOGUE: Have the others prospered?

DICKEY: Let's see. Eight volumes, that's twenty-four poets. And of these I'd say only three or four are, in any sense, names to be reckoned with. The rest you don't hear much about. A lot of them never wrote anything else. Louis Simpson, who won the Pulitzer Prize one year, was one of them and May Swenson is another one who is quite good.

LOGUE: At this time, Jim, were you writing advertising?

DICKEY: Yes. I was selling my soul to the devil all day and trying to buy it back at night. I'd come home and write poetry.

LOGUE: The first book, did you break away after that?

DICKEY: Well, yes, in a way I did. The first book came out in 1960. I left advertising in August 1961. By that time, I had another book ready to go. It came out on my birthday, the 2nd of February, 1962.

LOGUE: Was that a collection of poetry?

DICKEY: Yes, called *Drowning With Others*. On the strength of the first book, *Into the Stone,* I applied for a Guggenheim Fellowship and sent the book in as evidence of the kind of thing I wrote. Anyway, I was given the fellowship and that was kind of my escape hatch from the Atlanta commercial world. I told my wife that we wanted to take the money and go to Europe. I had been working pretty hard for six years in business, and I was thirty-seven or thirty-eight years old. I wanted to move on my own work, because I wasn't going to be one of these people who lives his whole life under the illusion that one of these days he is going to get out and do his own work. I wanted actually to *do* the work instead of talk about it.

LOGUE: Jim, will you give us a little chronology since your first two books?

DICKEY: We left for Europe in 1962, and we didn't have any job to come back to. I thought I would go, you know, into music or something. Give guitar lessons. I really didn't know what I would do when I got back.

LOGUE: You were in Italy?

DICKEY: The south of Italy. South of Sorrento between Sorrento and Amalfi. On those cliffs. John Steinbeck lived in the same village with us. We got a letter from Reed College in Portland, Oregon, saying that they did not have much money, but they could pay me a living wage if I would come out there and be the first writer-in-residence that the school had. We didn't have any other prospects; we went to Portland. I never regretted the decision. It is a rotating thing—they have different writers in. I was the first, and then they had somebody else after that.

LOGUE: What book did you write next?

DICKEY: I wrote—I was going to say, I have never regretted going to Reed because of the friends that I had out there, because the approach to education that Reed College has is the best one that I have seen in any school. I don't think it would be workable in a large school, but it sure worked fine out there. And the town is such a great town for folk music. You know, everybody plays a guitar.

LOGUE: Is that where you picked up the guitar?

DICKEY: That is where I got most of the guitar stuff: the basis for what I play, anyway. I was also working on a book called *Helmets*. I finished that, and one of the very enterprising students there calligraphed two poems and I brought out a gift book called *Two Poems of the Air*. There are only a few copies still around. It's worth a lot of money now, I'm told. There was an original edition of 300, and that was all. They destroyed the plates and everything. It was one of those kinds of things.

LOGUE: They didn't anticipate *Deliverance* or they would have made a few more copies.

DICKEY: Then my first book of criticism came out, printed by a small press, called *The Suspect in Poetry*. Then we had another job offer in California to teach at San Fernando Valley State College, and so we moved down there and we taught there for two years. I finished *Buckdancer's Choice* there. I wrote some more criticism. I did an edition for Macmillan of the poems of Edwin Arlington Robinson and wrote a long introduction to it.[20]

LOGUE: I always liked him so much and I always felt I was kind of lowbrow, or something, you know. Didn't he write "Mr. Flood"?

DICKEY: Yes. "Mr. Flood's Party."

LOGUE: And "To the Wall, Luke. . . ."

DICKEY: Havergal. "Go the western gate. . . ."

LOGUE: That poem always—

DICKEY: I could never figure out who the speaker is.

LOGUE: I felt like he had *me* to the wall!

DICKEY: I'll tell you, I'm crazy about Robinson. He is one of these reticent, Down Eastern types, you know. Then, let's see, in California I worked some more on *Deliverance*. We were going to come back east to be writer-in-residence at Hollins in Virginia. I took so many writer-in-residences that I began to feel kind of like a poetical bum. Not really a legitimate professor at any of these places, but just, you know, one of these people who arranges to walk across the campus at a certain time of day so people can say, "That's him." But before we were to go to Hollins we were offered the consultancy at the Library of Congress, which is the same chair that Robert Frost held and Lowell, and Randall Jarrell and some others. So we went and lived in Washington for two years, during the last part of the Johnson administration and also during the time of all the troubles after the death of Martin Luther King: the riots, the March of the Poor, and so on.

LOGUE: You were in the vortex of—

DICKEY: Boy, I *mean* I was in the vortex. Was it frightening, too. Terrifying. Anyway, after that we came down here to Columbia two years ago.

LOGUE: Your position now is?

DICKEY: Professor of English and writer-in-residence.

LOGUE: What do you teach?

DICKEY: I have two courses. One of them is a writing course, a workshop for poets, and the other one is just a reading course in modern poetry in English. The first semester is English or British Isles poetry and the second is American.

LOGUE: And while you were here, you finished *Deliverance?*

DICKEY: Yes, I finished *Deliverance* about a year ago, I guess. I was surprised by all the plans-making, publicity campaigns, and consulting editors and sales managers and all that. It's quite different from publishing poetry. Not that much attention is paid to poetry. I left Wesleyan Press, which did four of my books, and went to Doubleday, and they've done very well by the books that I have published with them or am getting ready to publish with them. But books of poems are just not in the same moneymaking category as novels. This last book of poems of mine is the best single collection that I have done, too, I think. I don't want it to get swallowed up in the hullabaloo about *Deliverance* any more than I want poetry generally to be swallowed up by the novel, generally.

LOGUE: This is *The Eye-Beaters, Blood, Victory, Madness, Buckhead and Mercy.* It's got, I think, of all contemporary poetry, my favorite poem, about the Buckhead Boys.

DICKEY: "Looking for the Buckhead Boys."

LOGUE: I don't know how this is going to work out, but it's impossible to talk about poetry and get poetry across. How about reading from The Book of the Dead?

DICKEY: All right, if you like. What you have to know is that this is about a fellow who went to high school in a town called Buckhead, and who goes back there as a middle-aged man. Everybody knows the feeling. You get that kind of desperate nostalgia for the old place, and you feel as though you *must*

Dickey Describes His Life and Works

find somebody that you knew in those days. You *have* to find him: *Some*body whom you recognize and who recognizes you. So this man walks around and goes to the drugstore where the fellows used to hang out and he goes to the pool hall, Tyree's, and it's been changed into a shoe store. He goes to the hardware store and there is an old guy there who used to attend the high school football games. A lot of the poem is a dialogue with the old man in the hardware store. The narrator asks him where all the fellows are: what happened to them.

LOGUE: The fellows were also teammates.

DICKEY: Yes, in track and football. The Book of the Dead is what the narrator calls the 1939 high school annual, where he can open the pages and see the pictures of himself and all these people as they used to be. One of the fellows that he remembers from the team is Charlie Gates, and the narrator asks the old hardware store man where he can find Charlies Gates, is he still around, and he's told that Charlie Gates *might* be working at the Gulf station, out north of Buckhead. So the narrator says: "O the Book / Of the Dead, and the dead bright sun on the page / Where the team stands ready to explode / In all directions with Time. . . ." [Dickey reads the last half of the poem with an increasing emotion.]

LOGUE: The only regret I have in this interview is that the written page doesn't articulate itself.

DICKEY: I believe very much that in all poetry, the *sound* of it is very important.

LOGUE: I think it is a great poem. This year you are coming out with a new book.

DICKEY: Yes, it is a kind of a crazy book of monologues and wranglings, called *Self-Interviews*.

LOGUE: When is this going to be out?

DICKEY: It will be out a month from today.

LOGUE: Is this Doubleday, also?

DICKEY: Yes.

LOGUE: Are all of your things going to be published by Doubleday?

DICKEY: Unless I write another novel and then I'll probably stay with Houghton Mifflin. But I might take that over to Doubleday, too. I really don't know yet.

LOGUE: Let's go back just a minute. You grew up in Buckhead.

DICKEY: Yes, I did.

LOGUE: You were a track runner and a football player and you had a brother who was a *great* runner.

DICKEY: Oh, yes, Tom was a very great runner. He ran all during the war. He just missed the 1948 Olympics. He had his track career at LSU uninterrupted, and he made the most of it.

LOGUE: Were you a sprinter?

DICKEY: No, I was a high hurdler. Oh, yes, in a way I was a sprinter, but the 120 highs was really my best event. I think if I could've concentrated on that I'd have done better than I did. I was always running on a team that needed me to do a lot of other stuff too. Run the 100 and the 220, the broad jump, and throw the shot, the discus, run on the relays. I stayed all tired out. I was glad the highs came early in the meet, usually.

LOGUE: Your class, of course, was cast into the holocaust of World War II.

DICKEY: Oh, yes, my whole generation—we just came along at the right time. We were born right after one world war and grew up in the Depression, and fought in another world war and it looks like we are going to die in a third. We haven't had it easy!

LOGUE: You were a flyer.

DICKEY: Yes, I was in night fighters, the 418th Night Fighter Squadron. We flew P-61's, the old Black Widow.

LOGUE: And it made a few widows, too.

DICKEY: I guess so. We had an awfully rough row to hoe. The Pacific war was so much more (I don't know whether to say dangerous)—I don't know what the figures of the people killed over there were—maybe there were more killed in Europe. But I would have gone to Europe anytime in preference to the Pacific. Man, that was rough.

Dickey Describes His Life and Works 63

LOGUE: How many missions did you fly?

DICKEY: I flew about 100, I guess.

. . .

LOGUE: You came back and went to Vanderbilt.

DICKEY: I came back to Vanderbilt under the GI bill. I went through on that and took an M. A. the next year, and then I took on my first job, teaching freshman English and "Technical Composition and Report Writing" at Rice in Houston. I wasn't there for more than two or three months and I was recalled into the service again—Korea—in 1950. I was an instructor in the training command. Then my first boy, Chris, was born. He is married now, and I'm a grandfather. He is in his junior year at the University of Virginia.

LOGUE: And your other son is Kevin?

DICKEY: Yes.

LOGUE: Let's get your wife's name in.

DICKEY: Maxine. But then, let's see, when I came back out of the service from the Korean War, I went back to Rice and I was still a freshman teacher. I was writing a good deal. I had had a poem published in the *Sewanee Review*[21] while I was in the service; I'd written it in college when I was in graduate school. I kept on writing, but nobody would publish anything I wrote. I didn't really care that much about publishing—the thing that mattered to me, as it has ever since, was the doing of it, the writing itself.

LOGUE: Can you put your finger on your first impulse to be a writer? Does it go back to high school?

DICKEY: No. All I was interested in was sports in high school. I think it was in the service. You have time for an awful lot of introspection in the service. A certain kind of person in the service becomes excessively gregarious and another kind withdraws; I had periods of both. I used to read an awful lot. In the barracks of various places where I was stationed, you know, I used to sit and read. A lot of fellows read in the service who never read anywhere else. I've never liked a specific thing without wanting to see if I couldn't do it myself. Same way with playing music and anything else. If I like it, I want to try to participate; no matter on how low a level of participation, I do it. I think participation is better than "appreciation." I like to do it—try to do it. I'm like most American writers—I just kind of backed into writing. There is very little tradition in this country, say, such as they have in France, of a family being "in literature"—like the Mauriacs, for example. Most American writers I know have just drifted into literature from other things, as I did.

LOGUE: Did any particular person at Vanderbilt or anywhere else—

DICKEY: Yes, at Vanderbilt. The first fellow who helped me was a freshman English teacher I had named William Hunter, now head of the English Department at Macalester College of St. Paul, where Hubert Humphrey taught. He was very encouraging to me. But the most influencing was the man who taught me eighteenth century, named Monroe Spears, who later became editor of the *Sewanee Review* and is now teaching at Rice. He wrote, I think, the best book on W. H. Auden.[22] He is really very good: a very reputable, intelligent, resourceful, literary man with a mind like a laser beam. I thought if anybody *that* smart sees anything in what I do, there may be something in it after all! He had me writing long verse satires and couplets and things modeled after John Dryden and Alexander Pope. I don't have any abilities along the eighteenth-century line, but I tried; it was good discipline. I suppose I am more or less, for better or worse, a romantic poet, for whatever these categories may mean or whatever value there is in them. I really began to write, to break through to something else, when I saw the creative possibilities of the lie. You know, I'm like you. I mean, you are from a rural background and all my people are from North Georgia up in the mountains—I mean I am just sort of first-generation suburban. And we always had this thing about lying and about telling the truth; and I thought, boy, if I write poetry, it has got to be absolutely, literally, factually true. And I remember Spears saying to me—he was reading something of mine—"Well, this would be better if you had the narrator do such and such, or this would be better if you said he did such and such at this point." I said, "Well, that's not the way it happened." And he said, "Well, what difference does *that*

Dickey Describes His Life and Works 65

make?" I saw what he meant like a blinding light! I *could* do it that way; it would be better, and it *was* better.

LOGUE: And an invention can make it truer.

DICKEY: That's right. That's what Picasso said. Somebody asked Picasso (can you imagine somebody asking Picasso such a question?) "What is art?" And he had a great answer ready for them. He said, "Art is a lie which makes us see the truth." And he is exactly right. That *is* what it is.

LOGUE: Well, do you think the accelerating effect of living under a war gave you insights?

DICKEY: Oh, yes. I look at my existence from the standpoint of a survivor, which is kind of like being a perpetual convalescent. When the sun comes up every morning, I'm awfully glad to be around. I just feel awfully lucky. I'm here by what amounts to being just vast historical luck. That's all that accounts for my presence on the scene.

LOGUE: You know Hemingway once said about Tolstoy that it was just amazing that he survived to write.

DICKEY: Same thing could be said of Hemingway. I wish he *was* still around!

LOGUE: I think maybe your great discipline—give me your schedule of what you do each day—in wanting to get all you possibly can out of every day—

DICKEY: That comes from the war. I mean, I would be foolish and I would feel that I had betrayed myself and everybody else if I didn't do my absolute best to *use* my time. But there are a lot of places that I fall short. I don't think I have had, since I started this particular schedule (I started it about eighteen months ago), I don't think I have had more than seven or eight days in which I did actually everything on here for these lengths of time.

LOGUE: This is what you are aiming at?

DICKEY: Yes. And the fact that you are trying to do it still enables you to do an awful lot. I get up around six and get dressed and come in and start working on whatever short poems that I am working on, until Maxine calls me for breakfast. All this takes about two hours, and then I start work again at eight and work on the same poems until I begin to lose interest in them, or finish them, or get to a place where I can stop, or whatever happens at nine o'clock. I work until nine o'clock and then put the poems away. And I'm sitting there in a warm-up outfit with tennis shoes on, so that I can just get up from the desk and run around Lake Katherine, here where I live. I just walk out the door and take the dog and start running, and run until I get tired.

LOGUE: Your dog must be in the best condition of any dog on Lake Katherine.

DICKEY: Well, anyway, it takes me an hour—really my record is forty-seven minutes, I think, or something like that.

LOGUE: About three miles?

DICKEY: Three and a half. I don't punish myself. I just run until I get tired, and then I walk awhile and when I get my breath back, I run some more, until I get all the way around. Then I come back and I sit down with a guitar and play an hour. I do the kinds of things in the first hour that I don't like to do—that is, I run scales and do chord work and that sort of thing. I'd like eventually to have a better command of the instrument than most folk players have, so I'm trying all the time to build up a chord vocabulary. I get that out of the way first. And then I start back working on poems, long ones this time. I've been working on one for years called *The Indian Maiden*[23] which is about the splendors and horrors of adultery and being in love with and taking up with somebody you are not married to. That's a subject much explored in fiction and in some poetry, but it has never really been "got." The heights and depths of it have really never been understood. I work on *The Indian Maiden* and another one until 12:30, and then have some kind of light lunch, and socialize a bit with my wife, and I take some kind of physical workout with spring cables, or weights for half an hour, just to be doing something bodily, physically, and then for half an hour I get out books from four or five languages and translate poetry from them, maybe just a line at a time, looking up stuff in dictionaries. I like languages and I like writers in other languages, so I enjoy that. Then I play the guitar again for an hour and at 3:30 I get down to working on a novel. I was working on *Deliverance* when I made

Dickey Describes His Life and Works 67

this schedule, but I am working on one now called *The Field of Dogs*.[24] It's about flying, and the protagonist is a blind man.

LOGUE: Just before World War II?

DICKEY: The early days of the war. Then at 5:30 I knock off and play the guitar again. I like to get in three hours of playing a day. You really can't play an instrument unless you play it that much. And then at 6:30 I watch the Brinkley show. Maybe shave and get cleaned up around that time. At 8:30 I sit down with the books for the next day's class for an hour and make some notes, and then I write letters, or dictate letters, from 9:30 until 10:30. At 10:30 I read for an hour and read myself to sleep. And that is *it!* That's all I can do.

LOGUE: That's a fantastic schedule. Let me ask you this, Jim, before the tape runs out. Of course, this is for a Southern publication—we circulate in fourteen states, basically from Texas to Virginia. You rather represent the emergence of a new generation of Southern writers, and Southern writers rather dominated the landscape in the generation before. How do you see yourself? I know you are not a Southern-oriented writer in terms of your subject matter.

DICKEY: The only way in which I am a Southern writer is that I am simply a writer who happens to come from the South. I don't have any doctrinaire feelings about this at all. I surely couldn't be considered as a regionalist or an agrarian. I don't have any particular ax to grind. On the other hand, it is inevitable that a good deal of my outlook would be colored by the fact that I *am* a Southerner and that I was raised here and was raised according to a certain way of life and a certain outlook and a certain set of values that are peculiar to this region. All this inevitably gets into the writing in some way—in ways that are so subtle that I don't even know what they are.

LOGUE: Do you think the South, with its emphasis on family, has had a great influence on developing writers—a sense of place in history?

DICKEY: Yes, I think that is very important, indeed. New England and the South are the only regions in this country which have any sense of the past at all. In some ways I guess this is damaging, but ultimately it is better than not having it. The whole trouble with the modern world is that people do not know how to *behave*. This completely laissez-faire kind of thing—this California anarchy—is exhilarating for a while, but after that it leaves you with this dreadful emptiness. You have nothing to draw on.

LOGUE: We were taking about your literary posture for the next decade and the fact that you are working (or beginning to work) on a new novel.

DICKEY: Well, I'll tell you what I want to do—what I hope to do. I have about a half of a new manuscript of poetry. I'll try a couple of titles out on you. The first one is taken from Neil Armstrong. I read with him in Milwaukee, and I took from his speech to the joint Houses of Congress a phrase that I thought was very good. "The Earth is traveling in the direction of the constellation Hercules to some unknown destination in the cosmos." I thought I might possibly call my new book of poems *Slowly Toward Hercules*. That was one, and then the other one is taken from a folksong, like *Buckdancer's Choice*. I got it from an Atlanta street singer named Oliver Smith. The name of it is "Just a Closer Walk With Thee," so I thought that I might also call it *A Closer Walk*. But I'm not quite sure that I want to call it one or the other or either. I just have those as working titles. But I have, as I said, about a half of a manuscript. Then I want to do this other novel, *The Field of Dogs*.

LOGUE: It is going to be entirely different from *Deliverance?*

DICKEY: Yes, completely different. I just have some notes. Some sequences of events, and so on. I also want to do an original screenplay: that is, not adapted from anything but written explicitly for the screen. I have another book of essays coming out. I want to write some more literary criticism, and I want to write a play based on this material that I spoke about earlier—*The Indian Maiden*—a play about taking on the commitment to some person that you are not supposed to have affiliation with. I got the idea from a New York taxi driver. I remembered him because he said to me, "Young fellow" (he is the last person who ever called me "young fellow" and that would be enough to make him memorable to me), "I just broke up with my girl friend." And I said, "Does that mean your mistress?" And he said, "Yeah, I guess you could call her my mistress—she was my mistress for sixteen years. I just broke up with her this morning and I feel like a free man." I said, "Why did you consort with her for sixteen years if you wanted to be free?" He said, "Well, you will find out about all this yourself—you don't have to have me tell you, but I'll tell you one thing about taking on obligations outside your family, as far as having a girl friend or a mistress is concerned. Young fellow," he said, "don't do it, because she's always got a brother who needs an operation." Isn't that great? You see, you take on all their troubles, and their human frailities, and all of that, in addition to those you already have. And it becomes intolerable.

LOGUE: You were telling me earlier that you really feel that everything you have done to this point and what you may do in the next ten years will be a preparation.

DICKEY: Yes, it's just a preparation.

LOGUE: In the back of your mind, do you have some *Report to Greco*[25] that you intend to write?

DICKEY: No, no, nothing like *Report to Greco*. I don't know exactly what it is I want to do. Whatever it is, though, is going to be the product of an enormous amount of digging, and an enormous amount of introspection, and I expect an enormous amount of living that I haven't yet done, and generalizing and trying to think things out, trying to figure out what it is I think is desirable for me to do. . . .

LOGUE: Let me ask you this. I don't mean for it to be a deadly question. But one hundred years from now—do you have *that* as sort of an operating standard that you work against; that what you have to say, you want some of it to survive?

DICKEY: No, I'd like for it to, but the literary sweepstakes are mighty unpredictable. What determines lasting value in a writer has never been formulated because so much depends on the temper of the times. The great tastemakers, say, like T. S. Eliot and Ezra Pound, come in and the whole literary picture changes. John Donne, for example, who was just kind of a literary curiosity up until the time Eliot began to write about him, has now become a very great poet because of Eliot's championship of him and his pointing out qualities in Donne that nobody had ever noticed before.

LOGUE: Like Herman Melville?

DICKEY: Melville. He's the *perfect* example! Lewis Mumford and Raymond Weaver and these people discover (and I put that in quotation marks, "discover") Melville, who is actually one of the most boring writers in the history of literature. The big literary game gets to be symbol hunting, and people discover that Melville is very fallow ground for symbol hunting, so everybody takes him up and by now he is a great genius, a stupendous world figure. This boring, sententious person! Taste varies and fluctuates. But I would like to think there would be a few things of mine that would speak to a human being in almost any situation. No matter whether we are flying to the moon or to Venus or wherever we go, or whether we are living on the ocean floor. I would like to think that at least a few things of mine deal with those human constants that are really not ever going to change much: love, life, death, disease, decline, joy, ecstasy, sex, childbearing. All the things we all know. Allen Tate once told me that he thinks of his poems as commentaries on those human situations from which there is no escape. Me, too. I'll go with those.

6
AN INTERVIEW WITH JAMES DICKEY

DAVID L. ARNETT / 1972

ARNETT: Could you give some background on the writing of *Deliverance?*

DICKEY: Well, it would begin with the time I lived in Atlanta. I worked in the advertising business, and fell in with a remarkable group of men—Lewis King and Al Braselton, to whom I have dedicated the book. Lewis King especially was a fascinating character to me. He is kind of similar to the Lewis Medlock of the novel, but also in some ways very dissimilar. But what fasincated me about Lewis King is what fascinated Ed Gentry about Lewis Medlock. He's the only man with the private means to do what he wanted with his one human life and also the ambition and the willpower to realize it.

So, Lewis King, and I, and Al Braselton, who worked with me in the advertising business, used to go on these long canoe trips through North Georgia. North Georgia is largely untouched, and people are moving out of it now. There are some places that Lewis King and I have been—say, in the Chattahoochee National Forest, up in the north central part of the state on the Tennessee border—that I would guarantee nobody has ever been to before. No Indian has ever seen some of those places. And it struck me that with the automobile there is this strange kind of schizophrenic or dual existence possible, where you are in a white shirt and a tie in an office one day, and then late that afternoon you can be in a canoe in an almost untouched kind of wilderness. And it seemed to me that a kind of balance of values would be possible to show in a novel, where

Reprinted with permission from *Contemporary Literature,* 16 (Summer 1975), 286–300. Interview conducted on 26 March 1972.

fellows who were decent suburban householders and commuter businessmen during the week would then be out in a totally different situation or in, as the hippies say, a different "bag" in just a few hours—you know, where they would be up against a situation of primitive survival that nothing in their upbringing or their contemporary, quotidian situation could ever have prepared them for.

It seemed to me that in a situation of this sort, which really just does come down to gut survival, characteristics in these people over whom the veneer of civilization has placed a kind of patina would then link up with the age-old preoccupation of men to preserve themselves—that they would feel that linkup with human-necessity situations that goes all the way back to the caves. And Ed Gentry, the guy who is a decent fellow and an art director and so on, sees what the situation is after Lewis, the guy who rather self-consciously trains for a situation like this, is injured. Ed Gentry, because of the circumstances, is thrown into the situation where he's got to be the deliverer. Either he does what he has to do—involving killing somebody—or they all die, including himself. And I would like the reader—or the viewer of the movie, as the chance may be—to sort of get the idea that this guy who sat in an art direction chair for years and has never suspected that he had any such qualities as these at all, is really kind of naturally good at this.

ARNETT: I have read that the idea first occurred to you in 1962 in Positano, Italy.

DICKEY: Yes, that's true. After one of those big Italian meals, I was lying in bed in the full southern Italian sunlight, which is really tremendously pleasant, and it occurred to me that some events that I had undergone, or lived through, I guess you could say, plus some things that I had heard about and some things that I could invent, would go together into a kind of unified or coherent story. I had never written any stories or novels or anything like that before, but it occurred to me that it might just work out fine. So I got up from bed, reluctantly, because I was so sleepy, and I made a few notes—I'd say half a page in longhand—and went back to sleep contented. And that was the beginning. I mean I knew the whole story in five minutes. The whole thing! And where it would take place and who the people would be. And the general outline of the action

I knew in five mintues or less, or maybe even one minute. But I didn't know *how* the people would be.

The hardest character for me to fix—or to find out about, or to make like I thought he should be for the novel—was Lewis. I knew how Ed would be; I knew how Bobby would be—we've all seen many of them. And I knew how Drew would be—I mean, he's the guy next door to you cutting the lawn. But I didn't know Lewis with his strange, enigmatic personality. Is he a phony? Or is it all just a put-on with him? Or is he a paranoid? Or what is he? You should think maybe one or the other. But the thing about Lewis is that he does what he says he can do! If he says he can put up 180 pounds in a military press, he can take you right out there and show you that he can do it. If he says he can shoot 180, 190, 200, or 220 on an archery field range, he can demonstrate that he can do it.

Lewis doesn't claim to be able to do anything that he can't do. And this, coupled with the fact that I gave him a tremendously impressive middle-aged body, would—I thought then, and I still do—would be so impressive to these guys that they would take his advice on anything, including questions of morality. Whether or not to bury the guy that Lewis has shot, for example, or to make a clean breast of it and stay within the law. He says, "No, no, we're not going to do that, we're going to go outside the law. We're the law!" And Lewis is the college athlete who still can outdo almost any college athlete at the age of thirty-eight. You see, he intellectualizes about it, which gives him even more authority. And then he says somewhere in *Deliverance* that the body is the one thing that can't be faked—it's either there or it's not! And his is.

. . .

ARNETT: The transformation in Ed Gentry is prefigured, I think, by the description of the linden moth early in the novel.

DICKEY: I don't know what that symbolism means, if there is any. It's just the linden moth, this thing, this little larva hanging down on threads, is an extraordinary thing to see. It's an extraordinary visual image. And I just thought it would give Lewis a chance to talk a little more, to talk about that, to show his expertise about the woods and also to have some kind of prefiguration of death and execution. That's really all I thought about.

ARNETT: Yet, also, there is the uncollected poem "For the Linden Moth,[26] in which the moths are described as "Struggling to change in midair, / On their monofilament threads, / To their other and better selves." And that certainly parallels Ed Gentry's struggle, I think, in the tree.

DICKEY: Who wrote that?

ARNETT: You.

DICKEY: That's damn good! Why didn't I ever collect that one! Well, that's right, I agree. I love to agree with critics—especially when they're this perceptive. But, believe me, much writing is subliminal or unconscious. That's exactly the same scene—the scene of the linden moth struggling to change.

ARNETT: We're also told in the poem that "They struggle, contending with / Themselves, and sentenced justly / To writhe until glorified." Resurrection is also mentioned in that poem. So, I think the same is true of Ed Gentry. Several of your poems, including "Sleeping Out at Easter," "The Lifeguard," "A Folk Singer of the Thirties," and "The First Morning of Cancer," describe the transformation of men into Christ figures.

DICKEY: "The First Morning of Cancer"[27] was an ambitious and kind of pretentious poem that I wrote when I really didn't know what I was doing. I'm glad I wrote it. And that poem brought about—in New Orleans, by damn! You see how everything comes together? The first mention that I ever had in print was by a man in *The New Orleans Poetry Journal*[28]— named Ashman, I think.

ARNETT: You mention that in *Self-Interviews*.

DICKEY: Did I? And he says, "This is very imaginative, but we think no poet has the right to be as obscure as James Dickey." I had no idea I was obscure, but I was glad to find it out. But, yes, I think that we all yearn to be something other than what we are. I'm really very dissatisfied with what I am. This is the whole secret of Lewis, because he despises himself. Lewis is no more or less than an intellectual and physical counterpart of Charles Atlas, who was once a skinny, ninety-seven-pound weakling, but now can be proud of himself, because he's put all this time in on his body. He is a victim of a crushing inferiority complex, so that he spends enormous amounts of time on himself, making himself impressive intellectually—physically first, and then hopefully intellectually—with all his theories and mystiques, so that he can make other people feel inferior. And Ed is sort of taken in, and this is why Lewis browbeats Bobby—this fat, out-of-shape businessman—all the time. That's much more prevalent in the movie than it is in the novel.

We see a little bit of this when they are driving. Lewis and Ed are in the car with the canoe on top, and Lewis says, "Hey, can that fat friend of yours handle himself?" "What do you mean, Lewis?" "Can he handle himself in a canoe, Ed, is what I'm talkin' about?" Lewis is always a little bit impatient—you know, always forcing you a little bit. Ed's used to it, he likes him, he's fascinated by him, but he's not taken in more than, say, about halfway by Lewis. He says, "Well, Lewis, I don't know whether he can or not. I've never seen him in a canoe. But he's very well thought of in his profession." And Lewis says, "What is his profession?" And Ed says, "Insurance." And Lewis says, "Shit! I've never been insured in my life. I don't believe in it! If you're insured, Ed, there's no risk."

The trouble with Lewis, which I did mean to show, is that he is almost totally without humor. He's so serious about these things and about this self-image of his. But at the end that breaks down some, and he becomes more fully human, as when he's lying on the bottom of the canoe with his leg broken, and Ed is trying desperately to figure out what they're going to tell people when they get back to civilization. And Lewis says to him, "You've got it figured, Ed. You're doin' it better than I could do." And there's a scene in the movie where they're desperately trying to get the change in story over to Lewis, who's lying in the hospital with his leg in traction and that sort of thing, and Lewis says, "I gotcha! I don't remember a thing!"

ARNETT: Ed Gentry hangs from a tree with a wound in his palm, and as he destroys evil in the person of the mountaineer, he receives another wound in the side. Now, are these conscious Christ symbols equating Gentry's better soul with the divine—Christ being the supreme example of the divine existing within the human?

DICKEY: No, if those things have any relationship to the Christ business, and again it comes as a complete surprise to me, it's through, I suppose, what Jung calls the "collective unconscious," because it surely was not conscious at all. What I thought about when I wrote those sequences in the novel was that when he's in the river and he's desperately trying to hold on to the bow and slide over the rocks without bashing his brains out, it seemed to me that his relationship to the arrows would be something dangerous to himself. And it seemed to be this business of grabbing for the bow and catching the arrowheads—these razor-sharp arrowheads—and cutting his hands on them would be a very good way to deal with this business of physicality in chaos—hurled and thrown around in the river. The real precedent for that—and I don't mean to be pretentious at all—was Milton's voyage of Satan through Chaos, which is the best thing in *Paradise Lost*. That's wonderful action writing. I've never read better anywhere. You wouldn't think that of Milton, whom you generally think of as being kind of inert. But that journey—

ARNETT: Satan spreading his wings and sailing across—

DICKEY: Well, no, and he goes through Chaos, in which there's nothing to grab hold of, and things sink away under him, and he flounders and just tries to make it any way he can. That was what I was thinking about then. But the wound in the side I got more or less from the Council of Archery hunting accidents—about people falling on their arrows and what that would feel like and what would it do to you to see an arrow come through your own flesh and that sort of thing.

See, these men—especially Lewis, and Ed who follows his example—they've taken the toys of civilization to play at the wilderness. Especially Lewis. He thinks there's some kind of metaphysical value at playing at being a survivalist, and he's an impressive guy in some ways—especially physically—and mysterious. And fellows who work in offices and live in the suburbs at that age—say around thirty-seven or thirty-eight—begin to feel like they've missed the whole thing. Something has happened; their lives have gone by. And here's Lewis; he's got deathly notions about what life is about. He can do something about it, and he *will* do it, and he *does* do it. Well, why not? If this guy thinks that there's something for us up there in those woods, damn! we ought to go. What else have we got? And it might be fun, too. We'll take some whiskey, and they're going to destroy the wilderness, anyway. The river is going to be dammed up. Why don't we have a little contact with the

An Interview 77

primitive? And that's essentially the motivation for the trip. Lewis has his own private demons that make him do it, and they go with him.

ARNETT: Can you detail the relationship of "On the Coosawattee" with *Deliverance*? For example, the first part was published in the *New Yorker* in 1962—"By Canoe Through the Fir Forest."[29] Were all three parts written separately? And were they written before the novel itself?

DICKEY: Oh, yes. Much, much before. Actually, they were written when I was in the advertising business in Atlanta and had just come back from the trip. That was an horrendous trip! I mean, that trip down the Coosawattee through the fir forest and those other places was the grimmest physical experience I'd had since I was in the service. Lewis King has the same characteristic as Lewis Medlock—that is, he thinks he's equal to anything, and he thinks you ought to be equal to anything if you go with him. So, he plunges himself and the other people with him into situations where he doesn't know what the outcome is going to be. It was one of those trips!

Actually, the Cahulawassee, the river in the novel, is a composite of several different rivers that we've been down and were lucky to escape from. The Coosawattee—that was the one that the chicken heads were on, and that was the one we ran up on the terrifying characters. They were not like the ones in the book. And then the cliffs—the gorge—was on another river, and the cows, the cattle and things that they see finally when they're coming down to civilization again, were on another one. It's really kind of a composite river, but it's mainly the one where the actual film was made. It was mainly the Chattooga River. That's the one where all the bad rapids are—the one that's so dangerous.

ARNETT: About the poultry incident in "On the Coosawattee" and also in *Deliverance*. Were the poetic and fictional treatments written separately? Or does one depend upon the other?

DICKEY: The novel depends on the poem, and they both depend on the incident. That was one of the most memorably disgusting things that I've ever seen. I think that is in Ellijay, Georgia. Either that, or it's north. I don't remember whether we put in at Ellijay or whether we got out at Ellijay. Ellijay, Georgia, is really the model for Aintry in the novel. We went down there—and it's just like in the poem and the novel. We said, "There's something wrong here." And then we saw all these feathers and things and chicken heads. I changed that in the novel to make it show just one chicken head, because I thought the focus would be better if we just showed one—lots of feathers and one head.

ARNETT: When you wrote the fictional treatment, did you have the poem in front of you?

DICKEY: No, no, I just recalled the incident. I remembered using it, but I used it in the novel in a different way for a different purpose. This business of going down past the chicken heads and so on is supposed to serve in the novel as a kind of symbolical way—I suppose you could say, I hope without being too pretentious—of showing them leaving the detritus of civilization behind and getting back into the primitive through that. It's like when they have all the junk at the side of the river, and there's this electric blue plastic jug—or whatever it is—and Ed is kind of offended by it, and Drew says, "That's plastic. It doesn't go back to its elements." Ed says, "As though that were all right." He's like the rest of us; he's kind of vaguely disquieted by this.

ARNETT: Are you implying also that man should go back to his elements? Did you have that in mind?

DICKEY: Yes, I supopse. I wouldn't deny it.

ARNETT: I had thought of the chicken head as a death symbol.

DICKEY: That, too.

ARNETT: Very much like the pig's head in *Lord of the Flies*.

DICKEY: *Deliverance* is a better novel than *Lord of the Flies,* if I do say so. *Lord of the Flies* is too contrived. *Deliverance* could happen.

. . .

ARNETT: You mention the Osiris myth in *Self-Interviews*. Were you referring to that myth in Drew's body floating down the river, foreshadowing the rebirth and regeneration of Ed Gentry?

DICKEY: Well, in a way. If there's any literary or mythological precedent for *Deliverance,* it comes from a review I read in the

Kenyon Review in the summer 1949 issue, when I was a senior in college. It was an enormously impressive thing to me, and it's been in my mind ever since. It's a review by Stanley Edgar Hyman[30] on a number of books on myths and rituals, and he quotes Arnold Van Gennep's "rites de passage" and cites "a separation from the world, a penetration to some source of power, and a life-enhancing return." If there's any literary precedent to *Deliverance,* it's that passage as I encountered it quoted by Hyman, referring to Van Gennep's concept of the "rites de passage."

ARNETT: Many of your poems, particularly those dealing directly with death, contain images of water directly overhead—"The Movement of Fish," "Winter Trout," "The Driver"—and sometimes of water rising, "The Dream Flood" is an example, and, of course, in *Deliverance* the water rises to form a lake, and everything is hidden beneath the surface. Traditionally, water has signified both death and rebirth, but why does it have such great meaning for you?

DICKEY: I don't know, except to say that I just like it. As I said somewhere in *Self-Interviews,* I think a river is the most beautiful thing in the world. Any river, even polluted, is beautiful. I feel very much like Heraclitus does about rivers and like Hermann Hesse did in *Siddhartha,* where the guy learns about the secret of everything by sitting and watching a river. That does it for me! Rivers always did it for me. Much more than oceans, although I like them, too, or lakes, which I like in their way, too. I'm so glad—if I never write another novel, and *Deliverance* turns out to be the only one—I'm so glad that I wrote about rivers.

ARNETT: Is "The Driver" based on personal experience?

DICKEY: Yes, pretty much. On one of the invasion beaches at Okinawa there was a lot of old, rusted equipment sitting around under water—amtracks and so on. The water is very clear. It's a very beautiful sea around Okinawa. And I remember going down there and getting into the driver's seat, just to see what it would be like.

ARNETT: There's another uncollected poem that I'd like to question you about, entitled "A Beginning Poet, Aged Sixty-Five."[31] Now that poem is equated in the Glancy bibliography[32] with "To Landrum Guy," but it's entirely different.

DICKEY: It is different, and I've done that more than once. I don't even have a copy of the one that was published in the *Quarterly Review.* I don't remember what it was like.

ARNETT: It seems to be a compendium of your most familiar themes and images. Everything seems to be collected in this one poem.

DICKEY: It's funny. I like to think of beginnings and rebeginnings, but all of it's in the question of approach and the question of form that the poem takes in which you talk about these things. And in this case, as you very rightly observe, there are two completely different approaches and ways of talking about the same guy and the same situation. I don't really know. The perspective of time has made it so that I don't even remember what the differences are. I know that one was collected when Richard Wilbur was my editor and told me to do the one that I did rather than the other one, so I did that one. But I often write poems on the same theme. I feel like I didn't get out of it the first time. I had the wrong approach, and there's nothing says I can't go around and try again. It's like when the tower waves you off on a landing, you go around the pattern and come back again. You try it another way. Any subject has an infinitude of possibilities, and if I'm not satisfied with the way I did the first time, I just take the whole thing and start in from another angle.

ARNETT: The epigraph to *Deliverance* is derived from Obadiah. How about the title?

DICKEY: Well, you pointed out to me—I'm very grateful to you—that the word "deliverance" is used in Obadiah. But I was so struck with that part of Obadiah having to do with the climb up the cliff and lying in the cleft of the rocks and all of that sort of thing. It just fascinated me. I didn't want to read any more. I just wanted *that.* But the original title of the novel was *The Deliverer,* and it's from the biblical quote. I don't know exactly where it occurs, but it's the quote "Who shall deliver me from the body of this death?" It was originally on the basis of that quotation called *The Deliverer,* but then I also remembered that the word "deliverance" and "the day of deliverance" and phrases of that sort are relatively frequent in the Bible. And

I've always like one-word titles, and *The Deliverer* did not seem to me to be as dramatic as *Deliverance,* so I just changed it.

. . .

ARNETT: You mention in *Sorties*—this is a direct quotation: "The phantom women of the mind—I speak from a man's standpoint only—are a great deal more important than any real woman could ever possibly be. They represent the Ideal, and as such are indestructible. It is quite arguable that poor mortal perishable women are just as dust before these powerful and sensual creatures of the depths of one's being." Coupled with this, we often find in your poetry a search for the Ideal—and this seems to point to Shelley.

DICKEY: Maybe it does, but it points way back beyond Shelley to Shelley's own master—Plato. I guess essentially I'm a Platonist, rather than an Aristotelian. Yes, sure, I think we're more or less lost without impossible ideals. Like in the novel there can be an enormous dramatic conflict and play between, say, a character who conceives of things in this kind of idealistic or eternal way and what he must settle for in the mundane human world. The Greek tragedies really are largely based on this idea, and so is a great deal of Shakespeare—people who will not bend, Coriolanus for one, who have that flaw of expecting too much and not being able to function when that condition cannot be fulfilled.

You can take a more modern instance—*All the King's Men* by Robert Penn Warren, where the guy is anything but an idealist—the politician, Willie Stark. But he is given this power, and he begins to conceive that he can be, with all the state power, a force for good. He can build hospitals, highways, and bridges, and do something about the plight of the poor people. And he really can. But in order to get the money and to do these things, he's got to compromise with these other forces, which are not good, and it's this business of effecting good ends by bad means that makes up the dramatic conflict of the book. And I think it's really unsolvable. I mean, should he bribe this guy, or should he make a deal with this other political faction in order to get these funds to build this hospital? Which is fascinating, which is really the way things are done.

ARNETT: Do you think of Robert Penn Warren as one of your teachers?

DICKEY: I wish he had been, but he's only a teacher to me through my reading of his works for a number of years and then very lately—the last five or six years—knowing him and corresponding with him. But in my formative stage as a writer, Robert Penn Warren was known to me only through his works. *All the King's Men* came out when I was in college, and I read the poems because I went to Vanderbilt, which was his old school, and he was talked about; and Donald Davidson was my teacher, who was his teacher.

ARNETT: You mention in *Self-Interviews* three of the writers that you consider to be your teachers—of a sort—or certainly whom you admire—Malcolm Lowry, James Agee, and John Keats. Would you add anyone to that?

DICKEY: Well, no. I suppose I could, but those are the ones that I like maybe more for their attitude toward experience—which seems to me to be an extremely creative way to take the act of living—than for what they actually wrote, although I like very much what they wrote. In the case of Keats, for example, I like *him,* John Keats, and what I know about him and what's been recorded about him a great deal more than what he wrote, although I like what he wrote. The same to a lesser extent is true of Malcolm Lowry. I like the way he experienced existence and the terms on which he took existence more than what he wrote, although I like what he wrote more than I like what Keats wrote. James Agee is exactly the opposite. He is a born, sovereign prince of the English language. He was self-destructive, say like Dylan Thomas was or Theodore Roethke, too, and many another. But James Agee—what little there is of him—is of an order of genius far beyond Malcolm Lowry, or John Keats either, as irreverent as that may seem. But Agee's style—and that really hyper-intense kind of verbalization that he has—is not right for me.

What I like about Agee more than anything else is his ability to place an unusual word in a sentence. Just to take an example, not from the prose works or the poetry either, but from directions in a screenplay for *The African Queen.* You know when they're mired up in the weeds, and Charlie has to go to clear the propeller, and he comes up with leeches all over him, and then they're just exhausted, and they're lying there on the floorboards of the boat, and the directions are: Camera pulls back and shows panoramic view of boat and the weeds and so on. And then he says: "And then there is a vague splintering of rain." It's just that "splintering of rain." Now, my God, who would have thought of that? That's just absolutely wonderful—at least to me it is. That's why I admire him so much. And he doesn't do it as a kind of a gimmick—that's just the way he sees the rain. Or hears it—maybe both.

ARNETT: You've mentioned several times that you're about to move into a new area of poetry—or at least a different area from what you have been working with before. Can you clarify that?

DICKEY: I'm just feeling it out. I get a glimpse of it now and then, but whether the promised land is there or not, I don't know. But if I can't find it, I'll try to invent it.

7
INTERVIEW: JAMES DICKEY
UNMUZZLED OX / 1972

DICKEY: My feeling is this about *Self-Interviews;* we live in an age of the interview, and I kept getting asked the same questions over and over so much that I thought it might be a good idea to lay that ghost to rest for all time and do a book that had all the questions that kept coming up and just let people go and buy it and read it. I don't have to be again and again on Johnny Carson and Dick Cavett and the *Today Show* and do the same thing over and over and over. . . . Everyone thinks that the interviewee is going to have the secret, the be-all and end-all of existence, you know, and they better listen to him because he may know something they do not know, which he frequently does, but much more often does not.

UNMUZZLED OX: I was wondering about some of the new poems that you didn't discuss in *Self-Interviews,* say, for instance, "Blood."

DICKEY: I think of all American poets, I've explained myself overly much, and it probably doesn't do very much for anybody for me to keep on doing it more and more and more. In "Blood" I tried to get an enormous dramatic compression in just a few lines. That's what I was trying to do in that one. Again, I believe my days of self-explanation are over. I just want to write poetry now.

UNMUZZLED OX: What have you been writing lately?

DICKEY: I have a couple of long overly ambitious novels working and a couple of films with my son, who was the first graduate in film from the University of Virginia. I want to do

---

Reprinted from *Unmuzzled Ox,* 3, No. 2 (1975), 74–85. Interview conducted in 1972.

some critical pieces, some more poems. These will take me up to the age of sixty-five, which should just about do it.

UNMUZZLED OX: In the *New York Quarterly* interview[33] you said there were some things you were absolutely dead, one-hundred percent wrong about in *Babel to Byzantium*.

DICKEY: Yes, yes, but I believe the critic should be prepared to take that risk and to reverse his own judgment. I don't believe in any kind of absolutism.

UNMUZZLED OX: I was wondering what specific opinions you had reversed.

DICKEY: I was wrong about Billy Merwin. I thought he was going to be a big writer and a good writer and he is good but he's not going to be big. On the other hand, I was absolutely, one hundred percent right about James Merrill. He did change, and he's emerged as one of our finest poets.

UNMUZZLED OX: Auden when we interviewed him said Merrill was superb.

DICKEY: Oh, yes. There's no doubt in my mind now. So the critic is sometimes wrong, sometimes right, but I'm very happy I was right about Merrill. I was half wrong about Kazantzakis. He has more brio than verbal ability. He's a writer you *want* to like. I was right about Edwin Muir. I was wrong about Vernon Watkins. But I don't mind admitting that at all.

UNMUZZLED OX: You're the last writer in the great Southern tradition of Faulkner and Warren and Tate, and I was wondering why that tradition seems to have so attenuated.

DICKEY: I don't think Faulkner's a great writer. I do think that Warren has got elements of greatness, moments of greatness. I think Allen Tate is a great man of letters in the old tradition. But I do not think Faulkner is. The Southern ethos is vanishing as the culture gets more homogenized; we're all going to end up in a gigantic Rexall's. Those fellows were lucky, Faulkner, Erskine Caldwell, Allen Tate, Red Warren, Andrew Lytle; they were lucky to have been able to get in on the last gasp of the Southern verbal tradition: in the storytelling, you know, where you had time to sit around and just talk.

UNMUZZLED OX: That's really interesting. Few other contemporary poets tell stories.

DICKEY: Well, that is important to me, but I'm trying to do something different now. The business of the narrative element: you take a novel, say, like *Deliverance*. It goes all the way back to the caves where the primary feeling in people is wanting to know what happens next. They don't want a lot of literary complications such as in *Finnegans Wake,* really they don't. It's like what Samuel Johnson says of *Paradise Lost,* "Its perusal is a duty rather than a pleasure." What they really want is a good story. And I had sense enough in *Deliverance,* in the novel and in the film version as well, to go right along with that.

. . .

DICKEY: So old Ezra's dead.[34] I was just reading through all the stuff to see if there were some part of the mystery that I might not have apprehended at the time, but I haven't been able to find it.

UNMUZZLED OX: Pound had a couple of lines in "Mauberley" to the effect that his goal was to maintain the sublime.

DICKEY: He believed in the sense of consequence, the sense of living the kind of life in which there are values and in which you don't have the prevailing twentieth-century sense of "what the shit does it matter? What does it *matter*? Who gives a shit?" He believed in trying to have some kind of cultural, political system in which consequentiality had a place. I think that sense is what we are all losing; we're *all* losing it. Nobody cares. You don't even care about your own life anymore. But people do need to have some sense of consequence, and that's what Pound was after.

UNMUZZLED OX: What kind of contact did you have with Pound?

DICKEY: I just went out to see him a few times at St. Elizabeth's. We had an enormous correspondence,[35] which is now in the archives of Washington University in St. Louis. I couldn't make head or tail out of what he was talking about half the time. The letters are just like the *Cantos*.

The kind of contact I had with Ezra Pound was simply the contact of an older dad who talked to you like, like you would be talked to by your own crackpot father. He would say, "Now son, I'll tell you, you're not going to find this in the history books—Now let me tell you what happened in 1877." The thing that's disturbing is that you don't know what Pound knows, you are not sure that there might not be a certain amount of truth in what he says. He operated that way.

UNMUZZLED OX: With that kind of ambiguity.

DICKEY: Yes, that's right. I mean, you don't know what the contribution of Martin Van Buren was to the American economy—at least, I don't. *You* might, but *I* don't. Martin Van Buren to Ezra Pound was a great, mystical kind of genius of American political life, a prophet. But I don't know that much about him. Seems Pound has always got some kind of an "in," some kind of an angle that you don't know anything about, and he was going to explain it to you; he was going to tell you all about it.

UNMUZZLED OX: That's the way with people who have a philosophy.

DICKEY: No, no, this is the thing. Ezra Pound is like your own crazy, intelligent father. You can't disprove him—at least, not quite.
 I don't have the integrity of Pound, at least, not that kind. I think integrity and fanaticism are probably two sides of the same coin. I don't have that at all. My orientation is completely different from his. He fails as only a large figure can fail, you know?

UNMUZZLED OX: Yes. I was delighted some place where you quote somebody saying that André Breton was an idiot for taking things to such an extreme.

DICKEY: Yes! This is right. Actually, I was quoting John Berryman, my poor good buddy who dived off a bridge. I don't understand. I see the fellows, the good guys of my generation—I don't mean to paraphrase someone like Ginsberg, you know, and say the best minds of my generation—but I see the best guys going down the drain. I see John Berryman kill himself, I see Randall Jarrell kill himself, I see Weldon Kees disappear, I see Dylan Thomas die, I see Jim Wright drinking himself to death, and I see people going downhill on alcohol and dope, and I see their inability to control their sexual and their family lives. Now listen, I am no exception to this, I don't stand high on a mountaintop. I mean, I am just as subject to this as they are. But because I am in there with them—with the Jim Wrights and the John Berrymans and the Randall Jarrells—I know what the hazards are.

UNMUZZLED OX: This room is really interesting—the guitars there, and the bows and arrows. I just felt a sudden connection of Odysseus and the lyre and the bow—

DICKEY: I don't know. Believe me, it never occurred to *me*! Archery companies send them to me all over the place. I love to hunt, but I am very, very mediocre.

UNMUZZLED OX: Is that the way you're escaping the dilemma of those people?

DICKEY: Well, in a way. The deep pit is writing. That's the deep frustration. It's like T. E. Lawrence said somewhere, "This everlasting effort to write is like trying to fight a feather bed." And the guitar or whatever, or running, or—

UNMUZZLED OX: Do you do much running?

DICKEY: Yes, and weight-lifting and all that. But these are all escapes out of the pressure cooker of writing—to work out an interesting tune on the twelve-string guitar; for example, I suggested the music for *Deliverance*.

UNMUZZLED OX: Oh, that was really fine.

DICKEY: It's wonderful to be able to turn to something else, with an entirely different set of problems, because when I am writing poetry I don't really think of the relationship of C major to A minor. It's a completely different set of problems. When you give yourself another set of problems, then you are temporarily relieved from whatever has been bugging you with the first set of problems.

. . .

UNMUZZLED OX: Have you written any more poems about reincarnation?

DICKEY: No, I was going to do that, and I hope to do it yet. I hope to do a whole series of those. I would want to take the whole evolutionary scale, and be reincarnated as the lowest form of life, and then take it up the scale, from the mollusks and whatever, until the last reincarnation is the guy reincar-

An Interview 89

nated as himself. I'd have to do some research. It's like any other poetic form or structure. It's all to do yet. All to do yet!

UNMUZZLED OX: It sounds like the structure for a long, major poem.

DICKEY: We would start out under the sea, where life came from originally; we'd start out there, and we'd gradually work the evolutionary reincarnation of the same soul in a fish, for example, or in a dinosaur. It just becomes a colossal undertaking!

UNMUZZLED OX: I thought "Madness" might have initially been conceived as part of that reincarnation sequence.

DICKEY: No, that was what you would call a sketch—about a dog that has hydrophobia. The dog's bitten by a fox in the rutting season, and he goes mad, and they have to hunt him down.

UNMUZZLED OX: That poem was a marvelous image of pathos.

DICKEY: I am glad you like it. It has a peculiar rhythm to it, which I haven't managed to reproduce anywhere else; I don't know whether I would want to. The technical problem was to write a poem without any pronouns.

UNMUZZLED OX: I didn't notice that.

DICKEY: I am not sure whether it was pronouns or verbs or whatever, but I set myself the technical task of writing. No, I think it was writing without any nouns. Oh, I don't know, you tell me. It was some kind of peculiar linguistic structure.

UNMUZZLED OX: I have recently been setting myself similar formal challenges. One was to put a foreign word in every line. I hedged a bit, and decided obscenities could be used as substitutes.

DICKEY: I challenge my classes with the peculiar and technical. I don't feel I should give them anything that I wouldn't be willing to take on myself. You know, to write a sestina with only one adjective. But the question is, where do you place *that*?

Poetry, like any art form, is dependent on the means at hand. I am trying to write a long thing now, a kind of collaboration with a dead man. He is a Dutchman named Marsman who was killed on a refugee ship in 1940. I am trying to connect with him. I did the Phi Beta Kappa poem for Harvard two years ago,[36] where I held a colloquy with a dead man, Trumbull Stickney, whose poems have since been reissued. He's a marvelous poet. But it's a collaboration between someone in 1970 and someone who died in 1904. You take his lines and then answer them back. Like we did in *Deliverance,* where there's a kind of musical dialogue. I thought that was a wonderful scene. I can't wait to see it again.

UNMUZZLED OX: Yes, I think that was the best scene.

DICKEY: When I have Drew say, "Go on, will you!!!" Pam, pam, pam. That's nice. Good things can happen between human beings.

But poetry—I've been working on this long thing called *The Zodiac*. My minor at Vanderbilt was astronomy, and I have always wanted to energize what little I remember about the stars and the galaxies into poetry. It's hard to do because the bloody thing is so vast. The universe is so vast, and how do you tie something as big as the universe—the Milky Way, the solar system—into something that's so small and intimate as human life on earth?

UNMUZZLED OX: What about the poem "Apollo"?

DICKEY: Well, I met with the astronauts; Walter Schirra, especially, I knew and liked. But *The Zodiac* is a completely different approach to the universe. . . .

UNMUZZLED OX: Speaking of the universal and the neo-primitive, I was fascinated by the Freudian "The Eye-Beaters."

DICKEY: That's one of the best ones I've done. I think it's wrong for a writer—although I am certainly guilty of doing it—to over-intellectualize and over-explain his own work and so on, but "The Eye-Beaters" is—well, *you* tell *me*.

What I want to do in poetry is to connect people to their deep, instinctual sources, whether they lie in the stars or in the caves. It important to recognize that as we exist in an atmosphere of glass and chromium and steel, we still have access to the things that underlie all those so-called civilizational advantages. You can sit out on the edge of a hill when the night comes, and it's as though you'd never seen a piece of glass or a telephone in your life. That's why I have Jon Voight say in *Deliverance,* "Night has fallen, and there's nothing we can do about it. No matter what's going on in the world, no matter what disasters befall in history this fall, no matter what petty little things are going on in Atlanta, night has fallen."

UNMUZZLED OX: The audience took that line as comic.

DICKEY: Yes. That's the point. "Night has fallen and there's nothing we can do about it."

    He is the best, the finest young screen actor in the world. My God, he's good! I just marvel at what Jon Voight does. He got the right part, and by damn we got the right man. He's so bloody good, and he was so deep into this thing, it was almost mystical. Whenever he got a day off, infrequently, Jon would get a canoe and go out on the river. He didn't have to, but he did. Everybody was terrified that he was going to get himself killed.

. . .

UNMUZZLED OX: What do you think of Denise Levertov's work in general?

DICKEY: Fair only. She has a little ability, but she has so incarcerated herself in political action that what little that's there is kind of sublimated in a general effort to be productive and to be an influence on the Scene (with a capital S), which is a mistake. She has a little something. But not much. She is not the really good lady poet around which she has long posed as being. The good one is Mona Van Duyn from St. Louis. She's got infinitely more talent than Denise Levertov. Or Ann Stanford out on the West Coast is good. They are real craftsmen, as well as being—as the Southern gentleman gallantly said—fine ladies.

UNMUZZLED OX: I liked "Turning Away" in *Eye-Beaters* very much.

DICKEY: I am glad you did, because nobody else did, or they never paid the slightest attention to it. We've all turned away from people that we cared for when we saw that it was no longer possible to swing. You turn away and things happen to you, you know? They don't know why you're turning away from them. They don't know why, but they've sensed it coming for a long time. And you turn away and things change. Everything begins to look like a military battlefield. It's a perfectly placid scene, nice country, beautiful weather, but because you did your act of turning away, the thing becomes a battlefield, and somebody behind you is crying.

UNMUZZLED OX: I made a guess in reading "Turning Away" that you had been reading *Modern Love,* you know, George Meredith's sixteen-line sonnets.

DICKEY: *Modern Love* is a very great piece of writing, I think. Meredith was married to Thomas Love Peacock's daughter, and a marriage break-up was going on between Meredith and her. "We eat our pot of honey on the grave."

UNMUZZLED OX: What about "Diabetes"?

DICKEY: As you get older you have a terror of things getting at you from the inside. Cancer, heart disease, diabetes, kidneys, your eyes, you know. I am writing a novel about a blind man. And you can't account for these things—they seem so bloody unfair. . . . How would you like to be hung up in one of those hospitals, where they say they've got to take more tests? You wouldn't like it. You know, eyes, ears, nose, throat, esophagus, stomach, body chemistry. I'll be fifty on February 2nd, and the hypochondriac tension builds up incredibly, because you wonder what's going to get you. You don't have to contend with that yet, but you will.

UNMUZZLED OX: There are very few instances of irony in your poetry.

DICKEY: Well, I don't think about it in abstract categories with capital letters. In other words, am I going to use irony with a capital I? No. If it comes in, fine.

UNMUZZLED OX: Are there any Canadian poets you particularly like?

DICKEY: Yes, there is one very good one. In fact, I think he may be the best of all of them around. He is David Wevill. Do you know him? He was involved with the tragic business of Sylvia Plath and Ted Hughes.

UNMUZZLED OX: There was a passage in *Deliverance* which I thought typified in many ways the value of your work. It runs, "What I thought mainly was that I was in a place where none—

An Interview

or almost none—of my daily ways of living would work; there was no habit I could call on. Is this freedom? I wondered." Can you comment on that?

DICKEY: No. I would just leave that to the reader, or to the viewer of the film, to figure out for himself whether it is or whether it is not, or whether habit is one of the best things you've got going for you, or whether it's a thing that's been screwing up all your life. William James says somewhere that it's just as easy to form good habits as bad, but there is a question as to whether it's desirable to form either one. I don't know. The thing about *Deliverance*—and indeed about most of my work—is to put the reader in a situation and then leave it up to him.

8
JAMES DICKEY: THE ARCHER'S AUTHOR
GLENN HELGELAND / 1973

James Dickey would thoroughly enjoy one-on-one football pass coverage, or a little of the same in basketball. And if anyone ever chronicles an actual meeting of The Irresistible Force and The Immovable Object, Jim Dickey will be the man to do it. He likes to set up those classically simple collisions—or tests, if you prefer— and see what happens. Which is probably the reason he likes archery.

DICKEY: The first time I picked up a bow and shot an arrow, I thought "this is for me." That was twelve, fifteen years ago. A couple of guys I knew in Atlanta took me to a field range. I didn't have any idea of the existence of such a thing, but I shot one of their target bows and some aluminum arrows.

I like the idea that a bow is not a machine, but a kind of primitive instrument. It doesn't require a lot of things from American technology like cartridge manufacturers and manufacturers of special sliding bolts and those things you have in guns.

The main thing is the interaction of the human body with the weapon—that you have to get strength from your own body to draw the thing and hold it still and shoot it right. It's tougher to do, but the aesthetic reward is so much greater.

You see the flight of the arrow, which for me is the prettiest thing in sports. There's nothing to compare with the sail of a really nice sixty-to-sixty-five yard shot. The arc of the arrow at that range is almost unbearably beautiful. It gives the illusion of predestination. It seems to be following a string right to the

---

Reprinted with permission from *Archery World*, 22 (April–May 1973), 34–37.

place you want it to go. That's *you* going out there, you making that flight!

It's classically simple. In sports, simplicity is the key to the kind of aesthetic enjoyment I get out of any activity.

The painters I like are those who just work on a few lines, a couple or three colors. The same with poetry and story-telling.

And in archery, you just crank the bow back and you get what you want for elevation and you let it go and see whether it goes in or doesn't go in.

Archery is a hell of a good sport—a beautiful sport. So why make such a desperation thing of it like some people do. If it's so serious, then it's no bloody fun. Americans get too mad for perfection. Imperfection is not bad though.

Dickey leans forward, hair askew and eyes piercing like diamond fire. He searches the air with his hands, and you know his mind has just kicked in the afterburners. Then he settles back. The intensity has been challenged, has responded; he's found what he wants.

DICKEY: There's a marvelous complexity to archery: with the mechanics of a bow, an arrow, a string, with the physical complexity of your bow hand and arm, your drawing hand, anchor and release. But if you can keep it simple in your own mind, don't let the elements run away with you, it all ends with a surpassingly beautiful simplicity—the simple shooting of an arrow.

I don't want to be counting backwards from perfect. I don't want to get mad at myself or the other guy because yesterday in practice I shot a round three points higher than the score with which he beat me today.

I like to come up to a certain level of competency—the level that gives me satisfaction and lets the game be fun. I don't want to shoot 280 on fourteen field targets, or something like that. Then I'd be miserable if I didn't do it every time. I wouldn't get any great enjoyment out of making one nice shot, say, out of a series of four at a fifty-five yard target.

HELGELAND: As an author and poet, Mr. Dickey, you work with words both precise and ambiguous. You know when you put down a word whether it's right or not. Isn't that perfection?

DICKEY: I don't really know. I only know that it seems right at the time. I'm not a great believer in perfection, because then there is no place to go. I didn't know whether the notion of perfection is not an impossible kind of abstraction anyway. What is the criterion? The ability to shoot 280 on fourteen targets? That's just an agreed-on assessment of what constitutes perfection.

He shrugs. You can boost the criterion to ten arrows per target, then that score would be the standard.

You know, I've never been to an archery range that has not been in the most beautiful area available. Archers have a natural eye for terrain, and they somehow come up with the nicest places for their field ranges. Archery, to me, is outdoors. It gets you into a natural environment. I think the best thing that could be done for a field archery range would be to leave it exactly as it was before the targets were set up.

And then just have fun—not competition. I'm glad I'm not a very good archer. I'm not a good pressure shot, and I don't want to subject myself to the intense psyching up necessary to hold absolutely still every shot and give perfect releases and so on. I won some local tournaments a few years ago, but that ceased to be fun. Competitive archery is not what I like.

But that dilemma is not as large as the hunting dilemma. The tide of public sentiment is against killing anything—men, deer, rabbits, or whatever. Yet I believe that hunters are the wisest conservationists. Hunters simply haven't been able to convince the populace that the deer will die by themselves like they've done in the past on some of the islands off South Carolina and like they do in the winter yards up north.

Game departments seem to have done good jobs informing people about special situations; now if they—and hunters—can just get that across for *all* sport hunting.

I like hunting, not only in practice, but in theory. I like to be out there with the wild animals in the situation they understand the best, which is that of life and death. I would much rather be out stalking a deer with a bow than giving one a lump of sugar in the zoo. Because he has you in *his* condition: his condition as a wild animal. Any animal senses that the condition he lives in from day to day is the condition of life and death. Animals understand that things are trying to kill them.

And men should be in that kind of deep relationship with

animals at least occasionally to find out where the human race came from. Our ancestors had to hunt to live, and if you have even a faint inkling from engaging in this activity, a plain inkling of what it must have been like for them, then you know more about yourself than you did until then.

If you have been around animals very much, you know they don't have any humanitarian sentiments about each other. Some of them have to kill others to survive. They did quite well without us; I hope they'll do as well with us.

In my film, we have Drew as a kind of sentimentalist, a theoretical liberal and humanist, and he's anti-hunting. People like him don't understand how another person can kill an animal. The Drews of the world are this way not because they have really thought about what they are saying, but because it is fashionable to think this way among their group. They're supposed to be pro-animal, and if they are, they're automatically anti-hunter.

This is seeing the condition only through their experience, without even examining their roots in life, without even placing themselves face to face with the most elemental conditions of life and death. One-to-one relationships force realizations and decisions that may seem brutal to some. But they tell a man a lot about himself. For instance, two terriers at the corner of my block will stand across the street from each other with hackles up and defend their territory like two wolves.

The "humanitarians" will say that we're not like that, that we're men, not animals. But that's a false distinction. We *are* animals. And the sources of our animal nature go just as deeply as the sources of animal nature in wolves or dogs. We have a great deal more intelligence and we can make things that wolves can't make; but the violence in the human race is as pronounced as it is in any animal species. It probably always was that way.

The hunting situation reduces the action to certain basic elements. Hemingway says something about this in his bullfight book *Death in the Afternoon*. But compared to bowhunting, the bull fight is the supreme artificiality. You herd an animal into an arena and have some fancifully dressed guy go out there in silk pants and play with him and then stab him.

Hemingway was contemptuous of bow hunters. He thought a man should hunt with a gun, that archers were murderous dilettantes. Actually, the opposite is true. Put a high-powered rifle with telescopic sights in a hunter's hands and then see who is the dilettante. Hemingway was so high on courage, the courage of the matador; but if his doctrine of guns were true, then he ought to have sent the matador into the ring with a Thompson submachine gun. If he wants to test courage, send a man after an elephant with a bow.

And you believe that if and when James Dickey goes after an elephant with a bow, the matter will be resolved along direct, classical lines. All the intensity within him will concentrate on the fact that he's hunting an elephant. The act itself will radiate, unspoken, all the overtones of the situation.

James Dickey is a big man, lean and rugged. He projects a force that envelops you. He applies an intensity to subjects that can wring dry and exhilarate concurrently. Then he assembles what he's learned, and things he's searched for and found, and shoots them back for rebuttal and/or clarification.

That graceful power, physical or verbal, is beautiful, stimulating, exhausting.

So in an effort to recover, we threw some short questions at him.

HELGELAND: What's the most interesting recent development in archery?

DICKEY: The compound bow. I have a couple, and I love them. The human mind is just diabolical in what it can develop—the eccentrics, the peak resistance at half-draw, the way the full-draw weights fall off. The bow is also ugly. If somebody gets a really stylish one, and retains its shooting characteristics, that will be quite a bow. If someone could make a handle as beautiful as the Howatt bows—they're almost like musical instruments in their beauty—then he would have something. But compounds sure do shoot!

I know I may be contradicting myself, because one of the things about archery I've always liked was its simplicity. And maybe the compound is introducing elements that have been anathema to archers from the beginning. But, again, I don't get into all the engineering parts of it. I just like to shoot arrows.

HELGELAND: Why is archery not a major sport like golf?

DICKEY: Sports writers generally don't understand it, Robin Hood being about all they've known of archery, so it doesn't get much publicity. The sports writer doesn't know that people like Vic Berger and John Williams are solid craftsmen, great athletes in their chosen sport.

People think of archery as a static sport, that we simply set up targets, back off, and shoot arrows at them. There is something in the American psyche that wants a sport to have a great deal of action. Most people think golf has more activity than archery, but then they've never shot a couple of field rounds. I think baseball is losing its appeal because, compared to something like basketball, it's a fairly static sport.

HELGELAND: Do you relax with archery?

DICKEY: Yes, I do. There's really nothing more enjoyable than a field round that I'm shooting just for fun, being no competition to anyone other than myself. There's also nothing more exciting than shooting a range I've never shot before. I was up in West Virginia a couple of summers ago. Somewhere near Morgantown they have the prettiest range. I'd go out there, wander around and shoot some arrows, and sometimes even get lost; you can do that on a field range, you know. Especially when you have no more sense of direction than I do.

HELGELAND: Isn't it impossible to avoid comparing this easy enjoyment of the sport against the power of the movie, *Deliverance*?

DICKEY: I know. We worked a week just to get Burt Reynolds's stance right in the scene where the two mountaineers have taken Jon Voight loose from the tree. The camera pulls back and suddenly has Burt standing there in the background in that wetsuit top in the half light. He's just standing there in that wet black outfit like an avenging angel. He's not moving a muscle, yet you know he's at full draw. You know he'll stand that way as long as he has to, and you know that when he strikes, it will be sudden, violent, and fatal.

He did, and it was. A basic, simplistic element necessary to their survival. The four men on the canoe trip were putting themselves to the test against nature, receiving more than they bargained for.

You also get the feeling that when James Dickey wrote the novel, he in some way was putting himself to the test. It's a brutal book. Also absolutely fascinating.

Then, our talk concluded, Dickey picked up his guitar, a big bull of a guitar with deep wood coloring. He nestled it on his knee, tilted one foot up to keep vigorous time, and the main thread of the guitar-banjo duet—the main thread of the entire score for the movie—came ripping out of those strings. Several hairs on the back of my neck stood right straight out, and suddenly I wasn't sitting anymore on the peaceful shore of a little lake on the outskirts of Columbia, South Carolina. I wasn't in James Dickey's backyard.

I was lost somewhere between two violent stretches of Georgia's Chattooga River, and there was one hell of a tough canyon straight ahead. There's only one way to conquer a situation like that. Meet it head on.

—Ahh, but archery is the most beautiful, relaxing sport—

9
JAMES DICKEY AT DRURY COLLEGE

WAYNE HOLMES,
JOSEPH COSTELLO,
MARK GREENBERG,
RANDY MCCONNELL / 1973

HOLMES: I have a question I have wanted to ask Mr. Dickey for some time, and that is about the gamecock and the gamecock as metaphor. I don't know whether you noticed my game chickens when you were out yesterday at the goat roast. There are not many people—particularly artists—who articulate in terms of something as basic as I think the gamecock is. I would like you to comment.

DICKEY: I certainly will. On two levels. First of all, my father was a chicken fighter. And in his later years, I think he had serious qualifications for being the grand old man of American cock fighting. My whole early youth was conditioned by going around with him to his various walks.

HOLMES: Seeing the cock-of-the walk.

DICKEY: Exactly. That's where the phrase comes from. If your cock is not killed—which they almost always are—if you want to save him, you put him out on a walk with nothing but hens, because what makes them fight is sexual pride. You take a cock that's been defeated or pretty badly injured, and then put him out on a walk with nothing but hens and then you pit him—he is ready to tear 'em up. . . . I may write something about this

---

Reprinted by permission from the *James Dickey Newsletter,* 5 (Fall 1988), 16–25 and from Drury College, Springfield, Missouri. Interview conducted on 26 November 1973.

one of these days because it seems like a metaphor for something or other.

HOLMES: I think an important one.

DICKEY: Yes, I think so. As I said, my whole early life was conditioned by going with my father to the walks and with the various country people he had keep his chickens for him. That's one thing. That's one reason that it is important to me. I remember saying to my father, "Dad, why do you fight chickens?" I know my mother was telling me—my mother was a kind of religious fanatic who suggested that this was a disreputable business my old man was engaged in. When I was no more than nine or ten years old, I went to my father and said, "Dad, why are you doing this here chicken fighting stuff when you could be providing for the family a little better some other way than gambling on your chickens." He said, " 'Cause, I tell you, it's *inspiring*. Every man that ever lived would like to have the *guts* those chickens have." The other side of the coin is that I now live in Columbia, South Carolina, and—if this is not fate I don't know what is—the football team and the basketball team are the Fighting Gamecocks! And there are all kinds of metaphysical implications of that sort, you know. All the chicken fights that I've seen! It seems an awful gory business, but it seems to satisfy some kind of hidden instinct in people to watch this kind of thing go on. My father also bred fighting dogs, bull terriers, those kinds of dogs. You don't like to see a dog get torn up by another dog, but a chicken is just something you can't like. You don't care what happens to them.

HOLMES: I disagree. I've raised fighting cocks, too. I remember an old one-eyed cock hitting me in the leg, burying his gaff in my leg. And I thought that was really fine.

DICKEY: Are you a short-gaff or a long-gaff man? My father was a short-heel man.

HOLMES: It doesn't make any difference, but I don't like the blade that so many use.

DICKEY: You mean the slasher.

HOLMES: Yes, the slasher.

DICKEY: My father thought that was not a true test of the chicken's fighting ability—one shuffle and it's over. I'll tell you.

There are really roughly three kinds of chicken gaffs: one is the short-heel, which is a short, pointed heel; another is a longer one of the same kind as the short. The other is the kind of thing that the Mexicans and Filipinos fight with, something that is sharpened on both sides, the slasher—sharpened like a Gillette razor blade.

HOLMES: And it is so long that they can only put one on each leg. Generally, you put two on each leg, but the ones I saw in Mexico were long, curved, and, as you said, kind of like a razor blade. But my point is that they go together just one time and one is dead. That's no test; that's no fun.

DICKEY: Yes, my father always thought that was not a real test of either the gameness or the fighting ability of a chicken. When you get those on a chicken, the bad chicken is just as likely to win as the good chicken.

McCONNELL: Mr. Dickey, what was your reaction to the burning of your book *Deliverance* and Mr. Vonnegut's in North Dakota?[37]

DICKEY: Well, I think Kurt and I are probably going to go out there and make a public stand on the issue, because I think there are important concerns involved in such an event. We may not. But it seems to me that Hitler has risen from the grave. He surfaced this time not in Berlin but in Drake, North Dakota.

McCONNELL: An unusual place.

DICKEY: Yes, I think so. But the thing that bothers me about this whole business of book burning is that people can take it upon themselves to do this sort of thing, that they can take a man's works—something I took twelve years to write and Vonnegut took at least that long. We are reputable—I won't use that dreaded word *sincere*—artists who are trying to work in a vein of creativity, to try to communicate something to people that we feel is important as artists, something we feel is important to do. And then our work is greeted by yahoos who put it in the same category with strict pornography, hard-core pornography—something like the thing I read on the place coming up, called *Stud Hustler*. But Kurt Vonnegut and James Dickey are not going to allow themselves to be put in that category. The only consolation I have is that we are in very good company: Hemingway, Steinbeck, Faulkner—three Nobel Prize winners.

COSTELLO: Following that line of discussion, what do you think of the new pornography laws?

DICKEY: I'm not sure; I don't know. That is the most difficult and thorny question that could possibly be proposed, not only to me but to anybody. I must say I am of a divided mind. I mean, what is the relationship of the state, which is essentially what it comes down to, to what is published and comes out of the mass media—whether the work is by a highly talented and dedicated artist who feels these materials are necessary to his work, or whether it relates to the most errant, money-making smut peddler. But these are two things that are intertwined to an extent that it is almost impossible to extricate one from the other.

GREENBERG: It seems to me that such works should be allowed as long as they do not offend other people.

HOLMES: I disagree with Mark in terms of the very definition of offending. Somebody has *got* to be offensive. If you allow only the works that do not offend, then there will be very little written. I know a lot of people who are offended by the sodomy scene in *Deliverance*. It doesn't offend me. (It does a little in context since I am a hill person, but that may be my own defensiveness.) But it does offend a lot of people, surely those people in North Dakota.

DICKEY: Something occurs to me. A weird scene—this might occur in a novel by Kurt or Phil Roth—where people are forced under guard to watch pornographic films. We don't have that situation, actually, and I hope we never get it because most of them are awful. And I would say, parenthetically—contrary to what David Riesman, the sociologist at the University of Chicago, says—that pornographic material (books, films, pictures, whatever) contributes to something he calls, fancifully but with a certain amount of propriety, the enrichment of fantasy—contrary to that, the ones that I have seen are very much a turn *off*. They don't contribute to the enrichment of fantasy; they just make you bored with the whole subject of sex. And that is a catastrophe, in my opinion. There are no pornographic movies I've ever seen, or books I've ever read, or pictures I've ever looked at, that were nearly as good as my own private ones.

GREENBERG: You were a poet and then you made the transition from poet to novelist.

DICKEY: No, Mark; it's not really a transition at all. It's just a novel I wrote out of the particular sensibilities that I had accumulated as a poet. But anything I write is simply a spin-off from poetry.

COSTELLO: I am in dramatic arts—film, radio, and television—so I am interested in the screenplay and the screen aspect of your novel. Do you think your novel made a successful transition to the movie? I know that so often novels made into movies can have a pretty bad result.

DICKEY: Oh, yes. All you have to do is talk to American writers. I have heard so many horror stories from American writers about what awful things were done with their material. John Updike was unhappy with what they did with *Rabbit, Run*. Now here's the situation; you have one of two courses when you have a novel that's bought by the movies. You have the take-the-money-and-run syndrome, where your agent will tell you to let them do whatever they want to do with it. You get X number of dollars and you get out. And there is another kind of agent who says, "Hang in there; you don't want to see your story ruined. Let's get a contract for the screenplay and *you* do it. And you do it like you want to do it." Well, that entails a number of difficult problems. You might not have the time to spend and you might not want to spend it. But that's the course I took. I did the screenplay, and I think although there are certain minor discrepancies, there can be very few instances of a film being as faithful to the original story, preserving the integrity of the story, as ours was. I don't claim any particular credit for that, but I'm glad it came off that way. I went out to Hollywood and talked to the producers and the rest of them before we started to make the movie. They were determined to make it, but you never heard such a weird variety of interpretations among those writers and directors. First of all, one guy wanted to cash in on the racial thing. So he wanted to make the two guys on the river bank Negroes. Another one wanted to make them hippies, stoned on whatever they were stoned on. Another one wanted to make them Martians. We, thank God, successfully resisted those possibilities, and we made them exactly what they are in the book, degenerate hillbillies. But, again, that has repercussions. I can't go over in those counties now. I'm afraid somebody is going to shoot me because they said I portrayed all mountain people as degenerate sodomists and it's given them a bad name. But that's taking the short view. What about the people at the inn who try to help Jon Voight and Ned Beatty, who try to get them to eat something? Those are hill people, too. Hill people are not subject to anything less than the rest of us are. There are good ones and bad ones. And the bad ones are mighty bad, and the good ones are mighty good.

GREENBERG: How was the casting of the movie determined?

DICKEY: That was one of the most difficult parts. We had a professional casting director, Lynn Stalmaster, who traveled around with John Boorman. I wanted to cast it with four unknowns so that it would be like a wide-screen documentary and you wouldn't know that these guys were actually *not* the guys. Warner's wouldn't go for that, so we compromised. They said, "We have got to have two names. Voight wants to do it—the old Midnight Cowboy. And this new guy, Burt Reynolds, could play Lewis and he wants to do it. He's an ex-stunt man and ex-athlete, an old football player at Florida State. He's got the body for it."

GREENBERG: You were satisfied then?

DICKEY: Yes, I think so. It took a period of adjustment with what we were going to have to work with.

GREENBERG: Were you standing next to the director when production began, tapping him on the shoulder?

DICKEY: Not that much, because John Boorman belongs to the new breed of film directors who have to control every phase of the film, all the way from the logistical parts of it to the makeup and the wardrobe. He controls all aspects of the film. He insists on doing it that way, and I don't have any complaint about that. The only thing is that he's an Englishman. And it struck me that it was a little bit incongruous that he would come over here and live in the woods of North Georgia and feel competent to deal with that milieu. But he did, and I'm not at all sorry for it. There are some things about the film I would change, but there isn't anything I can do about it now.

McCONNELL: How long did it take you to make the movie?

DICKEY: About two years. We had to know what we were doing every day. The story, the novel, is set in the fall of the year—September 14, 15, 16—with a prologue and an epilogue. But we went up there in the fall to look over the Chattooga, and Boorman said, "No, no, we're going to shoot it in the spring." And I said, "Why? It's supposed to be set in the hunting season. These guys wouldn't be up here hunting in the spring." He said, "The trouble is that this foliage up here in the mountains, in the Appalachians, would detract from the story, from what's happening." And he was right, and I was wrong. So we shot it in the spring.

McCONNELL: Did you enjoy your acting debut?

DICKEY: Oh, I can't claim any particular credit for that. I just acted myself dressed up in a sheriff's uniform. . . .

HOLMES: I wondered if fame and money have worked against you as a poet.

DICKEY: No, I don't think so. No, as the folksinger Reverend Gary Davis says, it just makes me feel like going on. I want to do some more. I have another book of poems coming out that I'm very high on. It is far better than anything else I've done before. For any artist there has to be at least the illusion of getting better. You can't just feel that you're repeating yourself. You have to be excited about what you're doing now, not what you did then. I have a couple of long novels working. What I want to do now as far as novels are concerned is to write a resounding and interesting failure. Which I think this is going to be, but it's got some good things in it. I hope you're going to like it. And I want to do some critical articles. I want to do some film work with my son. I was looking at the William Holden miniseries the other night on television, that four-part thing, *The Blue Knight*. That's an interesting new idea on television where you tell a story over several episodes. So I think there are many, many stories that would lend themselves to that sort of thing. I'm going to get together with my great boy, and we're going to work something out on that basis,

I do believe. I've always loved animals so much; I had one offer from a producer—he must be a pretty savvy fellow—who said, "We want to do and we'll give you the money to do the real *Call of the Wild*, the Jack London story. That would be pretty tough to do and would take a lot of location work, but that might be worth it.[38] The reversion, that's something I've always liked, the business of an animal, an *animal*, that is partially civilized and domesticated going back, reverting.

HOLMES: You're using that partially metaphorically.

DICKEY: I don't know how I would do it. I don't know how I would do it. But that idea. I mean, you start with a central idea—you can work details out, at least I think you can, but that would be good. I've hunted wild pigs, for example, and most of the ones I've killed were domesticated pigs that had run off. And it is absolutely amazing how they revert. They grow that ferrel rough up the back, the tusks grow out, the snout elongates, and you can't tell them from a wild one, from a Russian boar. Except maybe if they have a ring in their nose or a notched ear or something. You can't tell them. The idea interests me because there is a kind of reversion, too, in men, but it interests me in animals, and I'd like to see this thing with a dog. It would have to be a kind of dog that was obviously domestic, obviously bred, who's running with the wolves.

COSTELLO: You like working with the mass media?

DICKEY: It's frustrating, but it seems to me that working with, say a film, you can just as well put good stuff before them as bad. Again, the question is whether the regular television fare and movies are so notoriously bad because the movie makers just don't know how to make anything better or whether it's feeding the populous, the multitudes, on what the movie makers think they want. But that's not the only possibility. You can upgrade them in some way by making good films that are also interesting and exciting. It seems to me that we did that with our film *Deliverance* and somehow or another the whole cultural level will rise. I don't mean to talk like McLuhan or somebody like that, but I do think it is possible, don't you?

. . .

10

PLAYBOY INTERVIEW: JAMES DICKEY

GEOFFREY NORMAN / 1973

PLAYBOY: There's a great deal about you and your personal life—your archery, your white-water canoeing, your weight lifting, and the like—that doesn't really fit with what people expect of poets.

DICKEY: That's more a judgment on the stereotype we have of poets than it is on me. If there's any one characteristic of good poets and good poetry, it's the unexpected. I *like* things like white-water canoeing and archery, and if that means I'm a poet who doesn't fall close to the stereotype, that's fine with me.

PLAYBOY: Do you think that kind of thing makes you a sort of Hemingway among poets?

DICKEY: I'm not trying for any such image. They're simply things I like to do. I don't know why we have to go through this endless analysis of motive the way we do. You can't do a simple thing any longer without trying to discover some dark reason for it. The fact that you happen to *like* doing it isn't enough. If you like eating ice-cream cones, it's because you're a repressed homosexual or something. It's all very destructive.

If I weren't a poet, nothing much would be made of the fact that I like doing things that involve the body. I simply happen to feel better when my body is in shape to do things. I was an athlete before I was a poet. My first love was football. In fact, I first went to college on a football scholarship. In those days, poetry was the furthest thing from my mind. There's some-

---

Reprinted from *Playboy,* 20 (November 1973), 81–82, 86, 89, 92, 94, 212–216. From the *Playboy* Interview: James Dickey, *Playboy* Magazine (November 1973); copyright© 1973 by *Playboy.* Reprinted with permission. Interview conducted by Geoffrey Norman.

thing about the body, you know; it's the one thing you can't fake. You go into a locker room sometimes where a bunch of old, out-of-shape men are sitting around and see what happens when a fellow who's really in shape comes in.

PLAYBOY: Do your physical activities tend to be competitive?

DICKEY: I used to feel that it was important to be the best and it would make me miserable to think I wasn't. There was a time when getting the arrow in the middle of the target didn't make me particularly happy, but *not* getting it there made me feel awful. But I've reached the stage now where I can do all these things just for the pleasure that's in them.

PLAYBOY: But you've won trophies in archery tournaments.

DICKEY: Sure. Lots of them. And that's fine and it felt good. But I don't *have* to be the best anymore. We're raised to think that, and it's one of the reasons we are a nation of hustlers and go-getters and so successful and rich. It's also the reason the alcoholic wards and insane asylums and suicide graves are so full. This mad competitive situation we live in produces great material benefit and happiness for some people who seem to have been born for it—but great misery for many others.

PLAYBOY: A great deal of your poetry shows a strong feeling for the outdoor world, for a primitive and violent kind of nature. Can you explain your fascination with the wilderness?

DICKEY: The reason nature makes such an impact on me, in relatively basic activities like hunting, is that I see so little nature that every time I do see it, it strikes me like a vision. It's like a glimpse of another kind of existence. I would never go out and live for months in the wilderness. I couldn't survive there. I'm not that good a shot with the bow; I'm not that conversant with the ways of nature. I admire people who are, but I could never be like that. I'm actually a bookish and rather shy person.

Another reason I'm so taken with nature, with the woods, is that we are steadily and irrevocably losing them. Once gone, they are not restorable. It seems to me that the symbols of twentieth-century destruction are not the atomic bomb, germ warfare, the B-52 bomber, the ICBM, or any of the other much-advertised weapons of mass destruction that are supposed to be hanging over our heads like the sword of Damocles. I don't think the true symbols of mankind's destroying itself are those things at all. The two most pernicious symbols of the destructiveness of man by the greed and evil in his own nature are the bulldozer and the chain saw.

PLAYBOY: Is this feeling about machines the reason you hunt with a bow instead of a gun?

DICKEY: I'm deathly afraid of guns. If I heard a sudden loud noise close by, even if I made it myself and knew it was coming, I would jump cleanly out of my skin. And there is something so final about a gun. People get hurt so badly with them: They shoot off their feet; they mistake hunters for rabbits or deer; they kill their sons.

I like to look at guns, but I don't like to handle them or be around them when they're being fired. I guess I've seen too many of them fired at men in earnest. They don't seem to belong in the kind of hunting relationship that I want. I like a bow because your body is involved in it. You have to exert your own strength. It's hard to hit anything with one. You have to get closer to the game; have to enter into his world.

PLAYBOY: Why kill the deer? Why not stalk them for close-up photographs?

DICKEY: It's not the same relationship at all. I would rather enter into the deer's universe of life and death, of survival, than stalk him for something as inconclusive as a picture. It seems to me much more a tribute to the deer to join him on his own ground, where he really has all the advantages. He can run a lot faster than you; his senses are much more alert; it's his territory, not yours. I think you do him an honor by entering his world of life and death.

PLAYBOY: But it's only his death that's at stake. He's not likely to kill *you*.

DICKEY: That's true. But Fred Bear, the archery manufacturer and master hunter and woodsman, tells me that the whitetailed deer is the most challenging big-game animal in the world; that if you can successfully hunt *him*, you can hunt anything. And he ought to know, since he's killed just about every kind of game animal in the world—including an elephant—with a bow and arrow. So hunting deer with a bow is not easy and not simple slaughter. And I can assure you that the deer population is in no danger from me. I hunt once every two years, and with very ill success at that. What I like is just *being* there.

PLAYBOY: You're not just gratifying some atavistic need?

DICKEY: How in the hell would anybody possibly know? But it strikes me that the people who actually live around the woods and actually *know* them are a lot less worried about the fate of a single deer than people who live in large apartment buildings in cities. When you're *there,* the circumstances seem a little less unfair and the whole thing takes on a kind of excitement that makes it seem perfectly natural. You get out in the woods and start seeing tracks and signs and there's not anything else like it. And you learn very fast just how out of place you are. I remember once when I was hunting in the mountains of North Georgia. It was warm and I'd been walking since dawn. In the afternoon, I found a comfortable place at the edge of a clearing and stretched out under a tree. I very quickly fell asleep in that warm sun. After a little while, I opened my eyes for some reason and saw several deer across the clearing. They were just grazing; several doe out in the clearing and the bucks back a little in the trees. I was so sleepy that I just closed my eyes again. I thought I'd get them in a minute. When I woke up about ten minutes later, they were gone. At first, I didn't believe they'd ever *been* there. But the other side of the clearing was covered with tracks. I'm sure that something changed when I woke up and saw them. Maybe I gave off a scent. Whatever it was, they could sense it and they got out of there.

PLAYBOY: Another side of your fascination with nature seems to be an interest in its darker aspects. Why is it that in many of your poems about nature—and in parts of *Deliverance*—there is such a strong sense of evil lurking beneath the tranquil and beautiful surfaces?

DICKEY: In my little bit of graduate work in American literature twenty years ago at Vanderbilt, I was a kind of two-bit Melville scholar. That was my only claim to fame after a year or so of working in graduate school, in those dark satanic mills. The thing that impressed me most about Melville was exactly the thing you described, this sense of an apparently serene surface which masks some hidden horror, some unknown universal evil. There's the great chapter in *Moby-Dick,* on the whiteness of the whale, when he develops the idea that white is kind of the color that masks all the darkness. He talks very eloquently in *Moby-Dick* about striking through this deceptively serene and even beautiful surface under which lurks the other nameless thing.

PLAYBOY: Sharks and snakes appear often in your poetry. Are they your white whales?

DICKEY: I don't know. I've always had a very strong attraction to the *other*—the thing that's most unlike humans and most unlike any kind of life that is close to us like, say, a dog is. A shark is a low, brutal, terrifying, unpredictable, and successful form of life. The shark hit the evolutionary jackpot the first time around. He hasn't had to evolve at all in millions of years. He is very alien. So is a snake. Both of them are, I think, just about as far away from human characteristics and appearances as has yet been got. Well, maybe some of the insects would be farther. But some of them I feel much closer to than I do to a snake. A bee, for example, which can sting you and be very painful about it, does not evoke in me the same sense of fear and awe that a snake does or that a shark does. A shark is nothing but sheer, one hundred percent senseless power and rapacity. They tear their own guts out, you know, when they get excited and are snapping at something—get to eating each other and end up eating themselves.

PLAYBOY: Your first published poem was about a shark, wasn't it?

DICKEY: "The Shark at the Window." It was in the early days of marine aquariums down on the Florida coast. My brother and I took a trip down there after I got out of the Service. I had never seen an oceanarium, or whatever they call them, before. I was fascinated by those huge creatures drifting by with that kind of blank look in their eyes. It's so blank that you're quite convinced they know a lot you could never know. And they know it in ways more useful than the things that you know are useful to you.

PLAYBOY: How important do you think it is for the reader of your poetry to know about the kinds of things—such as sharks and snakes, archery and canoeing—that interest you as a man? Would his appreciation of your work be limited if he didn't know anything about *you*?

DICKEY: My formative years of dealing with poetry were so tyrannized by the influence of T. S. Eliot that it has taken me—as I dare say a good many other poets—a long time to get over or around Eliot's ideas. His notion of art as completely sufficient unto itself, that the important thing is what's on the page and that it doesn't involve the guy's personality, since all you're reading is words in a certain order that have a certain effect on you, sounds fine. But, after all, the thing wasn't written by a machine. It was written by one human being to another human being—in this case, *you*. I like, much better than Eliot's rather bloodless notions of poetry, the feeling that Malcolm Lowry had about the writers he cared for. Lowry is one of my favorite writers. He had all the guts and gusto and the accessibility to experience that Eliot never had. Besides being an alcoholic, he was an enthusiast, and theres not a thing better in the world than a genuine alcoholic enthusiast. Lowry loved the sea. *Moby-Dick* was his idea of a great book. There was a fellow from either Norway or Sweden named Nordahl Grieg who wrote about the sea. Lowry's impulse when he read Nordahl Grieg was not to write a critical article about him to but go and *meet* him. I like that.

PLAYBOY: Would it make any difference to your appreciation of someone's poetry to know whether he was a Republican, Democrat, Socialist, or vegetarian?

DICKEY: No, it would interest me, but it wouldn't make any difference in how I read the poem. But the fact that Robert Frost had these terrible fears of death adds a dimension to my reading a poem like "Acquainted with the Night."

PLAYBOY: And knowing that Keats was a consumptive would enhance your appreciation of him?

DICKEY: Sure. How could you read Robert Burns without being aware that he was a Scotsman? Or Faulkner without knowing that he was a Southerner?

PLAYBOY: Are the kinds of political activity some writers get involved in equally important to any serious consideration of their work? Norman Mailer's running for mayor, for example?

DICKEY: Oh, that's just fun and games. Norman Mailer doesn't know anything about running a city, though he has a number of crack-brained schemes. Why he does these things is his own business, and he does them for his own reasons. I like Norman very much personally. I'm always amused and sometimes infuriated at his public actions, but the man himself is the gentlest and most companionable fellow imaginable. I sometimes can't believe that the Norman Mailer I know is the same person I read about in *Newsweek* doing all those ridiculous things.

PLAYBOY: Still, some poets—such as Robert Lowell—have been conspicuously political in a serious way. And there are those who claim that in these times the artist *must* take a stand. Do you have any definable politics?

DICKEY: I don't think poets have any particular inside track on political insight. History has proved the opposite to be the case. Look at Ezra Pound. I think any man who happens to write poetry and is also interested in politics is really engaged in politics as a citizen, not as a poet. The business of poets' using their reputations, such as they happen to be, to prognosticate on political affairs is not only unfortunate but silly. A poet has no more reason to be taken seriously as a political pundit or shaper of public opinion than a mason or a pipe fitter.

There's a dangerous tendency in American life to assume that because a person knows something about one field he can tell you all about everything else. My political opinions are no better than anybody else's. They are just my opinions as a private citizen. I don't claim any kind of clairvoyance in any matters at all, *including* poetry. Certainly not in politics or international problems or the problems of cities or racial problems or overpopulation, ecology, and all of those things. I consider myself, as Santayana once said of himself, "an ignorant man; almost a poet."

PLAYBOY: What about in extreme cases, such as the persecution of writers such as Aleksandr Solzhenitsyn? Do you think the artist has some sort of responsibility there?

DICKEY: That's quite a different thing. The business of persecuting a man for what he writes is obviously reprehensible. I've signed dozens of petitions in favor of the Soviet Jews and protesting their treatment over there. I don't think any of them have had any effect, but I always sign them.

PLAYBOY: You appeared with Yevgeny Yevtushenko when he was touring this country. Did you ever argue about this with him?

DICKEY: Yes. I don't like to see a country that I've been in two wars for run down by a man from a country that is systematically disadvantaging hundreds of thousands of Jews. When Yevtushenko and I appeared together at Madison Square Garden, I spoke to him about the line of his that says, "The stars in your flag, America, are bullet holes." I said, "Suppose I went to your country and got up at a poetry reading and said, 'Russia, your flag is red because it is dipped in the blood of millions of Jews.'" He said, "They would not like to hear that from *you*." And I said I didn't like hearing the same thing from *him*.

PLAYBOY: Did you part friends?

DICKEY: Yeah. We swapped hats. He says it's the custom of his country, but I think it's a custom he made up on the spur of the moment because he wanted to get my hat. I had a lot better hat than his. Mine was fox fur and his was Siberian sable or something.

PLAYBOY: Do you think that artists, when they do get into politics, can influence events in a significant way?

DICKEY: I don't think artists ever influence political thought much one way or another. Under any circumstances. They might affect things a little in the way of public action—such as the publication of Upton Sinclair's book about the meat-packing industry, *The Jungle*. That helped get better pure-food laws put in. But I don't think any novel or poem or literary essay would ever cause the fall of a nation. Or the rise of one either.

PLAYBOY: What about cases like George Orwell? Didn't he shape political attitudes toward totalitarianism?

DICKEY: Theoretically and probably in some practical ways, an artist's work can do that. But I think Orwell's influence is not as great as some people believe it is. The connection of literary people with politics *has,* however, resulted in an atmosphere of literary blackmail. Say someone has an opinion of the Vietnam War and someone else has another opinion. One is a poet in this hypothetical case and the other is a reviewer. What happens far too often is that the reviewer will use his disagreement with the poet's politics to put the poetry down. In other words, the unspoken attitude behind the review will be, "You don't agree with me on Vietnam; therefore, your poetry is no good."

PLAYBOY: You've experienced some of that, haven't you?

DICKEY: There isn't anything politically reprehensible that I haven't been accused of by the literary-sheep faction at one time or another. I seem to have become identified with intellectual support of Vietnam. Bullshit. I don't support Vietnam. People talk about my poem "The Firebombing" as though it were written by a man who loved to burn up children. They are either being perversely ignorant or just ordinary, run-of-the-mill ignorant. That's not what it's about; that's not the danger facing pilots. The danger is in the feeling of power it gives them to do these things and not be held accountable for the carnage and the terror and bloodshed and mutilation. To not even *see* it. I guess it's no longer the fire-bombing airplane that's the symbol of this sort of thing but something even farther removed physically from the victims. It's the fellow who pushes the button for the ICBM. He is never even going to see the *cities* he reduces to atomic ashes. He might read about it later, but he is not held accountable or even called on to witness the result of this action.

Now, that's the dangerous thing. That is what "The Firebombing" is about—that you'll never have to face up to the carnage and death and mutilation you have wrought. To you it just looks like a beautiful spectacle. And it *is* beautiful. It's not horrible, because you don't see the horror. You're far above it. You're looking down like the eye of God. It's really like fireworks. "The Firebombing" is about the worst guilt of all—the guilt of not being able to feel guilt over the things you ought to feel guilty about.

PLAYBOY: You've written several poems about the war—among them some of your best. Why is it that you and so many other American writers have made war a central theme?

DICKEY: For a couple of reasons. World War II quite literally determined the course of history for hundreds of years, maybe for thousands. If you're part of a drama of that global scope, it can't help but make some kind of tremendous impression on your personal life. It's the most important and profound historical drama that you will ever personally have a chance to play a part in. The bloodshed, death, disease, and mutilation are terrible things. No humane person wants that to go on. Yet when it does go on, it's no good saying that it isn't tremendously dramatic and far-reaching. When you have participated in it, you have been part of the historical process. One of the sources of disillusionment after World War I and World War II was that people who went back to their jobs and their ordinary lives felt like something was missing, some sense of belonging to a large historical action. John Hersey attempted to portray one of these men in his novel about flying, *The War Lover.* There were people who didn't want the war to end. They knew they would never again be so *up* or have such a sense of consequence. Some fellows in my squadron actually cried when the peace was signed. They didn't want to go back to driving taxis. They wanted to fly airplanes and be heroes.

PLAYBOY: We were talking about knowing the poet to better understand his work. One of the things you learn about contemporary poets is that they are, most of them, truly tormented, haunted men.

DICKEY: Yes. The occupational hazards for poets are alcoholism and suicide—usually in combinations of one sort or another. You could rattle off a whole list of American poets who have committed suicide just in my generation and the one before it. It's terrible. John Berryman, Randall Jarrell, Hart Crane. I read that big book on Crane's life, *Voyager,*[39] and I'll tell you, I have never read of such a hellacious thirty-three-year-long life. And Crane was a creature meant for joy and ecstasy and all that. But what he got was agony and terror and uncertainty and worry about money.

Or take Robert Frost. I happen to dislike very much what I know of Frost. But I love some of the poems very much. I read that big two-volume biography of Frost by Lawrance Thompson.[40] Although he doesn't emerge as a very likable man, I'm glad I read the book and I'm glad that I know him better. I'm interested in the struggles that this singularly sensitive and strong-willed man went through in order to be able to write his poetry *at all*. It's very encouraging to know that as big a son of a bitch as the guy was and as much agony as he sowed about, especially among his family, he could endure as much as he endured. That adds a great dimension to him.

PLAYBOY: Do you have any theories about the vulnerability of poets to these problems?

DICKEY: I think there is a terrible danger in the over-cultivation of one's sensibilities, and that's what poets are forced to do in order to be poets. You will find that poets, almost without exception, are cast into the most abject despair over things that wouldn't bother an ordinary person at all. Living with such an exacerbating mind and sensibility gets to be something that one cannot bear any longer. In order to create poetry, you make a monster out of your own mind. You can't get rid of him. He stays right with you every minute. Every minute of every day and every night. He produces terrible things—nightmare after nightmare. I'm subject to having them no less than any of the rest of them. But I don't fool myself. I know what's doing it. Writers start out taking something to aid the monster, to give them the poetry. Poets use alcohol, or any other kind of stimulant, to aid and abet this process, then eventually take refuge in the alcohol to help get rid of it. But by that time the monster is so highly developed he cannot be got rid of. There are a lot of people who believe that if they can just reach this kind of ecstasy, they will finally be happy. But it's not that way at all. Those who have these kinds of experiences aren't really the happy ones. The happiest people are the stupid ones.

PLAYBOY: Does all this make you worry for your own life?

DICKEY: Yes. There's not any more dangerous occupation in the world. The mortality rate is very, very high. Paul Valéry once said, "One should never go into the self except armed to the teeth." That's true. The kind of poets we're talking about—Berryman, Crane, Dylan Thomas—have created something against which they have no immunity and which they cannot control.

PLAYBOY: And there isn't really any going back?

DICKEY: It's like wanting to be a virgin again. It becomes your way of life. You're used to living in this over-intense reality. Novelists and prose writers who are essentially poets in their vision, like James Agee and Thomas Wolfe, undergo the same sort of things. Take a workmanlike novelist, C. P. Snow, who's almost the antithesis of the poetic novelist or the poetic *anything;* he's probably not bothered by these matters. But the people with the intense visionary kind of apprehension are subject to these things and, as I say, there is no more dangerous occupation. You feed the monster and he grows day by day, and there hasn't yet been devised any defense against him. Once you've got him, he's got you. And he'll never leave you.

PLAYBOY: Is it worth it?

DICKEY: You don't know if it's worth it. The question of value, somehow or another, doesn't seem relevant. I think, though, that most people who live in this kind of situation—like, say, Sylvia Plath, who, incidentally, I think is one of the lesser talents, one of the very slightest—would say they wouldn't have had it any other way. Because the moments of intensity which do lead to delight and joy and fulfillment are so much better than those that other people have. You would go through almost anything to do that again. Alcohol or heroin or whatever is nothing compared with the burst of glory that descends from the clouds when you say something that you didn't know you could say and it's just damn good. That's the only rule of thumb I have for judging anything I write: It's good when I say something that I hadn't any idea my mind was capable of producing.

PLAYBOY: But for that special kind of experience, you have to go through all the others, too.

DICKEY: Sure. That's why I used to drink a lot. If my constitution had been capable of holding up, I would have drunk twice as much as I did. Liquor has resulted in some rather embarrassing scenes for me. Some of them were downright dangerous to me and to other people. But aside from actual physical deterioration, I never had anything but good things happen from drinking. It just came time to quit. And it's not nearly as hard as I thought. The first week is awful hard, but after that it's not bad. You just get to thinking in different channels. But liquor was a good and faithful companion to me, and the great thing about it is that it never fails you. Never fails to do what you want it to do. If you're feeling bad, you feel an awful lot better if you have a drink. If you feel good, you'll feel twice as good.

PLAYBOY: Do you think you'll still be able to produce poetry without liquor?

DICKEY: I think so. I certainly hope so. I've almost lived past the age when most of the people we've been talking about went under. Like all drives, that one decreases with age. These days I feel like the grandfather I am, and I'm more willing to accept that. I'm still working and it's good. And I intend to keep working. I have to. I don't have to scramble so much to keep the family together and educate the children. These last few years, I haven't had to do that, and that makes life a little easier.

PLAYBOY: In terms of wealth and public attention, you have achieved more than most poets. How do these things affect your work?

DICKEY: Well, I don't know. You have to find devices for coping with public pressures that you don't experience when you're confined to the scholarly journals or the critical poetry journals—at least, not to the extent that somebody experiences who has written a novel that a movie has been made from. You have to find ways to cope with problems that never have arisen before and make public appearances and give readings, and so on. I began to give readings maybe ten or twelve years ago. The public image, whatever that may be, notwithstanding, I'm really a rather shy person. It made me very nervous to get up in front of even as few as ten or fifteen people. My wife noticed how nervous it was making me. We were on a relatively modest salary at the time at a small West Coast experimental school, and even though I got a couple of hundred dollars that we very much needed for a week's work, I just didn't know if it was worth what I was going through to get it. My wife said, "Don't worry about it. Just be yourself." That sounded like good advice. But then I got to thinking about it. "Just be yourself," she said. Ah, but which one?

PLAYBOY: Most people who have attended your readings seem to have come away enormously impressed. Do you ever have a bad night?

DICKEY: Oh, yes. I've had some when I was so drunk I couldn't pronounce the words. But even in England, where audiences are sometimes rather hostile to American poets—and especially to this one—that seems to make them more sympathetic. They feel sorry for you. But I don't want them to applaud because they feel sorry for me. I've only had that happen three or four times.

PLAYBOY: Have you ever felt that you might be better off if you went back to doing something else for a living and writing poetry on the side?

DICKEY: I believe that the American poet ought to be a tough son of a bitch. He ought to hold his own in this culture on his own terms and not compromise under any circumstances. I think that he can be like Ed Gentry in *Deliverance*—resourceful. He should live by his trade, should see that he *can* live by his trade. Now, that seemed impossible until recently, but it's not impossible now. Poetry readings draw very large fees for some poets. Who those poets are is determined by a good many factors. Word just somehow gets around the schools and the people in charge invite a given poet. Then more and more of them invite him. This is a spin-off from his profession of writing poetry that enables him to go on writing more poetry. He might supplement this with a teaching job. But I believe in a poet's living by his trade in *some* way.

I used to believe that you could do something that had nothing to do with poetry, not teach it or anything else, then write the poetry whenever you could. That you could be a professional fisherman or a game warden and write poetry in addition to that. At the age of fifty, I no longer believe that. I am all for the poet's being paid well and being proud that he earns his way. If he has to serve on prize committees, do consultation work, advise, give lectures, readings, or appear on panels—well, these are all things that pertain to his being a poet. They don't pertain to his being an advertising writer. They don't pertain to his being a professional fisherman or game warden or an insurance salesman. They pertain to his being a poet, and that is very important. Poets in America have always been hangdog. They have always been downtrodden, looking at you out of the corners of their eyes, ashamed and thinking that people believe they really don't work for a living.

Playboy Interview

PLAYBOY: Isn't there a tendency among poets to live on grants and that sort of thing?

DICKEY: If they can get them. They are fiercely contested for. Literary politics are very dirty. People aren't fighting for control of corporations; they're fighting for a $5000 grant or a prize of some sort. The prizes are the silliest things of all, but if you win a prize like the National Book Award or a Pulitzer, then the schools are favorably impressed and you can get your price up. If I've done any service for the poets of my generation, it's been to get those reading prices up. To give Al Capp $3500 for a throwaway evening such as he provides and then try to pick up a fine American poet for $200 is an insult to my craft. I won't move for any figure like that. If Capp gets $3500, that's what I want. And if they'll give it to me, they'll give it to somebody else. I will not have the poets of my generation picked up cheap. Sure I make money, but so do they. And they made it because I made it.

PLAYBOY: What about resentment and jealousies over other poets' successes? Is there a lot of that?

DICKEY: I never feel it. That's one thing that has been left out of my make-up. I am the complete opposite of somebody like Robert Frost, who didn't care anything about anybody's poetry; he just looked at the other fellow as a rival. If a new, good guy comes along, I want to get his book and read it. I don't worry about his reputation. People promote animosities, but I don't do anything to further them at all. I remember a few years ago Mailer came out with a book[41] and in it had a rundown of all the other writers he thought were in competition with him: William Styron, James Jones and others. If you want to write novels, why take time out for spiteful journalism about your contemporaries? I'll be damned if I can understand it. I don't want to indulge in literary battles. I want to get on with the job of writing poetry and novels. I've got a lot of faults, God knows, but I have never been prone to the kind of warping, self-destructive envy of someone like Robert Bly. And you can print that.

PLAYBOY: He's the one who criticized you personally for "The Firebombing."[42]

DICKEY: I think so. He writes so badly that I simply can't read him. I could take a high schooler with an average capacity for language and have him writing far better than Robert Bly inside of three months. Bly has an inferior intelligence and no imagination at all.

PLAYBOY: There is an American myth about writers' success: that F. Scott Fitzgerald was supposedly ruined by success, Thomas Wolfe partially so, Hemingway—

DICKEY: There were a lot of other factors involved in all those cases. But I would say the dangers of success are considerably less than the dangers of failure—especially as you get older. Success and money are important when you don't have them, but also when you do. You don't have to cultivate yachts and private airplanes and all that to want to give your children good medical attention if they need it and to be able to pay your bills. I'm uncertain about the values of success, but I can categorically tell you that success and affluence are a great deal better than poverty, obscurity, and failure.

PLAYBOY: What about material comforts? In *Deliverance*, Lewis shows a great deal of contempt for the kind of luxury most Americans enjoy, seems to feel it makes them soft.

DICKEY: I'm ambivalent about materialism. Certain things I like very much. I like good guitars. And I like very good archery equipment. I don't care very much for clothes. Automobiles I am relatively indifferent to. A lot of the things that *Playboy* readers seem to set great store by, such as revolving beds with built-in hi-fi, would interest me only as exotica. And very expensive, too, I expect. There's a limit. I don't mind being comfortable, and I don't want anybody to starve or not be able to get penicillin when he needs it. But beyond a certain point, you have so many things that you've got to look after them and they take you over. When we moved down here on this lake, I told my boy that I could buy him an outboard motor and a boat. He was overjoyed. He had a great time with it until it started getting dirty and he had to haul it up on the bank and Clorox it. He quickly began to have second thoughts on the joys of being a boatowner. You don't get one without the other. If you have a lot of goods and chattel—several houses, apartments in different cities—you either have to look after them yourself or pay somebody else to do it for you. Then *they* come into it and you have to contend with them. It's not all roses. I was reading the chronicles of some of the very wealthy families in England who have cottages on their estates with gardeners whose families have been with their families for five hundred years. They have definite duties toward them. They have to go around and visit the sick, and so forth. I don't know how well I could carry that off.

PLAYBOY: You probably won't have to worry about that, but you *have* made a good deal of money from *Deliverance,* first as a book, then as a hit movie. Were you surprised at how well it did?

DICKEY: I had no idea. There are thousands of novels published every year and I was just thankful that mine was going to be one of them. It was the first fiction of any kind I had ever written.

PLAYBOY: Didn't your reputation as a poet help?

DICKEY: No. In fact, that usually works against you. Every poet seems to think that he has to write a novel or a play, and most of them do. But the description poetic novel has become almost a pejorative. People think of adjective-heavy prose that you can get enough of in half a page, like eating too much fudge cake.

PLAYBOY: The book seemed to translate perfectly to the screen. Was this something you had in mind while you were writing the novel?

DICKEY: Some reviewers seem to assume that I started out to write a book that would be sold to the movies and, seven years later, did just that. If it were as easy as that, there would be many more people writing books that would be eagerly bought by the movies. It just doesn't work that way, I'm sorry to report.

PLAYBOY: To some people, the success of *Deliverance* lay in the fact that it was an adventure story with a message for the time. Did you intend it as such?

DICKEY: I never thought of *Deliverance* in philosophical terms at all. I don't really believe in beginning with some kind of philosophical notion and then trying to write something to illustrate it. I believe pretty much in telling the story and having whatever might be implicit in the story emerge from it. The story of *Deliverance* has been read as a commentary on questions theological, military, political—in so many ways that I'm completely bewildered by what people read into it. Surely, if it has overtones—and I suppose it must have some, most stories do—those are secondary, not primary. My whole purpose was to write a story about four fellows who have got themselves into a situation and then have to get themselves out. Now, whether this is a commentary on the human condition in general or the human condition in our time, or what, I don't really feel qualified to say. I suppose it has something to do with the price of survival under certain circumstances, but I think it would be a mistake to assume that the circumstances described in *Deliverance* are universal. If anybody wants to see it just as an adventure story, that's fine. That would please me more than all the philosophical interpretations in the world.

PLAYBOY: But isn't there an allegorical structure to the book? After all, there's the title, the river, the journey, and all that evil to be overcome en route.

DICKEY: People seem to insist on reading that into it. One of my favorite American writers is Wright Morris, and he had a story in which there was a trapped fly. Let me read you what he said about it: "A student of the modern novel recently asked me off the cuff and man to man if I didn't think the trapped fly in one of my books was a symbolic cliche. The Midwest setting of this novel simply buzzed with trapped flies and so did the book. Flies, when they came to my mind, were still flies when I put them on the page. They belong to the scene I was painting like the screen at the door, the way it banged when slammed and the view through the glass-fogged window. Flies dead or alive were among the first inhabitants, and that they might also prove to be symbols was not my proper business. When the writing is good everything is symbolic, but symbolic writing is seldom good. Symbol hunting is the fashionable safari for the vacationing writer and reader, a way of killing time. The overtrained symbol-haunted reader will not accept the fly for what it is for both the author and the book—an actual trapped fly."

PLAYBOY: Still, you can't help reading something into *Deliverance*. It's pretty clear that Ed Gentry is changed, perhaps for the better, after he's led the others safely down the river and killed a man to do it.

DICKEY: Yes. I intended something of that sort. *Deliverance* is a story of how decent men kill. It's not enough to say, as some of the shallower reviewers have, that the book tries to show how man's essential malehood depends on his going out and killing somebody. Of course not. Nevertheless, American life is so structured that a lot of areas of one's existence—or one's potentiality, maybe—for either good or evil never get a chance to surface. And sometimes these *are* repressed feelings of violence. That doesn't mean one must go out perpetrating violent acts. This wasn't the case in *Deliverance,* where the violent acts by Ed Gentry were forced upon him. It was self-defense. Knowing this, he can take even more of a kind of secret pride in what he's done because he's a peace-loving person. He's never had any record of any criminal activity, much less murder. It was forced upon him and he brought it off. He got away with it, and this is a kind of index of secret powers he never suspected he had. Now he knows what he's capable of doing. And this gives him a kind of secret power that he draws off of in other areas, in his own life.

PLAYBOY: Gentry does take a kind of pride in being able to pull it off. Isn't that some sort of acknowledgment of a survival ethic?

DICKEY: Well, to tell you the truth, if you want to look at larger implications, I suppose the book might raise the question of what makes people do what they do to preserve themselves and their friends and families, and so on. I've had peaceniks—among them some poets, but I'm glad to say not very good ones—tell me that they would rather be killed themselves, sent to a concentration camp and murdered systematically, than raise a finger against another human being. Even in defense of themselves, their children and their wives and the people who depend on them. That they would rather be killed themselves than offer any violence to another human being. I think that is the most absolute bullshit. Anybody comes after me and my people, I'll blow his head off.

PLAYBOY: So you obviously do see a place for violence in an ethical system.

DICKEY: Nobody can love peace like somebody who has been in a war. I love it. There isn't any machine or dial to measure this by, but I can categorically guarantee that I'm no lover of war, killing, pain, and suffering. The things high-speed metal can do to human flesh and bone are so horrendous that once you've seen one battle fatality or fatal aircraft accident, you are never quite the same afterward. You learn just how mortal you really are and how vulnerable your body really is. I like the way these people tell you nobly how they would choose to die rather than offer violence to anyone, not even the worst possible human monster who is going to cut their children with scissors or something of that sort. That is a completely abstract statement on their part; it has no relation whatever to reality. I know perfectly well that the eventuality of their having to make that choice is almost completely negligible.

PLAYBOY: But Ed Gentry did have to make a choice.

DICKEY: Yes, he did. The thing is that deaths go on. Women and children are murdered, people are shot down in the streets, knifed, raped. We all know that offering no resistance to these things just makes it easier for more and more of them to go on. I'm reminded of what Hilaire Belloc said in quite a nice couplet. It goes like this: "Pale Ebenezer thought it wrong to fight, / But Roaring Bill (who killed him) thought it right."

PLAYBOY: Some people say that one reason so many of these awful things are going on is that books and movies such as *Deliverance* have created a climate saturated with violence. Do you think there may be any truth to that?

DICKEY: I don't know. I'm not really competent to judge that. In my more prudish days, maybe twenty years ago—before the days of nudity in movies and even in *Playboy;* in fact, a little bit before *Playboy* began—I went to a French film with a French writer I knew. I told him, "Lord, you French certainly are dirty-minded to show these things on-screen. We would never do that in America. You certainly are immoral here in Europe." He said, "We don't think it's nearly as immoral to show a naked woman as it is to show a cleverly committed crime." So I don't know about violence in the movies. I hope people don't start killing each other with bows and arrows after seeing the film. But I will say that I'm all for freedom for the artist. Even for freedom for the hack.

PLAYBOY: Are you happy with the movie version of *Deliverance*?

DICKEY: Yes, very much so. I think there must be very few instances in the whole history of film making of a movie staying as close to the original novel as this one. I've heard so many horror stories about people having their novels taken by Hollywood, butchered, and changed around every which way. I certainly can't complain of that. Some things about it, of course, I would change a little bit. I advised them or asked them to do things they didn't do, but, on the other hand, they did some things that came off better on the screen than what I had projected. I wrote the screenplay, but there was also a lot of improvised dialogue. That's one of the things I suggested, especially at the beginning, when the men first get on the river. When they're whooping it up and carrying on: "Watch yourself, Robert. Keep your eyes open." They were just *doing* it. And it sounded great.

PLAYBOY: How did you come to play the sheriff?

DICKEY: I was in the director, John Boorman's, lodge. He and the actors and I were sitting around with the script girl and various functionaries. We were talking about the cast, about the people who played the townsfolk: the taxi driver, the doctor, the nurse, and so on. John turned to me and said, "Jim, we all want you to play the sheriff." I said I'd never acted in my life. "You can do it. We all want you to," he said. So I just played myself dressed up in a sheriff's uniform. After we made that scene, I wore the uniform back to where we were staying and had dinner. Somebody said to me, "Does your sheriff's outfit fit you OK?" I said, "Yeah, I haven't had it off all day. In fact, ever since I've had it on, I've been going around collecting graft from every whorehouse in Rabun County. And that isn't all I got, either."

PLAYBOY: Do you expect to do any more acting?

DICKEY: I don't think so. I've had a couple of offers. But they've only been bit parts, so there's no reason for me to do them. I think I'd better quit while I'm ahead. If that's where I am.

PLAYBOY: Maybe you're missing a chance to experience something you can use in your poetry. You've written about flying, football, archery, canoeing, guitar playing, and most of the other things you've done in your life. Aren't you tempted to try a little more acting so that you can write about it?

DICKEY: I'm not a believer in going out and deliberately seeking certain experiences for the purpose of writing about them. If you're naturally interested in things and have certain things happen to you, then you can make the poetry out of the circumstances of your existence—unguided, more or less, by the fact of your being a writer. I didn't go to war to learn about flying night fighters so I could then write about it. I went to war because the world went to war. *Then* I wrote about it. If your imagination is keyed up through application over a period of twenty-three, twenty-four, twenty-five years, you get the habit of mind of making connections and associations. And that habit of mind discovers your subjects for you. They pile up by the ream.

PLAYBOY: Like your poem that was inspired by the Army post across the lake from here?

DICKEY: "Drums Where I Live." It's that business of living close to the war machine and that ghostly cadence count coming across the lake in the early morning, the drums, and so on. Some of the neighborhood ladies said, "You know, it's very comforting to hear them over there, isn't it?" That's not the effect they had on me. I felt like I was right on the edge of a war. That they were going to be defending the neighborhood and people were going to be coming in. Paratroops landing. They represent to me some kind of tendency in mankind toward belligerence that is going to destroy us all. It sounds like a ghostly take-over army just waiting for the day. Like *Seven Days in May.*

PLAYBOY: What if the connections and associations hadn't come? What would you do it you weren't a poet?

DICKEY: I don't have the slightest idea what I would do. My life for so many years has revolved around the use of words and the connections between words and ideas and images and rhythms and all that. That's been central to everything I've done. If that were taken away, I suppose I would be a professional scholar. But if words and scholarship and criticism and writing and everything connected with words were taken away from me, especially at the age of fifty, I don't know *what* I would do. I'm good enough to be a professional musician. I suppose I could play guitar six hours a day for six months and get a job for twenty dollars a night in some dingy coffeehouse backing up some kid of sixteen who could play better than I could. Or give music lessons. Something like that.

PLAYBOY: If you could be young again, what would you do with your life?

DICKEY: Exactly the same, except that I would have started earlier. I don't really regret very many of the things that I've done. The things I've done that you're supposed to regret—I only regret that I didn't do more of them when I had the chance.

PLAYBOY: Such as?

DICKEY: Oh, I don't know.

PLAYBOY: Impulsive weekends?

DICKEY: By God, yes. I missed a lot of my youth in the war. I'd like to have it back.

PLAYBOY: You said once that if you were reincarnated, you'd like to come back as a sea bird.

DICKEY: Well, I would like to come back as an alien form of life. I wouldn't like to be anything like a barnacle or some stationary creature that sucks things in and blows them out; making a few pearls whose value he cannot assess. I would like to be something mobile. Maybe something close to the ground like a snake that could feel every little thing along his whole body and also carry some deadly venom and be very secret, beautifully camouflaged and all that. Or something that could fly long, long distances, especially over water, where there is nothing to look at except endless miles of empty sea, a wandering albatross or one of those migratory birds that navigate by the stars without knowing how. You know, they go thousands of miles from, say, the Galapagos Islands to way past the Arctic Circle and stay up there. When it comes time to mate, they go home by some instinct that will never be understood. Some things are not subject to scientific investigation, are absolutely and forever beyond any knowing.

PLAYBOY: Well, you're in no hurry for that next existence, are you?

DICKEY: Lord, no, but I do have an ending planned.

PLAYBOY: Can you give it away?

DICKEY: Sure. I want to be buried on the west bank of the Chattooga River—if the state will allow it. Just dumped into a hole with no coffin. On a plain tombstone there'll be this:

> JAMES DICKEY, 1923 TO 19 WHATEVER,
> AMERICAN POET AND NOVELIST,
> HERE SEEKS HIS DELIVERANCE.

11

"THAT PLAIN-SPEAKING GUY": A CONVERSATION WITH JAMES DICKEY ON ROBERT FROST

DONALD J. GREINER / 1974

GREINER: We're talking about a poet who was born a hundred years ago; I'm wondering how you would evaluate his status now that he's been dead for more than a decade. In other words, today, are these poems dated; is his poetry the kind that younger poets are going to repudiate the way he rejected the rhythms of a Tennyson or Swinburne?

DICKEY: No, I don't think so. Frost is a poet that the younger fellows may reject and turn their backs on, and so on, but he is a poet whom people are going to come back to. Which is to say that he is a real poet; he's arrived to stay.

GREINER: Your comment suggests that his poems appeal to readers and not particularly to beginning writers. Do his poems have anything to show beginning writers today? I mean, you're teaching students who hope to be poets—

DICKEY: Oh, a very great deal to show them. The plainness and the colloquialism of the language is a very great plus. And for a certain kind of poet, a poet who's learning to write, this may be the way for him.

GREINER: Do you think his poems still speak to the American reader today the way they did maybe twenty or even fifty years ago? Frost was worshipped.

DICKEY: You'll have to dissociate—you have to distinguish in

Reprinted with permission from *Robert Frost: Centennial Essays,* compiled by the Committee on the Frost Centennial (Jackson: University Press of Mississippi, 1974), 51–59.

the first place between the actual poem and the public personality of the man. And it's hard to make any kind of reasonable assessment of that because the majority of people who revered Robert Frost had read very little of his work.

GREINER: Right, they read only the anthology pieces.

DICKEY: Well, and not even that. No, they only knew him as a public figure, a consultant at the Library of Congress, someone who gave forth with "frosty," if I may be forgiven a pun, saws and cracker-barrel wisdom and things of that nature. But they, mostly the people who I would say—and God knows I don't know what the percentage would be—but I would say ninety percent of the people who knew who Robert Frost was would never have read any poems of his.

GREINER: Do you think we ought to reread his poems, or should his poems—put it this way—should his poems be re-evaluated now in the light of what we know about Frost the man?

DICKEY: Oh, I don't think so. I'm fascinated by Frost the man, and he certainly must have been one of the worst sons of bitches that ever lived. But what really matters is what ends up on the page—what he did as an artist.

GREINER: In your essay in *Babel to Byzantium* you've mentioned the "Frost story."

DICKEY: Yes.

GREINER: I'm wondering, will it ever be possible for us to read "The Gift Outright," say, without thinking of the context of President Kennedy's inauguration; or could we ever read "Birches" or "Mending Wall" or any other of what you call his "beloved" poems without remembering Frost on the grandstand before the worshipful audience, cracking up those in the front row with his little asides? Is it possible that there—

DICKEY: That's an awful hard question to answer. This is getting exactly back to my point. There's a dissociation between the man and his public image and what he actually did put down on the page. He's a remarkable poet. But he became a personality. And I don't think—I mean, I agree with you—I don't think there really will, at least in our generation, be the possibility of dividing Frost the raconteur and the public personality from the man who wrote some *very marvelous* poems.

GREINER: You know, I think in a perverse sort of way that the negative information which we now know about Frost may eventually help his reputation as a poet. I know students who have been turned off by this image of the white-haired old bard of the nation, who now say, well, this guy really was—

DICKEY: He was human after all.

GREINER: Right. He was not "preachy." He had problems.

DICKEY: And he created most of them himself. But he's—those Lawrance Thompson biographies—those books are fascinating because you get the dichotomy between the poems as they have come to exist in innumerable anthologies and so on and what went into the poems. I'm very high on literary biographies myself. I was fascinated by those books.

GREINER: They're excellent books. I hope he lives to finish the third volume.[43]

DICKEY: I think it will be finished from what I've learned—the information that I have. But maybe not by him.

GREINER: One more question in this line of thought. Do you think, maybe, in Frost's last years—now this is speculation obviously—he was pursuing finally the reputation more than the art?

DICKEY: Yes, I do. I definitely do.

GREINER: To turn to another idea. In your essay on Frost in *Babel to Byzantium,* you mention "Design," "After Apple Picking," "Provide, Provide," and "To Earthward" as "a few powerful and utterly original poems." A marvelous way to describe them. Would you revise that list today?

DICKEY: I might put in a few more, but I wouldn't take out any of those.

GREINER: Okay, that's fair enough. In the same essay you mention Frost's, what you call his technical triumph, a triumph of the highest kind. You define it as "the creation of a particular kind of poetry—speaking voice." Yet I note in your list of those four poems that you neither discuss nor name one of the longer dialogue poems in which he literally does have a person speaking. Do these poems seem—a poem like "Home Burial"—do these poems seem startling still, today?

DICKEY: "Home Burial" is a mighty good poem. But when I talk about a special kind of poetry-speaking voice, I don't mean that someone speaking the poem (whatever the word is), a persona is—necessarily has to be—involved. That's not what I mean. If I didn't get that point across—

GREINER: No, you got it across. My point is that these poems—"Home Burial," "Hired Man"—my point is that when Frost hit it big in England and the United States in 1913, 1914, 1915, he was making it with the so-called dialogue poems which were misread as free verse. I'm wondering if today these poems are no longer—obviously they're not as revolutionary—if they're no longer as interesting, or if they no longer seem as technically innovative? I'm thinking of a poem like "Death of the Hired Man," or "The Fear," or "Home Burial."

DICKEY: I don't know. I really wouldn't be able to pronounce on that because I'm pretty close to the poems, and they've meant to lot to me over the years. What they mean to this generation or that generation or for this reason or that is really not of any particular concern to me. To me personally.

GREINER: You say that Frost—and I agree—you say that Frost is at his best when he's "most rhythmical and cryptic." Are you referring to his well-known love of hinting, of metaphor? He was obsessed with metaphor.

DICKEY: Yes. Yes, he was. But the thing about Frost that makes him so good is that he's able to say the most amazing things without seeming to raise his voice.

GREINER: That's very well put. A poem like "The Most of It" would then— I remember that Yvor Winters didn't like Frost's poetry but thought highly of "The Most of It."

DICKEY: He didn't think *very* highly of it. But he didn't think very highly of Frost. Yet he liked that poem except that he then proceeded to pick it apart in the most pretentious terms. Let me read this because I don't think that this is a very well-known quote, and it's very quotable. Tom Priestley, J. B. Priestley's son, was the cutter on my movie, the film editor. And he sent me this.[44] I've just about read it to pieces, but it's a very good assessment, I think, of Frost. Priestley says Frost "is widely recognised as a major poet and is altogether an odd, original, unexpected figure. His poetry is, in his own phrase, 'versed in country matters'; it is not even national but local, New England in scene and manner; it is as frugal with imagery and metaphor as a farmer with his money; much of it appears to have the rhythm and tone of cautious conversation, spoken out of the side of the mouth by a man not looking at you—"

GREINER: That's good.

DICKEY: "—Yet through this stealthy rusticity comes almost everything, short of the depths of personal dissolution and the blazing heights of ecstasy, that the modern poet is trying to express—bewilderment and horror, wonder and compassion, a tragic sense of life, which he, however, suggests without bitterness or whining. This is a poet, using his poker-faced rural *persona,* who likes to pretend he is being simple and obvious when he is not, just as many other poets, going with the movement, like to pretend they are being profound when they are not."

GREINER: That's nicely expressed. The idea about the modern strikes me. To continue from what Priestley says, Frost, as you know, for years was criticized as a leftover nineteenth-century poet, as a watered-down Emerson.

DICKEY: Or Wordsworth.

GREINER: Right. As a man who should be back in the 1850s. Do you think it's Frost's dark vision that makes him modern, one of the qualities that makes him modern since his verse form may not be?

DICKEY: I don't know about that. But I do think that the speech which Lionel Trilling made about him,[45] which I quoted in my article—Frost as a poet of darkness and terror, fear—the motivating emotion in him was fear—is the correct Frost.

GREINER: I would agree. You know, that speech wasn't made until 1959; and while I'm sure isolated readers here and there recognized the element of fear, as you call it, or terror in Frost, for years he was considered a benign nature poet, a goody-goody, the kind of poet read to the Camellia Garden Club.

DICKEY: Yes, those readers might have his face put up on Mount Rushmore.

GREINER: Exactly, with his hair fluffed up. I'm wondering, have we only recently discovered these dark poems? Is it because the critic is always lagging behind the poet, or is it because in our age of continuing crisis these poems are now speaking to us more and more—"Neither Out Far nor In Deep," for example?

DICKEY: Yes, I think that's very well said. The best critic, the critic who has understood Frost most deeply, was Randall Jarrell.

GREINER: Yes, his work is wonderfully perceptive.

DICKEY: Because Jarrell was something of the same type of man. And he understood the depths under the still pools, you know.

GREINER: He's the one who wrote the long discussion of "Home Burial."[46] What about Frost's wit? his humor? Do you think poems like—I'm just throwing out some—like "October" or "One Step Backward Taken" or "Fire and Ice"—I'm not thinking of his less-successful attempts to be funny in those awful "editorials"—do you think those poems have a place in the final assessment of Frost?

DICKEY: That is the Frost who has a kind of an elephantine local New England humor. The ponderous attempt to be funny and witty is the Frost that I can most easily dispense with, you know.

GREINER: Most readers dismiss the "cute" Frost of the "editorials."

DICKEY: The Frost I like is the plain-speaking guy who can in the most conversational possible way say things that you wouldn't have thought of in a million years.

GREINER: You know, talking about the common way of saying something, I find so many students today relishing, understandably, Stevens, or Eliot—I'm thinking of the more famous modern poets—or Pound, and dismissing Frost, until they come upon a poem like "All Revelation" or "Directive." And I'm wondering if the so-called easier poems like "Stopping by Woods" or "Birches" have been so over-anthologized, so over-taught that students no longer respond to them and therefore end up with a warped view of Frost's achievement.

DICKEY: As a university professor, as you are, Don, I have become—I couldn't speak for you, but I can certainly speak for myself—I have become very wary and mistrustful of this insistent, universal "talking it" to death. Talking things to death. We are paid to do it, but as far as the art of poetry is concerned, I have very serious reservations as to whether or not this is desirable.

GREINER: This is what's happened, I think, to a poem like "Birches" or "Mending Wall" or "Stopping by Woods."

DICKEY: Well, that's what you have when you say you "get" a poet like Frost who's well known, who's taught, as they say, "in classes."

GREINER: And who has an easy literal level.

DICKEY: You get lots of people who get to competing in interpreting him.

GREINER: You remember that Frost's famous comment about "Stopping by Woods" was "All I meant was to get the hell out of there."

DICKEY: Yes? Well, he was right. Certainly. You read the commentaries on those things and they're so over-read and over-ingenious and so on that the poem just gets mangled and destroyed in the process.

GREINER: Someone in the late 1950s or early 1960s, I understand, actually counted and decided that "Stopping by Woods" is the most explicated poem in American literature, that it's been "done" so many more times—

DICKEY: Well, but of course it's got to contain a homosexual Freudian overtone, undertone, all that kind of business, you know. It's just a hideous business. But the poetry, the fun of it, the delight of it, dies when you indulge this over-intellectualizing about it.

GREINER: I like the way Frost hits me with an unexpected

word. For example, to pull one out of the hat, in "Fire and Ice," when ice "is also great / And would suffice"—the word "suffice," for example, surprises me, that kind of thing.

DICKEY: Yes, I agree, that's good.

GREINER: Some critics have argued persuasively that Frost is a good poet but not one to be read finally with Yeats or Stevens or Eliot. Now, get the reason: because he did not develop what they call a coherent vision or myth, and because he oversimplifies human experience by writing about modern crises from the vantage point of the rural world. Are those criticisms justified in your opinion?

DICKEY: Not in my opinion, no. I think that he has one virtue that overrides all of those things, and that is that he speaks to people on a very deep level. He speaks to them in a language they can understand, but the meanings of the lines in his poems go very deeply down. He's not a recherché kind of writer like Stevens who is always dealing in riddles and conundrums and that sort of thing. Frost has a great, great, wide spread on the popular world. He shows us here in America that a poet does not have to talk down to his audience, but that he can talk to his audience without condescending.

GREINER: The literal level in my opinion does not hurt Frost at all.

DICKEY: No, I think that's one of the best things he's got going for him.

GREINER: I have so many sophisticated graduate students, though, who feel that he is less than great because of the literal level.

DICKEY: That's one of the finest things about him. I mean, you take Wallace Stevens and you keep going round and round in circles, trying to follow his thought and so on, and it's the poetry of a very sophisticated esthete. Frost, whether or not you accept him, is a plain-speaking man, and you are interested in what he says because you can relate to it, whereas you cannot relate to "sixteen ways of putting a pineapple together."

. . .

GREINER: In your reading of Frost—I'm thinking of all of

Frost—do you detect any development, change, trying out of new things, or would you agree with those who argue that he develops, shows his all in *North of Boston,* which was published in 1914, and from there on out his poems go in generally a straight line?

DICKEY: Yes, I do agree with the latter.

GREINER: That's his serious drawback?

DICKEY: In a way, yes. He never learned the great lesson of Picasso, which was never to be trapped in a single style. He found a single style, and he used it and explored it for the rest of his life. But he was not a man who operated on the frontiers of consciousness, who was trying new things and doing new things, such as Picasso, who was continually trying to push out the boundaries of human consciousness. He found one thing that he could do. He didn't try to go out; he tried to go in, to go deeper into what he had already found. And that's another type of writer from somebody like Ezra Pound or Auden who do try to do these new things.

GREINER: How would you define that one thing? Is that a fair question? He found "one thing."

DICKEY: Well, it's a—to come back to what I said earlier—a plain-speaking style which could say profound things.

GREINER: He tried in later years to move into satire, political commentaries.

DICKEY: Didn't work! No, and there he engaged the worst side of himself which was this elephantine levity and this cracker-barrel philosophizing which is not only unpleasant but painful.

GREINER: One poem of Frost's—I would hesitate to say he was "done" in his early life—but "Directive" which was published in, what, 1947? saves his later poetry for me.

DICKEY: Yes, that's a good poem, and "Provide, Provide" is a wonderful poem. Boy, I'll tell you—when you read Frost, when you read that poem and you read some of the others of about that time, you know the full horror of being a human being, you know, and the real practicality and the practical solutions of how you provide for yourself.

GREINER: A better "proletarian" poem than those by some of the proletarian writers?

DICKEY: Oh, yes, far, far better.

GREINER: Let me ask you one final question which is strictly personal opinion. If—one of these "if" questions—if you had room to include one or two of Frost's poems in a world anthology, right off the top of your head, which ones would you pick?

DICKEY: Of Frost?

GREINER: Yes.

DICKEY: Oh, I'd say "Acquainted with the Night" and "After Apple-Picking."

12

INTERVIEW WITH JAMES DICKEY

L. L. SIMMS / [1976?]

SIMMS: What do you think of the growing academic trend of offering undergraduate and Masters courses in creative writing? What, if anything, is to be gained by the young writer by beginning his practice of the craft in academia?

DICKEY: Well, this is already a kind of loaded question because we all know that we should hate academia, but in the actual situation that exists, I would say that there's a certain promise for young writers around universities. But my whole emotional setup is geared 180 degrees to academia. I would say forge your instruments otherwise than in the university. On ships, sailing ships, being a harvest stiff in the Midwest, an advertising man somewhere. But again, this is only emotional on my part. Practically, I would say that the university would give you a better shake than the Merchant Marines as far as giving you the God-given equivalent of your gift, which is time to sit down and make mistakes and try to thrash out your own kind of poetic or prose destiny on paper. It takes an awful lot of time. This is the thing—money is a secondary consideration. The main consideration is time.

SIMMS: In your travels, what, if any, opinions have you formed on specific in writing, Iowa, Arkansas, etc.?

DICKEY: I don't know. I really don't know that much about programs at Arkansas and other programs, but there is something about that that goes against the grain to me; I am haunted by the possibility of Dylan Thomas's going to the University of Iowa to learn how to write poetry. There is a certain kind of officialdom about these situations, which is, I

Reprinted with permission from *Copula* [The Poetry Center: San Francisco State University], First Issue [1976?], 41–46.

think, maybe not so good. But I would say this, for the greatly, greatly talented writer, programs at the University of Iowa and so forth are not going to have anything and they would probably be detrimental. For the middling good writer, they would be helpful.

. . .

SIMMS: There is a certain spiritual primitivism in your work. I'm thinking of "Approaching Prayer" as an example. You have said that you have a "stick-and-stone" religion. Could you expand on that imagery?

DICKEY: Well, I don't know. . . . I would say that although one is conditioned by motor cars and television and so forth, there is a kind of residual thing in the human animal which has never heard of a telephone and has never seen an automobile. All one has to do is sit down on a hillside among the pine trees, or whatever trees you choose to visualize, as the evening is coming down, to know that there is some kind of residual thing in you which goes back to the beginning. That is the thing that I would like to write about.

SIMMS: The pantheism that you have described sounds rather serene. Where does violence come in?

DICKEY: Pantheism and violence are not antithetical at all. Believe me, they are not. All you have to do is look into the eyes of the cave bear.

SIMMS: Is that what you do?

DICKEY: I don't know. I aspire to it.

SIMMS: Do you feel that you write "public poetry" or that your work is read mainly by other college professors and their students?

DICKEY: I write exactly what I would under any circumstances and what I did write for years when nobody would publish anything and nobody read anything of mine. I write now what I would write otherwise. I mean people talk about public poetry. What the hell is that—"public poetry"? Is it the protest-against-Vietnam poetry? It dies with the occasion. No, no, no, I would not hook up with that at all; it would not appeal to me at all. I would never do it.

SIMMS: In a way, academia has become the major, almost the sole patron of poetry. Do you feel that this affects your position as a poet?

DICKEY: Well, yes, in a way. But again, if you want my own testimony, that's not so true as all that. I've done an awful lot of different things. I think if the rage to write is enough of a rage, you are going to do it no matter what. That is going to be the number one priority, in other words, and what you do for a living is going to be the number two priority. . . . I remember with great affection all the time I was in the ad business when I was writing ad copy all day and writing poetry at night. . . . And that is not so bad either. I mean it cannot go on infinitely long—it's a kind of schizophrenic existence; you try to split yourself up into two people—but for a while it is enormously exciting. And I would say, God save the mark, that one stimulates the other, that writing ad copy stimulates poetry and poetry stimulates the ad stuff, too.

. . .

SIMMS: In some of your later poems, it seems that you are using some of the flashy, adjectival language of modern advertising.

DICKEY: Why not? I'd say that everything and anything is grist to the mill. I don't know of any poet who is really good who would refuse an impulse from any direction whatsoever—no matter if it was from advertising, from movies, from *Harper's Bazaar,* or from any place that it announced itself. The mark of the real poet is to pick up on it and recognize and use it, no matter what direction it comes from; it doesn't matter what the origin is. It can be in a newspaper underfoot in New York City. A word can jump out of a newspaper, you know, which is full of horse piss and other detritus from the city. But there is one thing. It might have to do with Teddy Kennedy; it might not. It might have to do with a society wedding, you know, white lace. Hart Crane, a poet like Hart Crane, would pick up on that. He would find a place for it. If it didn't strike him, he would discard it; if it struck him, he would work it in.

SIMMS: I have heard it said that, when asked whom you consider to be the world's greatest living poet, you always answer "James Dickey." Is this so?

DICKEY: No, no. That will be answered for me. I would not say myself; I would say Eugenio Montale. I would defer to him.

SIMMS: Are you the greatest living American poet?

DICKEY: It's between Lowell and me, I'm told.

. . .

SIMMS: The type of writing that you do seems to require a tremendous amount of emotional energy. Peter Davison of *Atlantic*[47] says that he thinks you are in danger of "overblowing." A slight recession of energy, he feels, would ruin you. Do you feel frightened? Energetic?

DICKEY: Listen, the thing I want to do more than anything else is to "overblow" it. I can't think of anything that would please me more. . . . If time allows, I will give them something.

. . .

13
DICKEY

JIM TOWNSEND / 1977

CHARLOTTE: You've become a rather rich and well-known figure, more because of the movies and novel than for your poetry. Does that tell us anything?

DICKEY: I'll say this about it. I was a failure for so many years. I was a penny-ante English instructor—freshman English—in various small colleges, and *pore*—couldn't get my children's teeth fixed, that sort of thing. Then this tidal wave of attention and money came along after *Deliverance*. I shouldn't say that; it sounds fatuous, but its true, anyway, and it's the American dream, I suppose, of love and fame and notoriety.

CHARLOTTE: It doesn't bother you that you're better known as a novelist than a poet?

DICKEY: That is not so much a comment on me or my personal situation as it is on American culture in general. Novels are far more widely read. In my particular case the poetry is the center of the creative wheel. If you hold that firm, if you write the poems and take your chances in the marketplace, then whatever else you do in the way of writing will come.

Poetry is the most difficult of all forms of discipline. It is the most difficult, the most frustrating, and above all, the most rewarding. Poetry is the center of my particular creative wheel; out of that everything else is a spin-off. The novel is a spin-off—the screenplay, critical articles, short stories, even advertisements—all come from that center of the wheel.

CHARLOTTE: What led you, then, from your poetry to the novel form?

DICKEY: Almost any poet feels it's incumbent on him to try to

---

Reprinted from *Charlotte*, 9 (March/April 1977), 22–24.

write at least one. And, if you take enough time to try to write poetry, and you're serious about it, you build up an enormous linguistic skill. The poor human creature, the poet, cannot help thinking that, in a culture that rewards written things as it does the works of certain novelists, it might be possible for him to subsidize his poetry-writing out of the proceeds of a successful novel.

CHARLOTTE: You put about ten years into *Deliverance,* didn't you? And aren't you working on another novel now?

DICKEY: This novel won't take that long. I'll probably finish it this year. It's one of those books that seems to unfold of its own accord—when I am able to work on it. . . .

CHARLOTTE: Tell us about the novel. Is it an adventure story?

DICKEY: Not in the pure sense. What I'm trying to do with *Alnilam* is to go for some kind of enormous multifaceted, multilayered type of book, a Nobel Prize type of book, and it'll fail. Because I'm talking about a big, big book; it's rather like *Ulysses,* lots of layers to it. I want to see if I can do it. I know I can't do it, but I want to try.

CHARLOTTE: You seem to know the Bible.

DICKEY: I guess so. I love the Bible, but as a great work of literature only. I don't read the Bible for its holiness at all. Holiness is above and beyond all those angels appearing to all those old shepherds in the Old Testament. That's the kind of universe I'd *like* to believe in. But I don't believe it for a second.

CHARLOTTE: Let's get back to poetry. Is "Falling" a favorite poem? To you?

DICKEY: A lot of people liked "Falling," but it's a little too much a *tour de force.* Let me tell you a story about that poem. Flannery O'Connor was pretty well immobilized because of her physical afflictions, and she said she got much of the information for most of her stories out of the newspapers. She was an indefatigable reader of newspapers, which I've never been. And she put me onto it.

But what happened is, this girl, the original of the protagonist, the stewardess who fell out of the airplane, was a French girl who had come to this country to live. And she was a bit too old for a stewardess, something like twenty-eight or twenty-nine, so she wasn't with the major airlines. I learned much later that this girl had been undergoing psychoanalysis for several years and—this is the thing that caps the climax—her main fantasy, her obsessional nightmare, was that she was a bird. That is incredible.

CHARLOTTE: Wasn't this over Connecticut?

DICKEY: I think so, but I set it in the middle of the United States, in the heartland. It seems to me that if a girl is to be blown out of an airplane—the airlines demand they be girdled properly with all this rig—and she falls out and she knows she's gonna die, she tries to get to water. She tries to get to a river or lake; she's taking off her clothes—she wants to die not as a commercial entity, all girdled up in a uniform, but as a woman—and she strips herself in mid-air and falls in the middle of a cornfield. *Inexplicable!* Why would a naked woman be out in the middle of a Kansas cornfield? But that's the way she wanted it, and that's the way she got it.

CHARLOTTE: There's another story about your being aboard an airliner trying to read that poem.

DICKEY: It was on Eastern, and the poem was in the *New Yorker*,[48] and I wanted to see if they had set my poem up against a quality joke. And when they brought me that issue, they had cut the poem out. There was a hole where my poem was supposed to be!

. . .

CHARLOTTE: You once said that the best people you've ever known—and the worst—were all poets.[49] Does that—

DICKEY: *Writers.* I think I'd just say writers. The poetic sensibility, the artistic sensibility is very erratic; you touch the heights and also you touch the sad depths of existence. A lot of them are heavy drinkers, a lot end up as suicides. But the best of them—the best human time you can have as a writer is with another writer you respect and admire, that you can talk to.

CHARLOTTE: Who are some of those?

DICKEY: John Gardner is one of them. Robert Lowell, James Wright, Robert Penn Warren, Allen Tate. When you sit down and look into the fireplace all kinds of marvelous things come out. I don't think human beings can have a better kind of situation between themselves. I could name others, but those will do.

CHARLOTTE: How much time will you spend in writing a poem? Of course it varies, but—

DICKEY: Some people, some poets, must surely write quickly, but it doesn't work for me. I work on something a long, long time, and try it all different ways. Some poems go into the typewriter two and three hundred times. And people ask me, "How long did 'The Firebombing' take?" The answer could be years and years, and I have a poem that I've been working on for more than ten years.... I'm a plodding, searching writer, and I assume tacitly at the beginning that the first fifty ways I try it are all going to be wrong. It is an almost unfailing constant that I like to work on things an awfully long time. The poet *builds* the poem so that the passion is conserved and is always available.

CHARLOTTE: Let's talk about your new book, *The Zodiac*. You've always had a great fascination with astronomy.

DICKEY: I had a teacher at Vanderbilt, a really remarkable man named Carl Siefert, and through him I got a feeling of intimacy with the cosmos. I had never known anybody with any particular attitude toward the universe, but he was always talking about it. He was fond of quoting Edwin Arlington Robinson's line: "The world is a hell of a place, but the universe is a fine thing."

The Zodiac is a long poem based on another written by Hendrik Marsman, who was torpedoed in the North Atlantic in 1940.

CHARLOTTE: Your work reflects a wide range of your own personal interests, like flying and rivers, archery, astronomy—

DICKEY: Yeah, right. But a poet doesn't have to know a subject comprehensively for it to excite him. Henry James was once asked—I think he projected writing a novel on the British Army Coldstream Guards—how much research he was going to do, whether he was going to live in an army barracks. And he said that all he needed to write a novel about the Coldstream Guards was to have one three-minute look through the window of the Officers' Mess. This approach is especially true of poetry. But, yeah, I naturally deal most with subjects which have a unique fascination for me.

. . .

CHARLOTTE: Most of your work seems to have been published by Doubleday, but *Deliverance* was with Houghton Mifflin. Why was that?

DICKEY: Well, you have to understand something. The word "novel" is a magic word in publishing because that's where the money lies in this business; novels, followed, I guess, by travel books followed by cookbooks, and poetry is *way* on down the line. And the people who work for publishing houses are like sharks; they're constantly maneuvering to find out where the meat is [*he moves his hands like gliding sharks*]; they read the literary magazines [*hands glide*], they're constantly just under the surface of the water, maneuvering around. So I published a suite of poems in the *Virginia Quarterly Review,* and they read the contributors' items, trying always to get a line on some new guy who might write 'em a best-seller. [*Hands move more quickly now, but gracefully.*]

And they read that James Dickey, author of the prize-winning poem "Springer Mountain" is now living in Italy and working on a novel. [*Whack! like a shark striking*] The publishers descend on you. A guy from Houghton Mifflin comes out to Portland, Oregon, where I was teaching when I got back to the states, and reads the ninety pages I have done and says, "This novel you call *Deliverance,* I managed to decipher it. Let's talk about a modest advance." So we agreed on $5000, which was modest indeed but seemed large at the time.

CHARLOTTE: You are—we should say you've *remained*—a Southerner.

DICKEY: Well, of course. I like the sense of continuity, the sense of human family that is part of being Southern. There's a sense here of your life meaning something, a sense of consequentiality; those are the things about the South that appeal most to me. Since Jimmy Carter came into the incumbency a lot of people want to be Southern.

CHARLOTTE: You've gotten now to be, what? Fifty-four? What's the toughest thing as the poet grows older?

DICKEY: You have a horror of yourself being a bland, one of the bland leading the bland. I hope not ever to become a felt-slippered or old person, at least not somebody surrounded by his dogs and cats and not responding. Everything I've ever done depends on a certain rawness of edge. I think some people, as they grow older, grow too civilized inside. They lose some of the life-quickening juices that got them to the age they enjoy.

CHARLOTTE: What is missing from your work product?

DICKEY: Nothing is missing, though there are some things I've not yet done. The main problem with my life is that I'm playing catch-up ball. I need to do all manner of things that have been offered to me and I'm not quite sure of my direction right now.

CHARLOTTE: But your success brings an awful lot of offers. How do you handle that?

DICKEY: This too shall pass away.

CHARLOTTE: What is the toughest problem you deal with now?

DICKEY: Time, probably; and neither money nor diligence will buy it. But I find it nevertheless. I know a place in North Carolina that I can almost categorically guarantee nobody but me and two or three others have ever seen. I can go there now and again. I may even want to be buried there.

CHARLOTTE: Someone once said of you that your writing requires a vast fire to keep the cauldron boiling; that if you were to encounter a slight recession of energy, your value as a poet might easily enter into a decline.

DICKEY: The cauldron boils anew every day, and I love it yet. I feel good, think as clearly as ever. I am excited by so many things, depressed by much, turned on and off in recurring cycles, just as it's always been. I can say that I would have been assured a better future as an advertising man—or a janitor—than as a poet.

But poetry is just about the last repository of language, of depth language, where you offer some insights and a piece of yourself. Poetry, the discipline of learning to write poetry, is incomparably the hardest to do and the most frustrating—and the most rewarding. I will tell you as I've told others over the years, and it doesn't change: I want to say something amazing in an absolutely effortless way.

I am still working on that.

14

JAMES DICKEY ON YEATS: AN INTERVIEW

W. C. BARNWELL / 1977

BARNWELL: Jim, you once referred to certain absurdities of William Butler Yeats's work. What did you mean?

DICKEY: It seems to me that the whole situation with Yeats has got to be taken in its entirety—that is, if it's an absurd thing to begin with, the whole system of metaphysics and astrology and the rest and whether you are interested in that, or whether you just suspect that it's the business of a crank who happens to write marvelously. One thing I do like about Yeats is that he succeeded in making an authentically nonlogical way of reasoning. I mean Yeats will say something like, if Aquarius does not stand at the end of Leo, how can the Archer send an arrow through the heart of Sagittarius? You know what I'm talking about.

BARNWELL: Yes. Yeats remarks in one of his last poems about modern verse among other things being all "out of shape from toe to top." Somewhere you talk about the "conclusionless poem" as a positive value. Would you care to reconcile the two views of poetic construction or simply let them go their ways?

DICKEY: Well, I don't know about that; my own poetic stance—that's not really a nice word but somehow or another it fits—is quite different from his. Not that there is any value comparison implied. Yeats speaks in a letter to Dorothy Wellesley of the good poem having a conclusion like the click of a closed box. I don't want to do that myself, as a practicing poet. I want the poem to open out. I don't want it to be final at all. To quote the Bible, well, to paraphrase the Bible, the whole problem of

---

Reprinted with permission from *Southern Review*, 13 (Spring 1977), 311–316.

poetry and the way the human imagination works is like a house of many mansions. There's not anything that says if you like the tightly constructed poem that you dislike the Whitman type of long-lined, loosely constructed poem. There is not anything, there is no law of human behavior, that says you can't have it both ways.

BARNWELL: In this regard Yeats was concerned with what we may call a participational cosmic perfection. That is, a static design that yet involved itself in active life. Do you see any design in life that you'd care to write about? Is all that system-making gone for good?

DICKEY: I think it's a mistake. I'm a believer in William James's doctrines of the fluidity and flux and the flows of human experience, and I don't believe that there is any finality that can be found in it. If you would take a certain person's day-to-day life, you would see that contingencies arise which would not be accountable by means of a fixed system and I personally don't think they should be. They should flow. Everything should flow; as Heraclitus says, "You cannot step twice into the same river, for new waters are ever flowing in upon you."

BARNWELL: What then do you see to praise in Yeats's views of manners and courtly concerns, of preoccupation with a made art, with golden birds, and not the live birds and beasts of your own menagerie?

DICKEY: I remember what Auden once said about Yeats when he is contrasting him with Thomas Hardy. He says that (as I remember, I may be wrong), he said the darkling thrush of Hardy is something you can see. You can walk out on an evening and see the bird and you can have your conclusion about it; but when Yeats starts talking about the golden bird on the branches of Byzantium who talks to the lords and ladies of Byzantium, a kingdom that none of us will ever see, you know, as Auden says, "As my old nurse of my childhood said, 'It's just something made up.'"

BARNWELL: Jim, I can't think of two people so far apart personally. Yeats, a reserved aristocratic fellow, a teetotaler by all accounts, and you, an outgoing man who drinks almost in the Mailerian tradition of a moral imperative; that is, you drink to learn things as part of the creative process. In fact, you've called yourself a true "son of the grape."

DICKEY: Well, it seems to me that whiskey or any kind of alcoholic beverage used rightly is one of the greatest benefits that has ever been available to the poor, benighted human creature. Of course, in a great many cases, it has been disastrous to people, but in a number of cases it has been enormously beneficial, too. It has gotten rid of inhibitions, it has released a person to the potential he might otherwise not have had.

BARNWELL: Were you aware that Yeats once tried hashish?

DICKEY: No, I wasn't. One of the things I would like most about Yeats would be the person that would turn on to something like that. What I also like about him is that he succeeded, through many years of effort, in making of himself an authentically dirty old man. I aspire, we all should aspire, to that.

BARNWELL: Being a dirty old man?

DICKEY: Yes, right.

BARNWELL: In his Crazy Jane days of the thirties, Yeats mentions the "Black Mass of Eden," referring to sexual abandon among other things. How does his sexual work strike you, as a passing fancy or a permanent fixture?

DICKEY: I think it is extremely important, but we will have to remember the poetry of Yeats, as the poetry of anybody, as it relates to himself, his situation, and his hang-ups and phobias and so on. I don't mean to be psychoanalytical at all, but there is a tendency to rationalize an author's particular personal situation by abstracting these and putting universal credentials on them. And I think that Yeats was no more free of that than the next man you meet when you're walking down the street of Columbia, South Carolina. I do think—let me switch over from Yeats momentarily to Goethe. Goethe says that the true woman for a man is the woman who seems to furnish the answer to everything. Or, again, in another even more memorable phrase, "the right woman for a man is the woman who seems to tie him to the center of the earth." It seems to me, now, again, I can't really speak for Yeats, who's dead these many years, but from what I know of him, I would say that he felt something of this sort was going on between him and Maud Gonne who looked at him pretty much as a poseur and somebody she didn't really want to go to bed with, and didn't want to live with, and didn't want to marry. But *he* thought she did, and the important thing for his poetry is that he did think of her as the woman that would bind him, the West of Ireland boy, Willie Yeats, to the center of the earth. And he wrote many of his great poems out of that premise. It has been ever thus.

BARNWELL: Looking through your *Babel to Byzantium,* one contracts something like intellectual lockjaw, the wide reading implied, and so on. Yeats is like that. Do you believe that besides direct experience, a poet needs continual reading and thinking to exist?

DICKEY: I don't know about whether to exist, but it's damn good for him. I think that the flow of ideas, coming back to William James, the flow of ideas in the single mind, sometimes helped out by conversation, sometimes engaged in pure solitude in the middle of the night or maybe in the late hours of the night, is a good thing. A few words may result from it which are valuable.

BARNWELL: Somewhere, I think in "Barnstorming for Poetry," you refer to yourself as having two personalities: one at home working—quiet, productive; the other out on the road—impulsive, talkative, giving what it thinks people want by way of a poet. Yeats's self and anti-self spring to mind. Have you ever deliberately tried to use a poetic ethic on this basis as did Yeats?

DICKEY: No, I wouldn't say that, no. There's a long-forgotten journalist in Indiana named Kin Hubbard who delivered himself of a certain number of aphorisms over the years, in the twenties, in provincial Indiana newspapers. I've always been very much taken with one thing he said, and I believe that it would speak to almost anybody as we live in our human situations—as we go to SAMLA or sales meetings or on business conferences and so on; this would more or less characterize everybody when Kin Hubbard says, "We're all pretty much the same when we get out of town."

BARNWELL: Jim, what in your opinion should be the position

of Yeats from our point of view in 1977? Is a high place deserved?

DICKEY: Oh, yes; oh, yes. If you were to take what would by general consensus be the five greatest poets of the twentieth century, who would you say they would be? The most influential poet in England, in English, would have to be T. S. Eliot.

BARNWELL: And, of course, Yeats in Ireland.

DICKEY: Well, it really isn't a question of nationality, it's a question of influence. Those would be the two, Yeats and Eliot. Now, in other languages, the great intellectual, perfectionist, classicist Paul Valéry would have to be somewhere. After that, who would you say? In Spain, Federico Garcia Lorca would have to be amongst the five.

BARNWELL: In America?

DICKEY: There's nobody in America.

BARNWELL: Besides yourself?

DICKEY: Yes, present company excepted. No, there's not anyone here of that stature at all. I don't know, you'd have to go with something like that estimate: Eliot, Yeats, Valéry, Garcia Lorca—

BARNWELL: Would you place a Lawrence in there, for his Dionysian qualities?

DICKEY: Oh no; no, no. He's not of that category, no. D. H. Lawrence as a poet, no sir. Oh, Rainer Maria Rilke, in German. That would give us five, would it not? Yes. So it would be Yeats and Eliot in English, Valéry in French, Garcia Lorca in Spanish, and Rilke in German. All right now, who are we going to do away with first? I mean, it's a process of elimination.

BARNWELL: I would drop Rilke first.

DICKEY: Whooo. Well, I wouldn't. He's got a certain enormous influence, Rilke. I would think that Garcia Lorca, Garcia Lorca we have to get rid of, as good as he is, and he is *mighty* good. We have to, because he's a little bit too provincial and he's too much tied to a single continuous—what is the word that the women's lib people use, chauvinistic? He's too much limited to the Spanish. He is not broad enough to be the greatest poet of the twentieth century, would you say? Although he's awful damn good. He is good. I would say that Garcia Lorca would have to be the first one out of the five greats to go, because he is tied too much to the Spanish folk tradition.

BARNWELL: How about Valéry next?

DICKEY: He would have to go next. He's too much of an intellectual. He's too rarefied and abstract to speak to large portions of the population, which a great poet must be able to do. His insights are of almost a diamondlike astonishing brilliance, but he is extremely difficult to read, and as a great poet of the twentieth century, he is going to appeal to coteries—very much as Mallarmé, his master, did. We're going to be left now with three people—Eliot and Yeats in English, and Rilke in German.

BARNWELL: Who goes next?

DICKEY: The most influential poet in the whole history of poetry is T. S. Eliot. But his interests are extremely narrow. He speaks to a special in-group type of scholar-poet. He is essentially a poet of the library. And so, I would put him out next although some things of his I like very much; he is not really a finalist in the hit parade of poets in the twentieth century. No, although much has been written about him, he's not in *my* opinion, one of the top—as we ex-admen say—not one of the top people. As much as has been written about him, he does not have a human force.

BARNWELL: Then it's down to Rilke and Yeats.

DICKEY: That's right. It would be down to them.

BARNWELL: Whom would you choose?

DICKEY: Well, it'd be mighty hard to do. Rilke and Yeats. Rilke is an enormously wide-ranging writer. He can write about anything and make it interesting. He can write about washing a corpse for burial in a way that would make you feel that you've never seen the human body before in your life. He's a marvelous person and he translates marvelously, and he represents the extremely subjective kind of Proustian way of taking human existence. And yet, he's a little bit too much committed to that point of view, to the Proustian, extremely subjective type of life. He's too much committed to that. There's a certain amount of sickness about Rilke, where nothing is what it *is,* but is always what it seems to be. He goes. And Yeats, despite his quirks and his strangeness of outlook on the universe, is going to have to be the greatest poet of the twentieth century with his broad masculine free-thinking, free-speaking, outspoken way of dealing with things. He can write a simple lyric which will speak to somebody in a bar and next make the most strange kind of metaphysical proclamations about the nature of the universe and the nature of existence. He's going to have to be *the* great twentieth-century poet. It has to be Yeats.

15

INTERVIEW: JAMES DICKEY

PHIL PATTON / 1977

SKY: Some people feel that you have become a sort of poet laureate to the new administration.

DICKEY: Well, to read one poem at an inaugural gala is hardly enough to make one a poet laureate. I suppose that if I've ever had anything like that attached to my name it would be when I was the poetry consultant to the Library of Congress. That's the closest thing we have to a poet laureate, but it is quite different from the laureateship in England. I didn't have to write official odes for Lady Bird's wedding anniversary or that sort of thing, as John Betjeman is doing now, so disgracefully, in England.

SKY: *Should* there be anything like a poet laureate?

DICKEY: No, I don't like official art at all.

SKY: What did you do in the consultant's job at the Library of Congress?

DICKEY: It's a very strange job, and you can make about what you want of it. You can come in and talk to the people that want to talk to you, or you can close your doors and sit up there and write your own poetry and drink a martini if you want to. I never did *that* because when I took the job I thought it was capable of exerting a good deal of influence on the cultural climate of this country. I felt that I should get out and initiate various programs and make myself available as well as do my own work. I did a good deal of traveling. They'll give you whatever you need to get out there and do things.

SKY: Did you have money to bestow on promising young poets?

Reprinted from *Sky,* 6 (July 1977), 26–27, 42, 44–45.

DICKEY: I could invite them to give readings, but that was about all I could do financially. I would also advise endowment boards and so on that give grants.

SKY: Your background and the way you've made your living over the years has not exactly been that of the starving poet in the garret.

DICKEY: I've been pretty close to starving at times.

SKY: Do you feel that the government needs to supplement what private foundations do for poets?

DICKEY: As much as I've turned that idea over in my mind, I would tend to reject the idea of the government being involved. I know how much a Rockefeller grant and a Guggenheim grant meant to me—I would have had to stop writing, I suppose, if I hadn't gotten them. But there's something about the government giving it to you that brings you into the role of being an official poet. It takes away the most precious thing a creative artist can have—the sense of doing things his own way and having absolute freedom to create as he wishes to. You would feel that there were some strings attached to you, although there probably wouldn't be. A president like Carter, well, that would be the furthest thing from his mind. For the inauguration he just asked me to write about anything I wanted to write about. He didn't ask me to "write something for the occasion." As it turns out, I did write something that was sort of about the occasion,[50] but I was under no pressure to.

. . .

SKY: What is your working schedule like now?

DICKEY: I teach two classes, six hours a week. I don't have a rigid work schedule. I travel a lot to give lectures and readings and go on talk shows, so I can't ever establish one. I just work in bits and pieces as I can.

SKY: How is your second novel going?

DICKEY: Going along pretty well, but I've gotten involved in so many other projects. It's easier, though, to work on a novel than on a poem because you have a story line. A poem is just a hit-and-miss thing, like the proverbial blind man in a dark room groping for a black cat that may or may not be there. But with a novel you know the story is there.

And I just can't shake the film makers off me. They want original scripts. *Deliverance* was the one that bailed Warner's out that year, so I'm told.

. . .

SKY: A lot of people who saw and read *Deliverance* viewed it as an encounter with wilderness and some primal, natural force that was particularly Southern. Do you think that is so?

DICKEY: No, I don't think so. The Southern setting of *Deliverance* was more or less accidental; it's just the landscape, the riverscape. It's not really particularly Southern. What I was after was a more abstract projection of what seems to me the salient condition of our time—the thing we're most concerned about in our era of crime in the streets and random violence—and that is being set upon by malicious strangers. Whether its those two criminals in *Deliverance,* who were just degenerates, just mean, vicious, and perverted, real monsters, or some guy who sticks a gun in your ribs in New York City—it's the same thing. There are people who don't have anything against you but who would just as soon kill you as look at you—in fact, some of them would *rather* kill you—and they do all the time. All you have to do is look at a newspaper any day.

SKY: Does literature or art of any type do anything about this type of situation?

DICKEY: No, I don't think art makes anything happen. I think that is taking it the wrong way. Art to me involves a deepening of the beholder's personal experience. It's not propaganda, except maybe in some very deep sense, and if it is overt—if it has very direct designs on the beholder—then it usually is not going to be very good art.

SKY: But doesn't the wilderness in *Deliverance,* like the animals that frequently appear in your poetry, represent some of the violence in human nature?

DICKEY: In a way. I've read a lot of books and seen a lot of films that describe reprehensible humans as being no better than animals, as being like animals. But those two guys on the riverbank in *Deliverance* were a lot worse than animals. Animals don't kill and mutilate except to eat or to feed their young. Those two guys just set upon the fellows from the city because they wanted to humiliate and harm them—just for the fun of it, because they *liked* doing it.

. . .

SKY: Do you still play the guitar much?

DICKEY: Some, but I don't really have enough time. If I get a few minutes, I'll work out a wrinkle on some tune I've heard or can steal off a record. I play mainly bluegrass. I arranged for "Duellin' Banjos" to be the music in *Deliverance*. Nobody would have heard of it otherwise.

SKY: How have you reacted to the recent interest in the South and things Southern?

DICKEY: I think that the South is pointing the way to some new kind of future for this country and I think—I am both prejudiced and extremely objective—that it will be a good thing for the South to lead, at least for a while, and maybe for good; to set the trends and furnish the leading politicians and the leading writers and the leading artists. We've got plenty of them down here. This is the most fertile literary region that has ever existed in this country.

SKY: Why do you think that is?

DICKEY: One of the reasons for it is that people are so garrulous down here. They love to tell stories and anecdotes. Most Southern literature comes right off the front porch. People sitting and talking, long-windedly, but always willing to listen to each others' stories because they've all got good ones to tell. Look at the Southern writers—William Faulkner, Eudora Welty, Flannery O'Connor, Erskine Caldwell, Mark Twain even—they're all essentially storytellers, yarn-spinners. And the poets, too; they have that kind of gift of honey on the lips. Not so much the gift of the gab, but a touch of eloquence. That's just the way things have always been down here.

SKY: Do you think that people in other parts of the country now feel something in common with the situation of people in the South?

DICKEY: The South began as an agrarian region, a region, as Thomas Jefferson call it, of yeoman farmers—him with his three hundred slaves. But the increased industrialization and modernization of the South are things that will make the South more like the rest of the country. All those differences—the folkways and mores that distinguish the South—are eventually going to die out. And that, it seems to me, is one of the reasons why people have fastened on to Southern ways and elected a Southern president and so forth, because they feel that the South has preserved this individuality of region as well as of person and has not been homogenized to quite the extent of the rest of the nation. People want those differences.

But let me change the metaphor for a second. Say an American goes to Europe. He takes a tour and goes around to different countries. Now why does he go? He goes for the differences. He does it because the English thing is not the same as the French thing, and the French thing is not the Italian thing, and the Italian thing is not the German thing. He goes for the differences in the way people take life; for the customs and the local cooking and so forth.

These differences are the things that make life interesting. Now, with the heavy industrialization of the South and the awful proliferation of the automobile, things are being made more uniform.

SKY: Is there anything we can do about it?

DICKEY: I don't think so. I think the process is irreversible. But I don't claim any great insight into social problems. I would certainly not claim my prerogative as a poet, novelist, critic, and filmmaker as giving me any great authority.

16

AN INTERVIEW WITH . . . JAMES DICKEY

EARL TURNER / 1978

DICKEY: I remember a guy in a picture in *Life* magazine who was back home after the war. He was stretched out in a kind of a lounge chair in an American suburban back yard, having a beer—and I've been trying to emulate that guy ever since! It's not bad duty.

TURNER: Is it painful at all for you to talk about the war?

DICKEY: You have to come to grips with it in some kind of way. I'm writing a long novel now that deals with World War II. Some of it is painful, sure it is.

TURNER: I know that at the time you went to war—

DICKEY: I was just a young boy. I have some pictures of when I was in cadets. It hit my generation hard. Nobody knew what to expect. We just had to go forward. We didn't know if we'd win the war or not—whether we were going to be subjugated and have our mothers and wives and sweethearts raped by the Japanese. Nobody knew what the hell was going on. We just got in there and tried to do what we could do.

TURNER: You were a cadet? In pilot school?

DICKEY: Yes. Aviation Cadet School. In some way those were very great days. Everything was open-ended—we had the feeling that we were all in this together. I think that's the main feeling of the military anyway. Fort Jackson is right over here. I hear them drilling every morning. It seems to me that the

---

Reprinted with permission from *Vetletter* [University of South Carolina], 2 (October 1978), 2, and the Office of Veterans' Records, University of South Carolina.

stay against confusion that we are obligated to take care of is largely the military. I was flying above Nagasaki when they dropped the second atomic bomb. Nobody knew exactly what had been going on. We just thought that it was some kind of enormously powerful, super form of dynamite. We didn't know that the secret of the universe was involved! You know? The $E = mc^2$ equation—nobody knew anything about that then. It was only after we came home and were civilians again, and were trying to get educated and married and have children and all that we knew exactly what we were a party to.

TURNER: How did you feel when you realized this?

DICKEY: If there's ever been any meaning to the term "mixed emotions," I would say that's what I felt, because I wouldn't be sitting here on the dock talking to you if they had *not* dropped the bomb. After the war was over they released the invasion plans, and my squadron would have just been sacrificed. If Truman had not made the decision to do it, not only my life, but a lot of my American service compatriots would have been sacrificed. So what do you do? How would you like to have that kind of decision? Thanks to it, here I am, and here you are.

TURNER: What was your rank? You were an officer, I suppose?

DICKEY: I think I was a First Lieutenant. That was the highest I got.

. . .

I think of those other guys. God help them. God love them; I loved every one of them. The guys who were killed, the one's who were wounded, the guys who were beheaded by the Japanese, the ones who disappeared into the sea and were never heard of again—I feel very close links with them.

. . .

TURNER: In one of your poems, you mention sleeping under an army blanket. Did you do much of that?

DICKEY: Many a time—and was glad to have it! The worst times were when I couldn't find one. It was rough, but it was good.

. . .

TURNER: I've read that one of your freshman-year professors at Vanderbilt, I don't recall his name, had a great influence on you after he read a paper you wrote for him entitled "The Invasion of Okinawa."

DICKEY: Oh, yes, he's dead now. Puryear Mims. He was a very good teacher for me. But you see, the service, for my generation, turned our whole perspective around. You didn't come out of the service the same person. My values had changed, everything about me had changed, because of the war experience, and because of the new things that had come into my head. I no longer wanted to be a numbskull football player, which I *definitely* was before. Good God! The only book I read at Clemson was the play-book: "Cut right, three steps, cut in, hold up hands for pass." I didn't know mathematics, English, history, economics, and whatever else I was supposed to be taking. Everything was subordinated to football. When I came back, I had a glimmering, maybe just a dim glimmering, of what the life of the mind might be like. And I wanted to go where I could fertilize that and learn to do something. I was twenty-three when I got out, and I knew that if I was going to chart a new course, I was going to have to do it right then, and not at any other time. *Right then!* So I pulled up stakes, gave up my eligibility at Clemson, and went to Vanderbilt on the G.I. Bill.

17

A Conversation with James Dickey

Peggy Friedmann and Betty Bedell / 1979

KALLIOPE: You have said that some of your poems have gone through hundreds of revisions. "May Day Sermon," I believe you said, went through two hundred revisions.

DICKEY: At least.

KALLIOPE: Do you still revise extensively? How many revisions, for example, did *The Zodiac* take?

DICKEY: It's hard to say, but many. Many. A poem like *The Zodiac,* which is conceived as a major effort, cannot go wrong. But you don't know what right is, because there's not any precedent for it, so that you come out at the end of it in a situation very much like the great modern French neo-classicist poet, Paul Valéry, described when he said, "One never finishes a poem; one abandons it." But I don't think you should abandon it without a long and honorable fight, to help it or to make it realize its best intentions such as you see it. That's more or less the condition of *The Zodiac.*

KALLIOPE: Do you ever want to revise after you see a poem in print?

DICKEY: No, I never do. I read through my earlier work and I say to myself that I might have changed this word or that punctuation mark, but by damn, isn't it good! You know, you look at it and you think, I'd kind of like to get back to that way of writing. It's like it was written by somebody else. That person is dead, or gone, or skipped the country, or whatever. He's gone, the person that wrote that poem, and all you can do

---

Reprinted with permission from *Kalliope,* 1 (February 1979), 30–35.

is sit there and read it, and appreciate it, or depreciate it, or whatever; but you could never do that again, because you're a completely different human being by this time. Somebody mentioned a poem of mine called "Sleeping Out at Easter," which was written around—gracious me—twenty-five years ago, and I look at it, I read it, and I think, well, maybe I ought to try something like that again. But I know that I won't, and I can't, because another person with a completely different set of values, a completely different life situation, and so on, wrote it. I have another life situation, an older kind of personality. I've been through a lot of different kinds of experiences that bridge the gap from that day to this one, and what I write now has to draw on the new life instead of continually going back to the youngish fellow that wrote "Sleeping Out at Easter."

KALLIOPE: But you still read it and think it's good?

DICKEY: I sure do. Boy, if a son of mine wrote that, I'd quit. I'd say the same thing Andrew Wyeth said about his son, Jamie Wyeth, who's also a wonderful painter. He said, "I'm going to be known just as the father of Jamie Wyeth in art history." And I say, I'll be known only as the father of James Dickey—except that it was *me*.

KALLIOPE: You have said that the narrative poem has been lost in America.

DICKEY: Yes, I think this as a novelist, having written *Deliverance* and part of another novel, but being primarily a poet. I feel that there is something indigenous to the human creature—man, woman, or child—which goes back to the caves, as far as the story is concerned. Either in poetry or prose or novels or short stories—whatever—plays, there's something indigenous to the human creature that, when given a story, wants to know what happens next. And I think that the poets in my generation, and in the one just before and just after mine, have given away entirely too much territory to the novel and to prose fiction. They have given away too much of what could have been theirs in order to concentrate on the lyric flight, the pure cry of the soul, and they've let slide the long thrust of narrative, which they need not have done. I'd like to get a little bit of that back.

KALLIOPE: What about the inner narrative?

DICKEY: Well, it can be inner, or it can be outer, or it can be a combination. You can break it up, you know, different ways. But the lyric poem, the supreme concentration on a moment of intuition, is beautiful, it's good; there have been wonderful things done by poets who had that attitude, but that's not all that in poetry can be done. I think we've given away too much. So in poems of my own like "The Firebombing" or "May Day Sermon to the Women of Gilmer County, Georgia, by a Woman Preacher Leaving the Baptist Church," or one kind of, I suppose, neglected piece of mine called "Reincarnation (II)," about an office worker becoming resurrected as a migratory sea bird, I think all kinds of things are possible. I think the lyric poet of the small exquisite moment is not the only poet we can have. I would rather read "Reincarnation (II)" than any number of beautifully turned rhyming lyrics by other poets, or even by myself.

KALLIOPE: Do you think, perhaps, that people can relate more to the narrative poem than to the lyric?

DICKEY: I do indeed. I do think so. All you have to do is go to your turnaround rack in your nearest drug store and see that what people are reading, essentially, are narratives of some sort. They're detective stories, they're brutal sexual stories, accounts of political corruption, but they're all narratives of one sort of another.

KALLIOPE: You have been critical of some women poets for what you called their "habitual gravitation to the domestic and anti-poetic." Is anything inherently anti-poetic?

DICKEY: No. If there's any lesson that we have learned from Modernism in poetry, it is that there is no intrinsically poetic subject matter, and there's no intrinsically anti-poetic subject matter. This is the great lesson of Whitman, for example, who taught us—and I think to our very great profit—that in the Victorian or Swinburnian or Tennysonian or Keatsian sense, there is no elevated subject matter to go beneath which we are not being poetic. A latter-day follower of his, William Carlos Williams, can make a lovely poem about the reflections of light on a broken beer bottle in the cinder parking lot of a hospital. There's beauty there. There's splendor. As Williams himself said, the great lesson of Whitman, of post-Whitman poetry, is that anything is a subject for poetry if the imagination can grasp it.

KALLIOPE: Which contemporary American poets do you especially admire?

DICKEY: There are a lot of them that I admire. I think Roethke was a very good poet. I love Lowell—it killed me when he died. And I wish to hell that the press would give over the supposed rivalry between Lowell and me. I loved the man. I had no rivalry with him. I'm not his opponent, but it's so fatally easy for journalists to do that. Here Lowell is the New Englander, I the Southerner, he the Classicist, I the Romantic. It's fatally easy to do that, when it should not be done, certainly not in this case.

KALLIOPE: Are there any women poets that you admire?

DICKEY: Oh, yes, many. I would rather read them than the men these days. Jane Cooper is good, at Sarah Lawrence. Ann Stanford, at California State, is good. They have a marvelous delicacy. To me they don't have the force that some of the men do, and I think that the best ones among the men poets are those who have the most admixture of feminine sensibility.

KALLIOPE: Androgynous?

DICKEY: You don't have to put it that way. That has a kind of pejorative feeling to it; but somebody like Wendell Berry, for example, at the University of Kentucky, has got a very soft kind of feminine instinct. James Wright has very close to a feminine kind of feeling for experience. I think the men poets who have the woman instinct are better than the women poets who have the woman instinct.

KALLIOPE: Why is that?

DICKEY: You tell me. But Wendell Berry certainly does have it, and it's all to his credit, and to the credit of American poetry. So does James Wright. So does William Stafford. To some extent, so does Louis Simpson. The tough-guy poets are inevitably not as good as the ones who have allowed the feminine admixture to come into their work, who have consented to respond fully, rather than be Hemingwayesque.

18

AN INTERVIEW WITH JAMES DICKEY

RON MCFARLAND / 1979

McFARLAND: You've said so much about your own views and have been interviewed so often that it's difficult to find new ground. Some colleagues of mine suggested, though, that the "real James Dickey" is concealed by a self-created and media-assisted mask.

DICKEY: I suppose anybody would have a tendency to do that, would partially invent or would partially have invented for him a kind of persona. You don't know which the real one is. The person himself would be the least qualified to answer that. . . .

McFARLAND: When and where was your first reading?

DICKEY: Damned if I can remember. I think it was probably in Houston, Texas, when I was teaching at Rice. I don't think I had very many poems published, maybe just a few at that time. I remember I was sponsored by a ladies' church group and I gave the reading in the parish room or one of the Sunday School rooms in the bottom of the Baptist church. It was in our neighborhood in Houston, and the lady introduced me. They'd never had any speakers before in this group, except religious speakers, people with messages, good words and uplifting speeches, homilies, that sort of thing. So at that time I was on a kind of death and disease kick and was writing about nothing but cancer—

McFARLAND: I don't suppose you had your "May Day Sermon" poem.

Reprinted with permission from *Slackwater Review*, 3 (Winter 1979-1980), 17–33.

DICKEY: Oh, no, it was much before that. And then I read other poems about people dying of leukemia. It was the most gruesome kind of depressing subject matter you could imagine. So I finished. There were about four or five, maybe ten people in the audience, of ladies obligated to come, including my wife with a couple friends of hers. And when I finished there was a polite spattering of applause, very light indeed and short, believe me, and the lady that had introduced me got up and said, rather uncertainly, after I had given all this death and destruction, disease, "Ladies, I'm sure we all want to thank Mr. Dickey for that nice message."

McFARLAND: I wonder, though, if you've ever had your self-confidence severely shaken.

DICKEY: I've never had it when it was not shaken. But if you let all that bother you, you just can't write, you won't try anything. I figure everything I write, I'll stand or fall on that forever. I'm kind of a gambler at heart, and I believe in risking everything on one turn of the card, one throw. That's the way I write. I was reading, of all things for some reason the other day, the biography of Billy the Kid, and I was delighted to hear it said by the people who remembered him that his favorite saying and his only homily was "a chance in a million." I'm glad to be in such distinguished company.

McFARLAND: Your answer's interesting because you come on as someone very confident, at least, and someone might even say that you were over-confident.

DICKEY: Oh, no, that's just show.

McFARLAND: You're not really cocky, for example.

DICKEY: No, I don't believe so. Some people might think so, but I don't see myself in that way. But I've never been a believer in false modesty, or even in true modesty. I'd rather see somebody like Cassius Clay—he's refreshing to me—whatever he calls himself, Muhammad Ali. That's refreshing to me. He's good, he doesn't mind saying so. He is good, why not? I've never been this "aw shucks 'twarn't nuthin'" type of person. And I distrust people that are that way.

. . .

McFARLAND: Here's another question. In *Sorties* you said some pretty hard things about middle age, about the terror and sadness of it.

DICKEY: Yes. It's even worse now that I've lived through it than I said it was. There's only one excuse for getting old, and that is that you've put your time in and have achieved through the passage of years mastery of something that you would not without those years have been able to have in that degree.

McFARLAND: What if you fail? What if you haven't achieved mastery?

DICKEY: Well, you might not have achieved mastery in the world's eyes, but you can at least say that you were better off than you would have been without those years of experience doing something. Which is why old Ezra Pound was such an oracle, because he had all that experience behind him. He had known all those people, he had done all those things, and had accumulated, maybe not wisdom, but a lot of things that were worth passing on. Some weren't, but a lot were.

McFARLAND: What happens to the "edge," the "razor's edge between sublimity and absurdity," as you age? Is it still possible to maintain?

DICKEY: Oh, I believe so. You should always be prepared to make a fool of yourself. I don't know, it's these people who play it so close to the vest that—I look for something new from a challenging poet, something interesting. I think the business of playing out there at the edge of consciousness where you're trying to push things out a little bit beyond where they were before you made the attempt, that's the thing that interests me. That's why Hart Crane is such an interesting writer to me, and why these people who have a certain consolidated position and never do anything but the same thing over and over again—somebody like Louise Bogan, you can name any number of them—are not.

McFARLAND: Does *that* strike you as one of the real dangers of academia, of the college academic as a poet?

DICKEY: The thing about American poets is that the stakes are so pitifully small financially, and so far as notoriety is concerned, fame, that if they get any recognition at all, if they get asked to read fairly often, or if they have pretty good press and so on, they're afraid to change that little thing that they painfully acquired. And if they don't change, they just repeat themselves, and everybody pats them on the back for being such an "assured craftsman" and that sort of thing, and they never write anything memorable.

(Several minutes passed in talking of Robert Penn Warren, whose work Mr. Dickey praised as, at its best, "startlingly good, raw and powerful, moving." He told of finding a copy of *Understanding Poetry* by Cleanth Brooks and Warren after the hurricane on Okinawa in 1945, and of how important that book was to his interest in poetry. We also spoke of overrated poets, in the context of which Robert Bly received some buffeting.)

DICKEY: Now James Wright, who had some early affinities with Bly, is very good. The good ones around now? Wendell Berry is one of my favorite ones. He's a great conservationist, on the side of nature. He's a farmer and all that, and a real one; he's not a fake farmer.

McFARLAND: He's from Kentucky, isn't he?

DICKEY: Yes. Wendell Berry's good, Wright is good. I like a little of Louis Simpson, not a whole lot. I like Howard Nemerov very much. I like some of Ben Bellitt's work. Let's see, who else—

McFARLAND: Do you still care for William Stafford's work?

DICKEY: I like him, but not as much as I used to. Yes, I think he's good.

McFARLAND: Is there such a thing as a poet being published too much?

DICKEY: If there is he'd be a good example of it. Of the women I think Eleanor Taylor is very good, the one that Randall Jarrell thought so highly of. The best woman poet writing, I think, is Margaret Atwood. Jane Cooper, I think, is good, at Sarah Lawrence. Mona Van Duyn is good.

McFARLAND: That's a poet, I think, who has been much undervalued.

DICKEY: Underrated, yes. I can think of a lot of them. Eleanor Taylor is also much overlooked. If you except those cult kind of figures like Bly—

McFARLAND: Gary Snyder?

DICKEY: And Snyder. Snyder has a little ability. He's an old Reed College boy. He has a little something. Not much. But he's a slavish follower of Kenneth Rexroth who has little talent either.

McFARLAND: Rexroth's was one of the first poetry readings I ever attended, at Illinois.

DICKEY: Well, you probably had to be dragged by horses to another one.

McFARLAND: The next one I went to was by Ferlinghetti.

DICKEY: That lonely craft of poetry. Those guys are turning it into a kind of cheap, unimaginative circus set. . . .

(Mr. Dickey commented briefly on the "scene" in England: his favorite English poet now writing, Geoffrey Hill; his least favorite, Ted Hughes. . . .)

DICKEY: A certain section of the poetry world will attempt to "put over" certain writers. Stanley Kunitz is one of them that has been sort of put over, but he's only mildly interesting.

McFARLAND: I read some stuff by Kunitz taken from his *Collected Poems* in the last *American Poetry Review* and I was bored. I started building a theory of reading poems along the lines that if the first two or three lines don't grab your attention at all, why should you punish yourself by reading the whole poem? I guess this is unfair, but—

DICKEY: No, it isn't. . . . It's good to get into the subject fast. Just start fast and keep on going faster.

McFARLAND: That's right, these slow-boiling poems sometimes just don't boil at all, never even simmer. I wanted to ask you how you felt about *The Zodiac*. It got some mixed reviews.

DICKEY: I don't want to be embraced to death, especially for something like that. Warren had a damned good long piece on that in the *New York Times*.[51] There was another good one in the *Washington Post* by a guy I think is really good, though I don't know much about him, Stanley Burnshaw.[52] Some people liked it. I don't care who likes it and who doesn't. I don't write for people.

McFARLAND: I just wondered how you felt about it yourself.

DICKEY: I like it; I think it's good. I'd do exactly the same thing again.

. . .

MCFARLAND: Would you call *The Zodiac* a kind of indirect narration?

DICKEY: A sublimated narrative, yes. It's a poem on about as big a subject as you could try to write upon. The kind of half-mad, half-drunken afflatus that gets into a poet, or a certain kind of poet, when be believes that he can write the ultimate poem.

McFARLAND: Right; to create a new constellation, literally to create.

DICKEY: Yes. Not approximately, but in exactly the same way God does.

McFARLAND: A lobster appears.

DICKEY: That's right. It turns out it's a creature from delirium tremens.

McFARLAND: When I read that I wondered why you said a lobster. I decided there was the interplay between that and Cancer, the crab, and besides the protagnoist is a sailor, so what else could it be? A shark wouldn't be quite right. There's something spidery about a lobster.

DICKEY: Right. Lobsters always frightened me very much. You don't know what kinds of things come after you when you have delirium tremens. It's also a poem which tries to compare the line between being drunk, especially a poet being drunk, and his feeling that either what he's doing is something miraculous and relates him to the entire created universe, or that it's just silly.

McFARLAND: He vacillates himself in this.

An Interview

DICKEY: Right. And in the end he decides that he just can't go on. It's like the end of one of Samuel Beckett's books, *The Unnamable,* which might have gotten into this in some way, in spirit if not in actual phrasing, where he says: "You must go on, I can't go on, I'll go on." So he does at the end go on trying to write the impossible poem.

McFARLAND: I had a hard time with the narrator in the poem. There was an intrusion by you, or by you as the narrator.

DICKEY: Well, sometimes there's not any difference. Sometimes I'm the guy, Marsman, sometimes not.

McFARLAND: Will people go back to this book, do you think, as your *ars poetica*?

DICKEY: I don't think so. I don't know; it's just one other thing that I've written. I don't know where I would place it exactly, but I like it, especially the end. I can't write any better than that: About doing the European poetic tradition like a tuning fork with his bandless wedding finger. The whole thing comes into being because of that, the stars and everything else, and "So long as the hand can hold the island / Of blazing paper, and bleed for its images: / Make what it can of what it is: / So long as the spirit hurls on space / The star-beasts of intellect and madness."

McFARLAND: Good.

DICKEY: I've been in astronomy. I didn't have a father like this guy does. And I think that's another good section, as long as we're talking about that poem. It's where he goes to the home place and his mother is stretched out in space over the road and tells him to go away. "Don't put your prick in a cold womb, / Nothing but walking snakes would come of that."

McFARLAND: The speech is right. There's a lot of profanity in the poem, but then Marsman's a merchant seaman, not a college professor.

DICKEY: Yes. He's a sailor with a sailor's relationship to stars, navigation, and the ocean. I like the part in the last section where the revelation that he's godlike comes to him when he realizes, after all this time, that he can say what he wants to say. It's given to him as it was to God. He can put words down in a certain relationship and they will be those words in that relation.

McFARLAND: That would be the constellation.

DICKEY: That's it, that's it, he's got it, at least he thinks he has. He's writing about deserts and camels, and suddenly it turns into the ocean.

McFARLAND: And is literally metamorphosed.

DICKEY: Yes.

McFARLAND: Because otherwise the sea won't be the sea.

DICKEY: That's right. For only in its ships "the sea becomes the sea." It's a difficult poem, but I wouldn't have it any other way.

McFARLAND: I remember reading that you said it was wrong to assume that because the times were complex we must have more complex poems. You did qualify that by saying there was a certain type of simplicity you were lookng for. And then, I think toward the end of *Self-Interviews,* you say something to the effect that the new poems you write are going to have more abrupt transitions, will be much more difficult in certain ways.

DICKEY: Yes, it's what I've wanted to do ever since I started using this kind of split-line technique. That opened up an awful lot to me. I did it really because I'd begun to think about the psychology of the line, not the mechanics or the logistics of the line, but the psychology of the poetic line as it relates to the brain and how the mind actually does work, especially the way it works in images, and the way it works verbally, and the way it works with the two in conjunction. Now the mind does not work in direct lines, like iambic pentameter lines across a page. It works in jumps, in spurts, like something leaping, a spark gap. And I thought if I could get an effect of that sort it would give a new kind of sound to the poem, which it does do. And everybody and his brother is doing that now. I see it everywhere.

McFARLAND: It drives printers crazy though, I bet.

DICKEY: Sure. But good Lord, they just ought to be glad it's not e. e. cummings.

An Interview 181

McFARLAND: You don't use semicolons, though.

DICKEY: In a sense these gaps take the place of various types of punctuation. What I wanted to get also through that device—I'm always thinking of the possibilities of the line—I don't think they've really been tapped yet, even touched yet. But I heard a little boy who had been in an automobile wreck who had a natural stammer. I happened to look down the street where it happened and saw that there had been a wreck and he'd run to tell somebody about it. So I knew that I could go down and get somebody to help out. But he was trying to tell this policeman about it and the policeman didn't see the car down there, and this little boy was stammering and he was trying to tell that policeman, but he couldn't get the words out. But you could tell what that little child was doing. Two things were characteristic of what he was doing: first, that he was trying to say something of utmost importance, and two, that his speech was blocked. So with that split line I wanted to get something of that effect of saying something important against something that's trying to keep it from getting said.

McFARLAND: Yes, and the repetition that happens is the sort that actually occurs. I liked your anapests though.

DICKEY: I liked that, too, but that can get to be a drag. It was getting to where it was too easy, and I even began to talk that way, just like I am starting to talk to you now. And it's getting a little bit too mechanical when you get to that point. I may go back and do some of that. I like it. It has a very compelling kind of tribal quality about it. . . . Well, this is something you can certainly learn from Pound, the value for the truly creative mind of endless experimentation. So many things are dead ends, but you wouldn't find the things that are not dead ends unless you risked a lot of dead ends. The main thing is always to keep exploring. That first book of mine was mostly either in received forms like quatrains or couplets, or in invented forms, where I invented that kind of double refrain thing where the last stanza is just the summation of all the refrain lines. That's a lot of fun to do. I think the dynamics of language, including the rhythmical, maybe especially that. I'm like Pound. I believe in melopoeia, any kind of sound device. . . . I like the very heavily accented, strongly marked. I like bad poets who have strong rhythms. Bad poets. I don't care sometimes what they say. Poe was a very bad poet. Very bad, but he's also a real poet in the same sense that somebody like Robert Service, who does the same thing, is not—Dan McGrew and all that—is not a real poet. Poe is a real poet. Poe has one of the most evocative and beautiful lines I've ever read in any poetry. I tell you it's absolutely haunting. And nobody but he would've written it, either. It's in the one called "The City in the Sea," which is his best poem, I think, really the only one that has any touch of greatness. He's talking about the sea. I forget the first of the two lines I'm referring to, but there's something—the winds that pass "Along that wilderness of glass." That's too good to believe. I mean Hart Crane would have liked that line, or anybody would. Pound would've liked it. The sea—I never look at the sea without thinking of that "wilderness of glass." That's just a perfect poetic trope. It's perfect. If you look at the original thing itself, that's what it's like. . . . I'm not that much of a classical scholar; I'm worse off than Shakespeare whom Ben Jonson characterized as having "small Latin and less Greek." I have infinitely small Latin and no Greek, except a couple of words. But Homer—I like the simplicity. Those guys, those early poets, those tribal poets like Homer, had a tremendous advantage over us latterday folk in that they could compare one thing to another, and it could say the obvious thing, or point of comparison, and it would not yet have become a cliche.

McFARLAND: Right. To be able to say "the wine-dark sea—"

DICKEY: You just take that example, "the wine-dark sea." Now you go the Aegean and know what the ocean looks *exactly* like?

McFARLAND: Wine.

DICKEY: Right. It looks exactly like wine. Doesn't taste like wine, but it looks exactly like it, not approximately but *exactly*. I remember when we were on the troopships in the South Pacific for days at a time going from one invasion to another, I remember that the exact shade of the water in the part of the Pacific I was in, say down around New Guinea, was like blueing. Know what blueing is?

McFARLAND: For a gun?

DICKEY: No. For washing.

An Interview

McFARLAND: Oh, yeah.

DICKEY: Do they call it that up in this part of the country?

McFARLAND: Yes, but they don't use it much, I don't think.

DICKEY: It's exactly like that. Nobody else said that, but it's the same kind of comparison. If I compared the water in the South Pacific to blueing, it would be exactly the same perfectly demonstrable one-to-one correspondence as Homer's "wine-dark sea" for the Aegean looking like wine. It's exactly the same thing.

McFARLAND: Except that "blueing" would never fill the place of "wine."

DICKEY: No, no, not enough people use blueing and a lot use wine, in Homer's time as well as ours. But I like the fact that these guys had that kind of simplicity. "Came rosey-fingered dawn" or "swift-footed Achilles." You know why he was called "swift-footed?" Because he could run fast.

McFARLAND: Or "ox-eyed Hera."

DICKEY: Or "many-minded Ulysses," or Odysseus.

McFARLAND: The "man of strategems."

DICKEY: Or Hector being called "the horse-breaker," because he broke a lot of horses. Nowadays we're so trammeled with over-subtleties, like the evening stretched out "against the sky / Like a patient etherised upon a table," when there's really not any physical correspondence there at all. None.

McFARLAND: And you can't hope to compete in that kind of an arena ultimately because it becomes a matter of sheer ingenuity.

DICKEY: Sure. Now the modern poetry so-called, the latter-day scene, has done some remarkable things that Homer would not have been able to do, like some of Hart Crane's poems, or Arthur Rimbaud, for example. They would not have thought to see things in those terms. They would not have done something like seeing paradise reflected in the eyes of a seal in Hart Crane's "until / Is answered in the vortex of our grave / The seal's wide spindrift gaze toward paradise." Which is marvelous, isn't it?

McFARLAND: Yes.

DICKEY: Or Pound, who was great at starting off with the *Odyssey,* using the voyage all through—Pound has a figure of speech about the ocean that is as good as anything in Homer with his "wine-dark sea," which is from "Mauberley," talking about the shores of forgotten South Sea islands "Washed in the cobalt of oblivions." Of "oblivions," the plural; I mean it's so beautiful. That would not have occurred to Homer, or to any of the other earlier heroes of the relatively primitive. Of course I'm also a great believer in tribal poetry. I can't help in some ways siding with Lautréamont, in the most famous of his statements that has come down to us. He's a great favorite of mine. Have you read any of his work?

McFARLAND: No, I haven't.

DICKEY: He hasn't been translated much into English. He's really wonderful, a real authentic. If any one writer is responsible for the attitude known as "surrealism," it was he. Not much is known about him. He came originaly from South America to Paris and went mad, died at around thirty. He made up a phony thing as a nobleman, the "Comte de Lautréamont." Really he was a crazy Jew named Isidore Ducasse, from Montevideo. He's a really interesting guy, a wonderful writer. I might read a sort of Zodiacan kind of free translation from him tonight, one called "Mathematics." He's very good. Anyway, his most famous statement is that "poetry must not be made by one, but by all." Usually I would take exactly the opposite view of that, but I can see that there's something in the idea of a tribal poetry that's important. I used to teach a course at Reed College in world poetry, and we'd go back into obscure anthropological expeditions and the things they'd written down—tribal chants, Eskimo tribes, Bantu elephant hunters, different kinds of stuff, stuff that's fascinating—and American Indians, some of that's wonderful.

McFARLAND: Isn't David Wagoner doing something like that now?

DICKEY: Yes, but he's far too sophisticated, although he's very good and rather witty. He's one of the few poets that has any wit. But he writes *about* the subject, and that's not like the Indians really believing it. There was one expedition that had gone to collect songs and chants from the Eskimos, and this guy, one of the anthropologists, had some literary interests, and he kept going around to the members of the tribe and asking them which one had written this line or other of the song, or where it had come from, and they were surprised that he would even ask that, because they didn't know, nobody knew. They had an aversion to attributing anything to anybody. It just belonged to the people.

McFARLAND: Just like the question I asked you about the Coke jingle.

DICKEY: Oh, God, don't make that comparison. Yes, commercials are not made by one but by all. Same thing. But the whole business of poetry being something secluded—I think people like Pound, who want poetry to have this kind of greater accessibility, to contribute to people's lives and so on, I think that's very healthy and good.

McFARLAND: I think so. It's kind of ironic that Pound is not really considered a very accessible poet.

DICKEY: No, he is considered the exact opposite of that.

McFARLAND: And yet he really did want to be accessible.

DICKEY: I'm going to talk something about this tonight,[53] but ... the best things of Pound have a marvelous, imaginative primitivism about them, and the things that he likes, say in the Chinese poems, are in the English poems that sound like Chinese poems that he likes. They have this kind of quality where you can read the poem and then look at the thing or imagine the thing that he's writing about, and you see it with an intensity and you experience it with an intensity that you would not have been capable of had you not read about the subject in *those* words. Like Lionel Johnson's lines that he cites as having a beauty like the Chinese: "Clear lie the fields and fade into blue air." Simple. Now *that* (he's quite right), he says, has a beauty akin to the beauty of Chinese poetry and also Chinese painting, where the effect of distance is not given by perspective lines, but by a gradual fading out, and creating a background in the sense of distance by blurring it out, which is wonderful. Don't you like that?

McFARLAND: Any advice for young, aspiring writers? Are creative writing programs worthwhile, or should they be limited to a course or two instead of the M.F.A. degree?

DICKEY: I guess without being pretentious I could cite the way that I try to teach it, because obviously I would want to embody any principles I have in the way I actually do teach actual courses and actual students. I divide the course into two parts, a year's course. One of them is an intense concentration on the various received forms that are most used in English verse, the epigrammatic couplet, the heroic couplet, the extended use of it in satirical forms, the quatrain, the sonnet, and working gradually into more difficult French forms like the villanelle, Italian ones like the sestina and canzone, and so on. I just concentrate on forms. One assignment a week.

McFARLAND: Do your students like this approach? Do they write the poems?

DICKEY: Oh, yes, they write them, and we critique them, then I give them another assignment. We go on. They like it usually. You can tell the good ones by the ones that really look on it as a challenge. They like the resistance of it. The second semester I take the whole semester to have them write one poem, starting with the absolute beginning, the seed of the poem. It's either in the memory or in an invention of theirs, an invention of a situation or a line of thought, or a dream, wherever it comes from. I start at the beginning of something, the seed or the kernel of the poem, and then we gradually try to explore the possibilites of that, and then, the last part, define a form of it, see how it comes out.

McFARLAND: They usually create their own form?

DICKEY: They try it all different ways.

McFARLAND: I see, they try out various forms.

DICKEY: That's right. So that's the way I do it. . . .

19
JAMES DICKEY RIDES AGAIN
L. ELISABETH BEATTIE / 1982

LIFESTYLE: What sort of book is *Puella*?

DICKEY: Well, it's dedicated to the pubescent girl, and the dedication in the book reads "To Deborah—*her girlhood, male-imagined.*" It's my very subjective interpretation of female puberty. Because it deals with puberty, it sounds like it probably has a lot to do with sex. It's not really about sex at all except only in a fleeting mention. It's about coming into one's powers as a woman.

LIFESTYLE: It sounds as if you sense that as a mysterious time, and a time that is quite different for women than it is for men.

DICKEY: It must be radically different, I think. The woman's body chemistry is in touch with the seasons and the moon. That's something men don't know anything about—cycles.

LIFESTYLE: In what ways does your wife, Deborah, inspire your poetry?

DICKEY: In the way that any woman has ever inspired any poet's work, I guess. Just by the mystery of her existence, of her radiation, her mysterious radiation.

LIFESTYLE: What about your new daughter, Bronwen? Has she inspired your poetry?

DICKEY: She's great. I haven't written anything about her yet, but I will. It's wonderful for someone my age to have a child. It's a wonderful renewal. She's not my granddaughter, she's my daughter. And there's a vast difference. I have a grandson who's eleven. It's a sort of crazy mixed-up genealogy. My daughter is

---

Reprinted with permission from *Carolina Lifestyle*, 1 (May 1982), 42–46.

my grandson's aunt. She's a very pretty little baby—very pretty and very sweet.

LIFESTYLE: Has her presence affected your work timing any?

DICKEY: I think it's very interesting to have a lot of things going on at the same time, because energy for one project will give you energy for another. The British writer Herbert Read was wonderful to me in this regard. He told me about the years he spent working at the Victoria and Albert Museum as a curator of ceramics there. He carried out his literary work at night and on weekends and holidays, which is very much the same sort of thing I did when I worked in advertising. He said that it's just a matter of ordering your time. When you come home, you have a certain schedule for the day, and it's not a very difficult thing to tack fifteen or twenty minutes onto that every day. It's not all that taxing, and you can do it, and you can get a lot done.

When I have a lot of different projects going, I do that. I just travel from one to the other, and they sort of cross-pollinate one another, I find. And the criticism and the poetry and the travel and the movies and the essays and whatever else I do—everything just goes in together. I don't believe that much in compartmentalization. I believe in the creative process going on all the time and taking many forms.

LIFESTYLE: What projects are you currently working on?

DICKEY: I'm working on a novel about World War II. I leave it and then I come back to it; I'd like to finish a version of it by June. . . .

LIFESTYLE: How do you believe that you have evolved as a poet and as a writer? How have your priorities changed?

DICKEY: Oh, I don't know. I don't know about priorities, but I like to take in as much territory as I can. I had rather throw a wide net and take in a lot of different subjects than specialize in one. If that means superficiality, that's fine. I had much rather be broad than deep.

Broad in contradistinction to deep is supposed to be a rather pejorative term, but I don't look at it that way. I remember what Samuel Johnson said when someone asked him what the secret of living a successful life was. He said the secret to living

Dickey Rides Again

a successful life is to know something about everything and everything about one thing. I don't know everything about one thing, but I do know something about a lot of things.

LIFESTYLE: When the public hears your name, what sort of image do you think they have of the poet and of the man?

DICKEY: They probably think about *Deliverance,* because for every one person who reads a book of poetry, a hundred thousand will go to a movie. Of course, if you have a movie and a best-selling novel, they're going to associate you with that. But the audience that I really care for pays very little attention to *Deliverance,* as I do. I pay some attention to it. I enjoy *Deliverance. Deliverance* is very good. But the audience that I really want has been loyal to me from a long time before *Deliverance* and will be, I hope, for a long time after *Deliverance* passes into wherever it passes into—oblivion or immortality. It's over ten years old now, and that's a long life for an American novel, much less a movie.

LIFESTYLE: What sort of image would you like the public to have of you?

DICKEY: Someone who likes words and can work with them and who tries to see what he can make them do. Someone who has a notion of the mystical idea between words and things.

LIFESTYLE: What about as a person? The name F. Scott Fitzgerald elicits a certain image and so does the name Ernest Hemingway. Do you think the name James Dickey evokes a specific image?

DICKEY: I really don't have any idea what sort of image I would want. I don't try to second-guess the public. In an ideal situation I would like them to think of me like what I think my best self is like. Everyone has a best self, no matter how sorry he is. I would say that if I could project some sort of image of strength, of vitality, but above all, a sort of passionate and involved male tenderness, masculine tenderness, that is what I would like.

LIFESTYLE: Do you have what might be called a philosophy of life?

DICKEY: I don't think the greatest philosophers in the world have a definitive philosophy of life. I suppose I'm some sort of vitalist and a mystic, but I don't know of what specific sort. I believe in the life force and the mysteriousness of it. I believe in instinctual life and the unlimited emotional response to things. I believe in loving things and hating them because they're what they are and you're what you are. I believe in reason when it surpasses itself, not just conventional reason.

LIFESTYLE: When you say mystic, do you mean that in the Yeatsian sense?

DICKEY: Well, there are different kinds of mystics, as many different kinds of mystics as there are people. Yeats was a sort of systematizer of his own mystical values. I'm not that at all. Instinct is part of the mystery that intrigues me, that fascinates me the most. The instinct of migratory seabirds that navigate by the stars. How could they know how to do that? How could they possibly know? How could they have been taught? And yet it's incontrovertibly true that they do it.

There are all sorts of things in nature that are quite literally inexplicable, according to some law that's deeper than any law, inexplicable by reasonable process. The business of homing pigeons is as mysterious as it's ever been. I don't know that much about science. I know just enough about science to stay comfortably in the dark. My son is a medical student, and he decries this attitude on my part. But I believe that I have more satisfaction in mysteries than he will ever have in explicit knowledge.

LIFESTYLE: What things in the world make you happiest?

DICKEY: My family and writing. Anything in the arts that I respond to. Folk music. Some painters. I like astronomy very much. I like architecture and city planning—things of that nature. Things that are subject to reason.

LIFESTYLE: Many young writers today think you're fortunate to be able to make your living as a writer. Do you believe that it's possible for young writers who are just starting to publish to make a living in writing?

DICKEY: That's very difficult to say. I don't think there are many writers of any sort who make their living doing nothing but writing. There are a few, but they are not the writers of any quality at all. They are the writers of the sex books and best-sellers and Harlequin romances and that sort of thing.

But there are a few good writers in American literature who have made a good deal of money from writing. Hemingway was one of them. And Fitzgerald was one of them. Even though he did a considerable amount of hack work, he was, while he was doing it, a serious writer.

As far as poets are concerned, I don't think any American poets have made a living just from the work that they have written and published. A few, like Frost in his later years and Vachel Lindsay for a few years, and Edna Millay, and W. H. Auden when he became an American citizen, made a living from doing nothing but writing poetry and doing things that pertained to poetry. But the writing and publishing of poetry is not going to sustain anybody, no matter who it is. If I were to advise young writers, I'd say find something else to do. Teaching is very good for some people.

LIFESTYLE: You teach both undergraduate and graduate students. What do you enjoy most about teaching, and which of the courses that you teach is your favorite?

DICKEY: I enjoy the writing courses best because that's what I do, and I'm only secondarily an interpreter of literature or a critic or teacher of contemporary and modern poetry. Poetry, in addition to being my profession, is also sort of a hobby of mine.

I read a lot of verse. I enjoy it. It's like encountering another sensibility, especially if it expresses itself well or uniquely in some way. I like to read the old people. I'm always changing my opinions. I just reissued one of my critical books, *Babel to Byzantium,* with a new afterword in which I repudiate most of the views expressed in the book, or at least half of them. But that's all right. I think you should be open to change.

. . .

LIFESTYLE: Whose opinion of your work is most important to you?

DICKEY: The late Randall Jarrell's criticism. He's the best critic, I think, that we've ever had in this country. Allen Tate was good, too. Robert Penn Warren, among those who are still living, is the best, I think. And you could put him on one of these other lists, too, as a poet who will survive.

LIFESTYLE: Do you generally read criticism of your work?

DICKEY: No, I don't read any of it. If I ever see any of it, it's just by the merest chance. The few I've read over the past few years are so contradictory—they'll praise and criticize you for the wrong things. You can't trust even the ones that like you.

LIFESTYLE: If you had to choose one writing project that would mean the most for you to complete during your life, what would that project be?

DICKEY: A huge collected poems that would be a sort of monument and/or tombstone. But I want to write two more novels: one, the novel that I'm working on, and one, a sequel to that. And I want to make some more movies, too, and go on to write some more critical articles and essays.

LIFESTYLE: Is there anything that you believe has never been understood by the press or the critics or the public that you would like them to understand?

DICKEY: No, I don't think so. One or the other at one time or another has hit on a whole lot of sides of my curious personality; mostly the sides that are there, although they've also hit on a lot of sides that are not there.

But no, I don't think so. I would rather let the work express it. A writer's actual existence is private to him. His existence as a writer should be in his writings exclusviely, and whatever people want to find out about his personality and his sensibility should be in the words he puts on the page.

20
AN INTERVIEW WITH JAMES DICKEY
DICTIONARY OF LITERARY BIOGRAPHY YEARBOOK: 1982 / 1983

DLB: Your forthcoming volume, *Night Hurdling,* is really the first collection that you have done. You have published volumes made up of shorter pieces before, but they were all of a kind. *Night Hurdling* is the first time that you have assembled a variety of forms and types of work. What made you decide to do it now?

DICKEY: It seemed to me that I had enough different kinds—enough essays and enough literary criticism and enough odd forms, like graduation addresses and various interviews with various periodicals and people and so on—to make an interesting collection. As I said in the introduction, the main point of interest for a reader would be that the selections are all forms of my own particular reactive mechanism to things, and if readers are interested in anything of mine—poetry or novels or screenplays or essays or whatever the form—they might be interested in this. If they're not interested in my opinions, they wouldn't be interested in the book. If they *are,* they would.

DLB: Is *Night Hurdling* something more than an occasion to put together all of these things? Does the volume, as a volume, add up to anything? Does it make its own statement?

DICKEY: I think so. A book of this sort can't be themed as one would theme a book which is written around a simple central point, with various commentaries on a central position that

---

"An Interview with James Dickey," *Dictionary of Literary Biography Yearbook: 1982,* ed. Richard Ziegfeld (Detroit, Mich.: Bruccoli Clark/Gale Research Company, 1983), 142–147. Copyright© 1983 by Gale Research Company. Reprinted by permission of the publisher.

was predetermined. But one hopes, in a collection of this sort, that the thrust of a personality will be felt by the reader, even though the pieces have been collected from different sources and written and spoken over a long period of time, and for many diverse occasions. One would hope that the thrust of a personality would come through. Whether the personality itself is valuable is a question that I'm not able to answer.

DLB: Are there any pieces included in *Night Hurdling* that you are particularly happy to rescue from inaccessibility?

DICKEY: Surely; some more than others, surely. The essay about blowgun hunting for snakes—the one called "The Enemy from Eden"—I'm very happy to have in a book form. It was originally in a gift-book format, and it's been out of print for some time. I'm glad to have it generally available. Norman Mailer suggested that I collect it in some kind of way, and I asked him what type of book it should be in, and he said, "Any book, as long as it's available as the same piece." This is the book that "The Enemy from Eden" is finally appearing in. You don't have to dig back through the library and the back files of *Esquire* to find it.[54]

DLB: You have included commencement addresses in *Night Hurdling*. Do you have any special feeling about the commencement address, and why it is important to preserve them?

DICKEY: Yes, I think it is important. The commencement address is one of the most fragile forms of all, and the most perishable; the most likely to get lost in the general darkness that immediately begins to gather around any sort of utterance that we think is appropriate to a specific occasion. Richard Wilbur has pointed out that the commencement address is an extremely difficult literary form, and very demanding in its need for appropriateness. The hazard of the graduation address is that the things of permanent value will not get said and that hot air will be the main property of the discourse. Well, these are very real hazards, and I think the form demands that you try to transcend them and say what you have to say or think you have to say, hoping that it will be of some sort of permanent value to people. One of my addresses, the one I did at Wesleyan University in Macon,[55] has

An Interview 195

to do with a very topical kind of subject—which was more urgent then maybe than it is now, but is to some extent topical now as well—was on the assignment of guilt to other people because they don't agree with you politically or on certain public issues, such as the Vietnam War. It's to the eternal shame of some members of my generation that they seem to believe—either covertly or, in some cases, overtly—that poetry is simply a form of propaganda. In other words: if you don't agree with us on the Vietnam War, no matter what our opinion is (most of these people I'm talking about were against it), then we're going to shoot your poetry down in reviews as often as we can. This is a sad, weak, and cowardly position for people to take, I think: the assumption of virtue by yourself, and the corresponding assignment of guilt to other people who either don't agree with you politically or are in some sort of literary rivalry with you, and making the political issue either the main issue of a discussion of a writer's literary efforts or deliberately leaving it unsaid but still the main basis for attacking your literary work. This is an unfortunate practice, but it went on all the time, and to a certain extent still exists.

DLB: You are known in the trade as a generous interview and a good interview; that is to say, you make yourself available for interviews and you obviously try hard to give the interviewer something that he can use. You have long since passed the point in your career where you need free publicity, but yet you go on giving a great deal of your time to anybody who shows up on your doorstep with a tape recorder. What purpose do you see your interviews as serving? Are you contributing to the eventual biography of James Dickey, piece by piece, in these interviews?

DICKEY: No, I don't think so. I don't have that in mind, at least not consciously. I don't really want a biography. I did some sort of cursory research on literary people's biographies and found three major literary figures who refused to authorize biographies. One of them was Matthew Arnold, another was T. S. Eliot, and a third was W. H. Auden. I don't forbid it—and I suppose eventually that there might be some possibility that there will be a biography written—but I don't encourage it either. I don't have any official designatee, such as Frost had Lawrance Thompson. I'd just rather let the work speak for itself; but one's talk and opinions are part of one's work as well, it seems to me. . . . I think that the spontaneity of an interview can lead to valuable insights some of the time—with certain interviewers and certain interviewees—and that these might not ever get around to being made available in any other way. I think that a person should get everything that he has or wants to say in front of anybody who wants to listen to it. This assumption inevitably makes for some repetitiousness, because the interviewers tend to ask the same questions and the interviewee has the same answers, or roughly the same answers, to the same questions. But after a person does that a certain amount, he starts looking for different answers to the same questions, and a new aspect of the original subject comes into play, all from the need to avoid one's reliable stock answer. The interview is a variation on the Socratic Method, I guess: a question-and-answer attempt to get at the truth of something. Although maybe truth is not what you want to get either, but something that could be useful to the imagination in some way—something revealing.

DLB: Except for the four poems included in *Night Hurdling*, it is all prose. You are obviously a born poet. Nonetheless, you have written and published more than your share of prose. Do you consciously approach a prose job in some way different from the way you feel when you're writing poetry?

DICKEY: Well, yes, there's inevitably going to have to be some differences, although there are also some very great similarities. The kind of poetry I write takes off from a rhythmical premise. A good deal of the time I start with some kind of rhythm that doesn't have anything to it *but* rhythm. It has a *sound* or a sequence of sounds. And then the subject—I have initially only the vaguest notion of the subject—will sort of come out of that. As nearly as I can tell, this practice has no parallel in the way I write prose. When I write a review of, say, a book of poems or someone's work, like the piece I did on Robert Penn Warren,[56] I start out with an opinion about the work, and I try to articulate that. It's an opinion which I more or less already have as soon as I've finished reading the work in question. I have a definite position on it, and the prose work is an attempt to articulate that as best I can, when possible quoting from the work itself to back up the points that I'm making. But that's quite a different process from working out of a rhythm into a sequence of images and actions, as I do when I'm working on a poem. The form is different, the approach is different, and the possibilities are different, and above all the kind of concentration that I try to get into poetry would be detrimental to a prose piece, because the essential thing in the latter is discourse. It's not revelation by a juxtaposition of words in a rhythmical pattern, as poetry is; it's the development of an idea and a presentation of a sequence of thought which is directed to some subject which is previously present instead of discovered in the process of the writing.

DLB: You recently had a birthday (2 February 1983) which the University of South Carolina marked with an extended James Dickey festival, which brought distinguished critics and scholars to talk about your achievement. What's left?

DICKEY: Everything is left. At the age of sixty I feel that, through a great many vicissitudes and false starts and trials and errors and much frustration, I have finally arrived at the beginning. Now it takes me both longer to write something and not as long: I realize that's a paradox! I know now, though, after a good many years, when I'm into a subject that has potential for me, or not. I know now when I've got into a subject and a treatment of it that's right for me; in other words, that I haven't just got a piece of it, but have got something like the whole thing in view or just under the surface somewhere. I can tell when it's there. I spent so many years looking for it when it really wasn't there, or trying to will it into existence. It's the difference between making something—getting something—and discovering something. It's very largely a matter of intuition, but it's an intuition that develops with a great deal of trial and error, and I feel that when I write now, I have a better mode or means of choosing things than I used to have.

DLB: You don't agree, then, with James Gould Cozzens's complaint that the hell of writing is that the better you get at it the harder it becomes?

DICKEY: Yes, I do. But you have more confidence because you know you're not wasting—at least I feel like I'm not wasting—your substance in trying to evolve something that was never capable of evolving to begin with. I spent most of my early years trying to make poems work which never had the possibility of working, the potential for coming to something. And

I've now learned to say of a subject, I might get a piece of this, but I can't get fully enough into it to do it the kind of justice that I particularly and uniquely can do to a subject, so I won't try it. *This* one, though, I *feel* it; the thing is there for me; it's potential. Not for me in the sense of being potential for any poet (either a good poet or a bad poet or a mediocre), but for *me,* being the poet that I am, for better or worse: this is *mine;* it will become part of the kind of thing that I do best.

DLB: Are there compensations for a poet, for a writer, in getting older?

DICKEY: I think so. If I could maintain a reasonable level of health, I think this is the best age that I've ever had. It's a far better youth than the one I had! If I can remain ambulatory and perceptive for a reasonable time, I'll try to write the things I think are possible for me to write; I'll give it the best shot I can anyway.

DLB: Most people who keep track of what's going on in the literary world are aware that you're nearing completion of a big novel with the working title of *Alnilam.* This is your first novel in fourteen or fifteen years. Why have you returned to the novel form?

DICKEY: It's something I want to do. I'm not one of those people who are prolific about novelistic ideas. I remember reading some letters of Hart Crane when he was just a boy, eighteen, nineteen years old. He wanted to write a novel, and he tried for a while, but in the end he went back to writing poems. He said, "I just finally have to admit that I don't have the kind of mind that thinks up plots." I could see what he meant immediately, because I don't either; but to a limited extent, I guess, I suppose I do, after all. One or two or three ideas for a novel will come to a writer like myself in a lifetime. *Deliverance* was one of them, and this is another one, although it's a much more complicated book than *Deliverance* is. It's about the early days of the air force—back in the days when it was part of the U.S. Air Corps, the Army Air Corps—and that *is* a long ways back. It takes place in the early part of 1943. My difficulty with it is to know when to research the material and when just to remember or imagine. I went through the first draft of the book deliberately not looking up any aircraft specifications or any tables of organization for training-command bases, or any of those things. I just went with what I either remembered or figured out or imagined, and then went back and checked. I don't want the book to be overwhelmed with technical jargon and data about the air force doings. That could be boring. A book I read in connection with this, or reread, was John Hersey's novel *The War Lover,* which is about B-17's. I'm a great admirer of that book, but it has a defect that I don't want mine to have; this is the constant bombardment of the reader with the technical paraphernalia of the aircraft itself. That's interesting in a way, and John Hersey is a demon researcher; he knows what he's talking about, but all the information gets in the way of the narrative to a degree that I don't think is working for it. On the other hand, with the premier writer about the air, I suppose of all time, Antoine de Saint-Exupéry, you don't have even the slightest idea of what kind of airplane he's flying, most of the time. He says nothing about throttle settings; he says nothing about fuel consumption; he says nothing about any of the instrument flying at all. What he tries to give you is the sensation of flight itself, which is much more what I want to try for. The Bible says, "The letter killeth, but the spirit giveth life." I'm trying to get close to the spirit. What I really want to try to do in *Alnilam* is to write about the air itself. That's the element that we're in, you know, and it's maybe more dramatic to write about than water and the mysterious creatures that live in it, even Moby-Dick. Air is more fundamental than water. When we fly in it, we enter a new kind of existence. I don't want to talk away the book now, but it's about flight and about the human body taking off the ground into the element of the air, and into its particular mystiques. Saint-Exupéry is a good writer, maybe a great writer in some ways, but he does not have—even *he* does not have—the air thing really right. John Hersey's *The War Lover*—these, of course, are not the only two examples—has got part of it right, especially the air-war hysteria of technique and procedure, but there's still an area that has not been touched on yet, and that's what I want to try to get into. It's not done yet, but I'm closer than I was.

DLB: If you were promised that you would have time to write three more books—and only three—what would those three books be?

DICKEY: I'd like to finish *Alnilam,* and if I had a lot of time and if *Alnilam* comes off, not in a way that pleases the public or the critics or anything like that, but in a way that pleases me, then I would like to write another novel, a sequel to it, called *Crux.* The star Alnilam is in the middle of the northern winter constellation, Orion; and Crux, the Southern Cross, is south of the equator. I would like to write about the night air war in the Pacific. *Alnilam* first, definitely, and then *Crux,* maybe. And definitely as much poetry as I can write, according to my standards. And I think the book of poems I would really like to write would also be about the air: would be a suite of poems about bodily flight in things like engineless vehicles like soaring-craft or sailplanes or hang gliders; anything in which the human body on its own is in the element of air. I plan to call the poems "Peace-Raids," or at least right now I do.

21
AN INTERVIEW WITH JAMES DICKEY

WILLIAM W. STARR / 1983

STARR: Jim, you have a unique position from which to talk about the relationship of business and the arts. You started off as a businessman with several advertising agencies. What sort of experiences did you have in the business world?

DICKEY: I was in that business for just about six years. I started out in New York. I broke into advertising with Mc-Cann-Erickson just after they had been given the prestigious Coca-Cola account, which had been in the hands of an agency in St. Louis for thirty or thirty-five years, I believe. McCann had skyrocketed up the ladder of advertising on the strength of a "wildcatter" named Marion Harper, who was head of Mc-Cann and who had really created a huge conglomerate company, an octopus sort of thing. I came to them in the first flush of Marion Harper's meteoric rise in the advertising business.

They were hiring a lot of people at that time. They were so big, in fact, that they had gotten a new name, Interpublic. I quickly found out McCann was not an agency writers and art directors like to work for. Writers like to be individuals and feel they are creating, but McCann was research oriented. They didn't care who their writers were; all they wanted were people to handle computer-fed information. All the young and promising writers I knew were leaving for places they felt they could preserve a shred of individuality. But I was just breaking in and I stayed.

I wrote for a time for the *Eddie Fisher Show,* which was called "Coke Time." As I recall, it had about the lowest Nielsen

---

Reprinted with permission from *South Carolina Business,* Volume 3 (Columbia: South Carolina Chamber of Commerce, 1983), 39–41.

ratings ever recorded. We were on real prime time, about 6:00 or 6:15 P.M., I believe. We had a fifteen-minute format. Eddie Fisher was married to Debbie Reynolds at that time and was a nice fellow to work with. The show of course died, and it turned out to be the last network show Coke ever sponsored on television. They've done specials since, but maybe that experience convinced them to stay away from most shows.

Eventually, the radio and television operation was shifted to Atlanta and I went there. We had an operation which required us to individualize commercial spots for the 2,600 or so Coke bottlers around the country. Coke was in a real pricing war with Pepsi and had given autonomy in pricing to all of its local bottlers across the country. So we were turning out spots for little towns in Louisiana and Minnesota and Arkansas and California frantically. Our secretaries had a terrific workload; I don't know why they didn't commit suicide. I remember I put up a sign in the office which had Darwin's advice to the animals on it. I told our staff they'd better read it carefully. The sign said, "Adapt or Die."

I did that for three and a half years somehow. I had been promoted to senior writer, then radio-TV director, and I finally had enough experience to do what all agency people do—change jobs. I went to a smaller agency in Atlanta. We had some good accounts, Lay's Potato Chips was one of them, and I also had Armour Fertilizer and some banks. There was a little more individuality there, but basically there wasn't much creativity.

So I went to another Atlanta agency, one that had the Delta Air Lines account. I was riding high, I guess. I was named "Atlanta's Young Man on the Go" and some other things were going on. But I had just had a book of poems published, poems I had written at night and on weekends. I was thirty-eight and decided it was time to gamble, time to risk things. Fortunately, I got a Guggenheim Fellowship, so I decided to sell my company stock and take my chances at becoming a writer.

STARR: That gamble certainly paid off. You won some of the highest literary awards this nation confers. You could have taken your career to any of the logical places, New York or California, or to one of the major universities. Instead, you chose to come to South Carolina. Why?

DICKEY: For one thing, I was a Southerner. I was born in and raised around Atlanta, and my parents were very old and I wanted to be near them. That was one thing. The second was my best friend from graduate school was on the English Department faculty at the University of South Carolina, Calhoun Winton. He did a hard sell job on me. My family really preferred that we go back to California where we had been for a while, but I liked what I saw in Columbia and South Carolina.

STARR: Could you be more specific? I'm thinking that you could easily have been part of a large and well-known writing community elsewhere.

DICKEY: I've always been kind of a loner. You have to be if you write poetry—or if you work in the advertising business. You have to be self-sufficient. And it seemed to me that here I would have my own time.

I wrote an article for *Esquire* magazine in 1981 called "The Starry Place Between the Antlers"[57] in which I tried to describe why I came to South Carolina. Having been born and raised in the Deep South, I started feeling that magnetic pull that draws from pine roots and kudzu vines for those who were born among them. And Columbia had the perfect location, halfway between the mountains and the coast. The mountains are the deer, the mountain-deer, the coastal islands the sea-deer, and Columbia "the starry place between the antlers." South Carolina had everything I wanted. I liked the people, I liked the land, I liked the climate, I liked the connections that made it possible to get away when I had to. You know, I turned down a Switzer Chair in New York a few years ago at triple my salary. I don't want to uproot. I've got pretty much what I want right here right now.

STARR: From your experiences on both sides, do you find that business and the arts are necessarily incompatible?

DICKEY: No, not at all. Certainly not. I think a lot of business people are very much interested in the arts. That's a fact. Maybe a lot of them feel they might have gone in that career direction themselves if they had had the talent or enough of it. As in my case, though, you take a terrible chance when you give up everything for something untried. That's one of the good things about business—you learn to do things with dispatch and accuracy.

STARR: Are there certain things you learned when you were a part of the business world that you still carry with you today?

DICKEY: You'd better believe it. There are great lessons to be learned about human nature and, well, call it survival. I learned a lot in business. One is to move on things and get them finished. I've seen too many of those manila job jackets with those blue job descriptions on them mount up in account executives' offices. And if that happens often, that account executive is gone and the work is given to someone else to finish. You have to learn to be hard on people, sometimes, even when it hurts you. When work has to be done, it has to be done. The engine has to move, otherwise it will run over you like a juggernaut.

And there's one more thing about business. I learned there that you have to know about making deals with people, and not agree with the first thing offered to you. That's good advice for anybody. Editors and publishers are business people and they look out for their companies. The writer has got to learn to look out for himself. I never would have known about getting an agent if I hadn't seen first-hand how business people handled their own financial affairs. There's professionalism involved here. That's what you expect from the business community, and that's something everyone ought to learn and remember.

STARR: I rather imagine many people may be surprised to hear you talk this way about business. There's a suspicion that artists don't really care much for the business community; in fact, they rather despise it.

DICKEY: I love business people in some ways. If I could have shut out all of my own literary interests and concentrated on business, if my conscience hadn't been dogging me so much about neglecting my own writing, I would have been content to remain in the business community. The business world offers high drama, continuing drama, night and day. Coca-Cola and Pepsi are in a war that will probably go right on till the end of time. It's exciting, it really is.

The only quote I know from Calvin Coolidge other than his "I do not choose to run" is "The business of America is business." And it is. Anybody who hasn't worked in business doesn't really know his country or what makes it run or what its values are, its stresses, its frustrations, its rewards. Those people are outside the mainstream of what this country is all about. I'm happy I was in business for six years. I have no apologies for that.

STARR: Looking to the future, are you optimistic about the relationship of the business community and the arts? Do you see them closer, and is that necessarily a good thing?

DICKEY: I'm of a divided mind on this. One of the things I shy away from and react instinctively against is any sort of officialdom in the arts, especially for the American artist. American artists have always been "freebooters" and "outlaws," people who were "against," like Herman Melville. The idea of the community or foundations or business subsidizing the artist, sort of embracing the artist to death, making things very easy, too easy, goes against the grain. But, on the other hand, without getting two fellowships, I probably wouldn't have been able to become a full-time writer. It was a Rockefeller Fellowship that got me out of freshman teaching at Rice, and the Guggenheim got me out of advertising. I really shouldn't run down that kind of support from private groups or businesses.

STARR: But you feel strongly about business subsidizing the artist as a general principle?

DICKEY: As a general principle, the artist shouldn't be beholden to business or to a supporter in any way. There should not be situations in which he feels or business people feel that ought to be the case. The artist has got to be free to bite the hand that feeds him if necessary. And business has got to understand and accept that. I do feel that over-receptivity on the part of the business community to the artist deprives him of some of his freedom, some of his power. The artist requires absolute autonomy. It's a complex issue, and it requires understanding on everyone's part.

STARR: Even with the mixed emotions you talk about on this subject, do you think it's desirable to have this relationship or partnership continue and flourish?

DICKEY: Yes, and I do see a closer relationship between business and the arts in South Carolina, closer than we've ever had before. And I hope that's the way it turns out. After all, businessmen and the artists are one and the same; they are both human beings. The artist is interested in interpreting human experience, and business people—especially the more sensitive, intelligent ones—want to see what the "seismographic artist," the one with "sensitive needles" to register changes, has to say about life and experience.

I believe there are many people in the business community in South Carolina who have either a yearning toward the creative act themselves or a deep appreciation for it. They have found there can be a satisfying symbiotic relationship between business and the arts, one which is profitable and enriching to both the business community and the artist. I hope to see more of that in South Carolina.

22

RECOVERING THE COSMOS: POET JAMES DICKEY AT 60

LESLIE BATES / 1983

"I know what I'm doing, mainly, I think."

James Dickey rises slowly from the sprawl of papers and books surrounding the chair he calls the Cockpit.

"It's the rightest it's ever been. I think I'm going to look back on the time I spent in this room, in this chair, as the happiest time in my life." His voice grows soft. "It's quite possible. I'm doing what I want to do. It takes a long time to get to that point."

. . .

Inside the long, low house in Columbia, South Carolina, where James Dickey lives with his wife and baby girl, among animals skins, Indian masks, leather chairs, guitars, and archery bows, are the instruments which help Dickey know what he is doing. These are his sextants, delicate devices which navigators use to measure the angle between the sun and the horizon. Every day near noon Dickey "shoots the sun," measuring with precision to learn the exact latitude and longtitude *of where he is.*

Also in the house, amid the thirty thousand titles that make up Dickey's library, is a "time cube," a radiolike box which announces the time each minute. Dickey uses it to synchronize the two digital watches he wears—one on each wrist, one of which has a calculator *on* it—since the exact time he makes the sighting is one of the key variables in the calculation of determining place.

A cheap certificate over the door of his workroom declares Dickey to be an official celestial navigator. He's more proud of that document than of all the awards and honorary degrees on the

---

Reprinted with permission from *City Paper* [Washington, D.C.] 3 (28 October–3 November 1983), 1, 7, 9.

opposite wall. He received the certificate after completing a correspondence course from an outfit in California. It took him years.

Dickey knows how to navigate by the stars although he was never a navigator on an airplane or boat. His interest in determining place by the planets has to do with learning not where he is going, but where he is—*that* he is.

"I want God to assure me that I really am here, at thirty-four degrees, no minutes, and two-tenths north, and at eighty degrees, fifty-eight minutes, and five-tenths west," he has said. But he doesn't take the daily sightings only for that reassurance, either, but because of something D. H. Lawrence said about one's relation to what's *out there*:

"[Lawrence] says . . . that our main trouble," Dickey notes, "is that we have lost the universe, that we have lost the cosmos, we have lost the sense of correlation with the cosmos. But he says that it is always, at any given moment, recoverable. . . . He said, start with the sun and everything will slowly, slowly happen."

Dickey uses the sextant daily to recover that correlation. He says that the universe will disclose your position to you if you have the right key to it. And he says the first time he saw sextants in the South Pacific during World War II, he found them "certain proof of the relationship of human bodies to celestial: the compplex star-angled keys to everything."

The obsession with celestial bodies shows up in much of Dickey's work, most notably in the title of his seven-hundred-plus page novel-in-progress, *Alnilam*. "It's the name of the central star—the middle star—in the belt of the constellation Orion," Dickey explains, spelling the name of the hunter configuration for emphasis. "It means 'string of pearls.' . . . It's not a first order of navigational star, but tables on it are kept. The main thing is that it's in the middle." The fact that a star has a particular, identifiable location which relates it to other stars is important to Dickey. He applies the same principle to his writing of poetry in that words, like stars, have a place that is "rightest" within the poem. He even describes the writing of a poem in galaxial terms, using a line from Kenneth Rexroth: "It's like looking into an inkspot and suddenly finding yourself in the Milky Way." And he has referred to the pageful of words in his typewriter as a blueprint for the poem at hand. Since constellations and star tables are no more than blueprints of the sky, you might not be far off to say that in the same way Dickey studies the order of the sky, he searches for the correct configuration of words in a poem, draft after draft, until he finds it.

Because the writing is such hard work, Dickey wishes he could streamline his painstaking process of doing anywhere from twenty to one-hundred-fifty drafts of each poem. "I'd like to get into some sort of phase where I would write a whole lot of poems real fast and not revise very much," he says, "because if there's any defect in the bulk of work of mine, it's that it might seem overlabored. But I don't think so. I think there's a way you can labor to get spontaneity into it, rather than have the spontaneity evaporate because of the labor. I think Gerard Manley Hopkins did something like that. His is very worked-over and so on, but very rapid, and it seems almost breathlessly spontaneous."

The labor of fulfilling the blueprint of the poem, of getting it right, is, Dickey says, "a state of drudgery, which is very hard and, among other things, is very hard physical labor—long and time-consuming—and you have to find some way to circumvent the almost inevitable deadening process that goes on when you work that way. But if you love it enough, you'll do it."

How does Dickey circumvent the deadening process?

"I do it by having the house sort of booby-trapped with typewriters, with different things in different typewriters, and when I get tired of one I go do something else. I play guitar or fool around, or I take a walk and I'll come back and pass by a typewriter and whatever's in it, if it interests me, I sit down and work on it for a while until I get tired of it, and then I may go work on something else. One of the things I don't like about the writer's life is sitting in one place—the sedentary aspect of it—which is necessary to some extent, but I try to jump up and run around as much as I can."

The jumping up and running around includes comic relief. One day Dickey exited his workroom—the room he calls the Cave of Making—and returned in a magnificent garish purple suede vintage 1960s coat with fringe. "My wife won't let me wear it out of the house," he roared, "but I'm wearing it today!"

Another time he ducked into the hallway, out of sight, and exploded a paper bag. "I'm SHOT!" he cried, staggering to the carpet. Other times he did his uncanny Marlon Brando imitation, or shot blow-darts into the furniture.

Dickey likes action, which is why the passions for archery, hunting, lots of sports (he owns a javelin) and for collecting blowguns, knives, and other primitive weapons. He has two Soloflex weight-lifting machines and recently took up sailing, in a Sunfish he christened "the Omu," on the lake behind his house. He played football in college and buys season tickets to games at the University of South Carolina, where he teaches.

The activities Dickey throws himself into outside of his writing at one time evidently included those which made, or could have made, front-page headlines, i.e., the time, still legend in Columbia, South Carolina, when he wrapped a Corvette—"It was a Jaguar," he corrects you—around a telephone pole. But why wouldn't the excesses inside the poems spill over into real life? "I like to turn from writing, and getting such close focus on poetry and on any kind of writing," Dickey says. "You can't really see what it is you're doing, you just see little pieces of it, and bits of it. I like to turn to something with an entirely different set of problems, every now and then, like learning a few new chords on the guitar, or some new piece or something. It's something *else*, something that's not verbal."

Besides seeking action to offset the sedentary work, Dickey maintains his enthusiasm for writing by creating action within the poems. "Experiment is the lifeblood of what I do. That's necessary for me to do. Whether what I try to do will turn out or pan out to be good or bad or whatever it turns out to be is just a gamble we all have to take."

The gambling attitude is part of a desire Dickey has voiced before to strike out in a new direction, to use the English language in a new way. "I'm still working out an approach to that," he says. "I haven't done very much with it, yet. But *Puella* was a radical departure from the previous work, whether people like it or not. . . . You have to be prepared to make mistakes, partial mistakes, or total mistakes. You can't lose your sense of daring to try to do something else. *Puella* was essentially a linguistic experiment which I like very much; some people liked it a lot, some people were indifferent to it, and so on. But I liked it, and I learned a lot from doing it, and I would do it again, only more so."

. . .

Dickey works at keeping enthusiastic not only about the writing of poetry but about the teaching of it. He spends two mornings a week prowling through books and writing lectures in preparation for the two afternoon courses he teaches at the University of South Carolina. "I hate for any aspect of the canned to get into it," he explains. . . . "It's like the medical profession, or any literary situation, or anything having to do with any given writer: there's a lot of new material and new books always being written about them, and you have to keep up—you don't have to, but it's best to keep up—with the new literature on somebody like Dryden or Hopkins or Shakespeare, or anybody else you might be lecturing on."

Yet for someone so concerned with time and its use, Dickey doesn't begrudge the hours spent on teaching. "A lot of American poets and other writers complain about teaching or having to teach," Dickey says, "but I'm one of the ones who *should* be a teacher. Because I *do* enjoy it so much. I like the interplay of the minds, you know? I like to see what the students say, and how they respond to different poets and so on. I think it's very good. There sometimes will come along a student that you don't have the secret for. You can't be all things to all people or all students, but most of them, they're very eager to know whatever it is you want to tell them. And if you like the telling of it, and you like the subject itself, it's a very fortunate way to earn a living, as a writer. I don't feel that they consume my time unnecessarily, in any way. And if I want to curtail my activity with them, I do, and tell them, put limits on it. And try to work within those."

In the Cave of Making where Dickey prepares material for class and does most of his writing, one bookcase holds copies of most of his work, including . . . *The Strength of Fields* (1979), the title poem of which he read at President Jimmy Carter's inaugural ceremonies. Dickey's visit to the Carter White House "was limited to just that occasion, and just a few others when I visited up there, and took part in some occasions of state," he says now. "They had a big sort of rendezvous of American poets there, during the Carter Administration, and I went to that. And I was there on a few other occasions. The main one I was connected with was that inaugural situation. And I like Jimmy Carter very much. I don't know very much about politics or about people's qualifications for those huge jobs, but I will tell you that if all the American presidents had the personal integrity and human values that Jimmy Carter did, we'd be in very much of a better fix."

. . .

Also in the Cave of Making are shelves jammed with paperbound books Dickey brought back from Europe after a Guggenheim stint in 1955. Nestled among these is an old, but serviceable, Harmon-Kardon stereo and a reel-to-reel on which Dickey occasionally plays tapes of the original versions of "Duellin' Banjos" which inspired the familiar theme from the movie *Deliverance*. Below these are a huge collection of records by Delta blues guitarists and ancient editions of the *Sewanee Review,* where Dickey first published in his mid-thirties. In careful piles near Dickey's corduroy chair—the Cockpit—are manuscripts of the forthcoming book about Appalachia, *The Wilderness of Heaven,*[58] and copies of *Night Hurdling,* an assortment of essays and interviews published in October. Stacks of review copies of hardbacks clutter the floor. One entire cabinet is given over to storing the mailers these copies come in, and more mailers are stashed in Dickey's garage. He hates to throw anything away, and saves not only empty boxes but also ice: as pilots in the wartime South Pacific, he and his buddies never had ice, so these days, if he should drop a cube on the floor, he retrieves, washes, and uses it. The fascination with ice goes further; in a recent article[59] Dickey suggested that aspiring poets begin their first attempt by examining the properties of a piece of ice: "What more mysterious and beautiful *interior* of something has there ever been?"

This sense of the value of things shows Dickey's awareness of how easily things, and people, can be lost. "Everything is very fragile," he says, "very fragile. And people should be aware of that. If they don't lose their sense of daring and their sense of the fragility at the same time, then they have a good balance, I think."

At least one critic, Benjamin DeMott,[60] has picked up on the sense of daring Dickey's talking about which permeates his work. DeMott, Dickey says, "gave me a whole school, called James Dickey and the More Life School. I wonder what Benjamin himself wants: *less* life? As he's a very good critic, I'm glad he put a label that seems that affirmative on me and on my work. I think that's fine. I"ll go with it."

Daily he works on the poems, the novel, and various other writing projects in the Cave of Making. But every day he also takes the sextant, reaffirms his place on the planet, although he knows by now exactly how the calculations should come out, and reassures himself that not only is he here, but that there is indeed a Plan up there, an order, and that he is related to it.

"I get as depressed as other people do," he says, "but I think of myself as generally affirmative. I suppose that's the result of my upbringing, and the fact that my generation was a war generation, and the survivors still feel sort of like convalescents, you know? We're glad to see the sun come up in the morning."

Start with the sun and everything will slowly, slowly happen.

23

INTERVIEW WITH JAMES DICKEY

BETTYE GIVENS / 1984

GIVENS: In the first part of *Deliverance,* leaving the civilized world, there is almost a similarity to Conrad's "Heart of Darkness," where Conrad gradually leaves civilization behind.

DICKEY: That's right. It's an interesting theme: what happens to civilized men when they get into an extreme situation, what happens to values and goals? That's why Drew feels he has to hold on to the Constitution. There's nothing else.

My father was a lawyer. We used to talk a lot about this question when I was a small boy. My father was a rather unsuccessful lawyer, a born loser, a gentle, sweet person. He revered the profession of the law—not the letter of the law and the legalistic paraphernalia of the law, but the ethical qualities of the law. My father did not believe that laws were really lawful—the kinds of laws that exist. He believed that justice was very seldom done. He had his own ideas about what constituted justice. A lot of that debate business in *Deliverance* was based on conversations I had with him when I was a little child.

My father was a person who liked rhetoric very much. He had a series of twenty volumes around the house called *Classics of the Bar*; he would read the summation speeches of famous lawyers over and over again to me. I remember there was one speech he read to me hundreds of times, which was by "the great agnostic," a village lawyer, Robert Ingersoll. He was a predecessor and mentor of Clarence Darrow, who was classified as one of the most famous trial lawyers. Ingersoll was trying a case in California with a judge and jury and an audience of gold miners about a murder on somebody else's claim. I forget the exact circumstances of the trial. My father

---

Reprinted with permission from *Texas Review,* 5 (Spring/Summer 1984), 73–85.

read Ingersoll so much that he had memorized his speech. I remember him saying to the gold miners, "I'm very happy to be here today among you hearty souls who earn your precarious living by wresting the precious metal from the clutches of the miserly rock." My father would lean over to me; and I wanted to express myself like that.

GIVENS: Do you write poetry in your short stories?

DICKEY: I have never written a single short story. It is curious because I like the form a whole lot. It is much closer to poetry than to the novel, and I admire some short story writers more than I admire novelists who are supposed to be towering world figures. I like Chekhov because of his mastery of the short story better than I like Dostoyevski, who is a great novelist. A personal opinion.

GIVENS: Do you enjoy writing poetry more than writing the novel?

DICKEY: I put more store into writing poetry than I do into writing a novel. Novels have nothing like the resonance that poetry has. Poetry's got a great sort of shimmer to it. It can change meaning a great many ways. Nobody really knows what Wordsworth's immortality prose is all about. It's all things to all men. In prose fiction you have to go to the writers who write with a greater sense of being, like parables, some people like Kafka. Then you get this kind of multiple meaning or resonance of intent. This you can get in poetry, some of which is relatively mediocre. But the great poetry has such a great deal of that shimmer that you can live with it forever without exhausting it.

GIVENS: Your poems and your novel seem as though they were written in the same voice.

DICKEY: You couldn't say anything that would please me more. I like to think that the same sensibility gets into anything I write, even if it's a laundry ticket. What I want to do is to make life more vivid and splendid and mysterious. American life is often routine. Dominated. For most people a lot of the possibilities in life never do get energized. If I can say something about that condition to whatever readers I might have, that's sufficient reward for me.

GIVENS: Do you use your art background?

DICKEY: I love images of all kinds. I wish I could paint. I have less than zero talent as a painter. I do admire that quality in anybody who can do it. I try to supervise the covers of my books. I was an art director rather like Ed in *Deliverance*. I had that same attitude that he has about it. He feels that he's got a good sense of design, of balance and proportion, and that's all. No real creativity, but he admires and likes it in others and can recognize it in others. At the end of *Deliverance* he goes back to making art works, in a modest way, of his own. A kind of plastic art. Even his connection with that has been enhanced by the river experience. This doesn't make him a great artist. He makes a few things for his friends.

GIVENS: In your war poems, how much is based on fact?

DICKEY: I was with the 418th Night Fighter Squadron the last year and a half of the war in the Pacific, and we had some pilots and air crews that were taken prisoner and beheaded. One of those people was a boy I wrote about whose name was Donald Armstrong. He was a terrific fellow, and he was my best friend over there. It was a dreadful business. He went down in an island south of the island we were holding in the Philippines called Mindoro. He was making a raid on the islands south of us called Panay. Some labor Filipino troops were building an airstrip on the Japanese jurisdiction. He misjudged the distance. He hit the ground and tore up the airplane. He and an observer were taken out and kept prisoner for a night and beheaded the next morning. The Filipino guerrilla forces on the island radioed almost a blow-by-blow description of the whole proceedings. We knew almost exactly what happened. In the poem I lied about his doing handstands beside his grave. That's not true. You can't bear the thought of what they must have really gone through.

GIVENS: What do you mean by a poet being "typified" man?

DICKEY: It means he has regular human qualities to a stronger degree. I don't want to use the word "violence," but to a degree things hit him further and deeper than they do other people. He feels more, he lives more, I think. Any poet who deserves the name poet has some of that. Sometimes there is an exaggerated degree of it. Some of the best poets have curious ways about them. And obsessions. Theodore Roethke was a good friend of mine. The last year of his life I saw a good deal of him. He was obsessed with the idea that he wanted to become a business tycoon, or a gangster overlord. I think he was a very strange person. Actually, he was a tennis coach at Penn State, and evidently a pretty good one. That was before I knew him, though.

Delmore Schwartz wanted to be a movie producer like Irving Thalberg. Randall Jarrell wanted to be a sports car racer. He spent all the pittance he got from teaching and writing poetry on keeping up with sports cars. He liked to drive around in them. As I say, eccentric; some of the eccentricity was self-destructive.... Poetry is a hazardous occupation, very hazardous. There may be bad things in there inside you that maybe you can't handle.

GIVENS: Sometimes you hear a student say that the poet is writing about things that the student doesn't want to hear.

DICKEY: Poetry contains anything and everything that is possible for the human mind to conceive. It's as large and wide and deep as the universe, and the poet can see it his way rather than the way of the creator of the universe. This is what makes poetry important and unique. Don't let students fret about what is proper and improper.... This is one of the concepts that was destructive to John Keats. He conceived—because he was a Cockney and relatively low on the economic scale of things—but he conceived the poet as some kind of exalted creature who could only deal with exalted subjects. Milton, too, had a too lofty position. Then Whitman comes along and says in effect there's as much beauty in an ordinary action such as someone sawing a plank in two as there is in the wrath of Achilles, and that's true. If there is any great virtue to what the pioneers of the so-called modern phase of poetry have done, it's in destroying the barrier to, and false distinction of, what is a legitimate subject for poetry and what isn't....

GIVENS: Do you open all doors that are available to you?

DICKEY: I have a strong liking for the unexpected in human paths. I am a great worshiper of the God of Chance. It can do bad things to you, but it can also do wonderful things. I remember when I was driving through Edinburgh, Scotland, there was a girl with red hair that crossed in front of my car and turned and just looked at me. I'll probably never see her again, but that was the most electric, marvelous experience that I ever had in my life. Years later I read in a poem of the French poet Apollinaire, "It's that chance moment; she was so beautiful she made me afraid." You should have those chance things. Some of them don't have to do with encounters between people; it doesn't have to be based on that at all. When they come, you should realize what they are. They are what e. e. cummings would call natural miracles. I very much believe in them.

GIVENS: Many of your poems are about secrets, about things that people don't know that they know.

DICKEY: I'm naturally drawn to the mythical or the parable interpretation of things—the mysterious. This is why the writer Jorge Luis Borges appeals to me so much; he deals in that kind of apprehension. There's one story of his called "The Hand Writes of the Writing of God," which is supposed to have happened some time after the Spanish invasion of the New World and the wrecking of the Aztec kingdom by Cortez and of the Inca empire by Pizarro. The story is told by the last priest of the old religion, which has been deposed by Spanish religion, Catholicism. They have put him into a dungeon; the priest is getting old and dying. In the other part of the dungeon is a jaguar, a wild predatory animal. One day when the jailers let his food down, a ray of light comes into the cell. For an instant each day he can see the jaguar on the other side of the bars from him. The priest believes that the spots on the hide of the jaguar constitute a secret writing that God has written into the living flesh of the animal; that, as the last priest of his religion, he will eventually understand it and be able to read it. Finally, the priest does figure it out. The writing has been put there by God, and he is the one to understand the words. If one could pronounce the fourteen syllables, then the priest could restore the empire and the religion and defeat the Spaniards and change the world. And he who has seen everything and has apprehended everything knows that he doesn't know anything. He knows that everything is nothing. It seems to me that is a parable of time and religion and philosophy and of what the poet is trying to do. The poet is like the guy in the cell and the world is like the

An Interview

jaguar with the secret writing. The poet is trying to interpret the world in his own way and unravel the secret of the inscription of God that is on everything. And it could be anywhere.

GIVENS: How much of your poetry is based on actual experience as opposed to fantasy?

DICKEY: It's hard to pin that down exactly because you would have to define what you mean by experience. Experience, to me, is not only what you have happen to you insofar as actual events. Experience is everything that has been in your imagination or has made an impression on you in any way. That includes actual occurrences, things that people have told you, books that you have read, fantasies that you've had, dreams, free flights of association. All of that is experience and you should draw on it. You should not be limited; the word "truth" has only limited application as far as any art form is concerned. . . .

Do you think there was ever a prince in Denmark named Hamlet who went around talking like Shakespeare's Hamlet? No, of course not. But which Hamlet do you remember? Nobody knows what the real one said, but you remember what Shakespeare's Hamlet said because Shakespeare used the character as a dramatic pivot for saying certain things he, the playwright, thought. That's the point; you must bend language to the situation, to your own conception of what it is you're trying to say. I don't think there's anything I've ever written that was literally true or happened the way I said it did in the poem. Because the poet is not trying to tell the truth; he is trying to *make* the truth. There *is* a difference.

For example: When you read a poem, you say something like this to yourself, "Well, this is good; this fellow is saying something that I myself have often felt." This is the eighteenth-century interpretation of what constitutes poetic value. Alexander Pope, in his "Essay on Criticism" that speaks of wit or imagination as having certain qualities, says, "True wit is nature to advantage dressed, / What oft was thought, but ne'er so well expressed." This is a good, workable, rule-of-thumb criterion for a good poem, but not for a great poem. When you read a great poem, you say, "My God, I never would have thought of anything like this to save my life, and yet I can see that this way of saying this is better than my idea." So there's a real change of your interior barometer or emotional and intellectual makeup by means of the poem that you would not have had available to you otherwise.

It's really an enlarging and deepening of the personality. This is the magic of art. It reminds me of Rilke, the German poet. He was a great museum-goer. Museums are never an interesting subject to me to read about. But Rilke is different. He's a person who should write about museums because he gets so much out of them, with his extraordinary sensibility and responsiveness. Rilke says, "Why are you made uneasy when you go into a portrait gallery, with portraits of people by the great masters, or even very good painters? Why are you made uneasy? Because you are being looked at simultaneously by some of the shrewdest, most penetrating eyes in the world." Is that not true?

There's one great sonnet of his called "On an Archaic Torso, Apollo," which is about an archeological museum containing the torso of a Greek statue with no head, no arms, no legs, just the trunk of it. The speaker walks around looking at all sides of the sculpture. He gets this uneasy feeling, and he says in effect that the work of art is judging you. It's pronounced a judgment on you. In the end this is a chilling metaphor: "There is no place here that does not see you. You must change your life." This thing is in the world; as ruined as it is, it's judged you and you're not good enough. You've got to get better! You know you have to live better, you have to feel more, understand more, live more, because this thing exists. It has witnessed you and found you wanting. You've got to get better. You aren't living right! Which is wonderful. It's just terrific, that kind of truth. That's a kind of truth, the creative kind, I think.

GIVENS: Do you have a particular method of working?

DICKEY: I have only one method—writing poetry, novels, screenplays, or anything else—and that's to work on something over a long period of time, a very, very long period of time. I like to try a subject out all different kinds of ways, experiment with it. I go on the principle of the gold miner refining low-grade ore. Two weeks ago I went over in North Georgia and actually mined some gold, in connection with a new film we're working on. I worked five hours and I got thirty-six cents worth, a very low-paid occupation in my home state. Anyway, I go on the principle of refining low-grade ore. You dig several tons of earth for a couple of specks of gold. The process is very laborious and backbreaking indeed. But if you stick with it you have the satisfaction that the gold that you do end up with, by means of this laborious process, is just so much of the right substance. It's just as much real gold as it would be if you picked up a nugget.

I've got to dig for what I get. But I enjoy the writing process very much. I like to work. You discover so much in the process of doing it. You can take an analogy from music, or two kinds of talent. Compare Mozart and Beethoven. Mozart was one of these sunny, facile types of genius, something like Auden is as a poet, who is just naturally good. Mozart could go out for a walk and write out movements for a quartet, or a harp and flute concerto, or even scenes for an opera. He would come back and take a piece of music-notation paper and write it down, just like he thought it up.

That would be wonderful. I don't have that. Beethoven, on the other hand, worked in a series of notebooks, and he would compare the last versions and the version that he was finally satisfied with, and they would bear absolutely no relation to what he started out with. There seems to be no connection. You have to go back through all the notebooks and see how he changed keys and modulated in different ways and tried out this and tried out that and then came up with something completely different.

It's sort of an alchemical process of metamorphosis, a constant and continual change and experimentation, that finally yields the final result. The methods of working, the Mozartian or the Beethovian, which are the two extreme kinds, are not all that important. What really matters, and the only thing that matters, is what ends up on the page. The end result is what matters—what you're left with after the process you've gone through has exhausted itself.

GIVENS: When you start out writing, does your work change, turn out to be something different?

DICKEY: I don't really commit myself emotionally to the poem unless it turns out to be not only different but a lot better than what I originally had in mind and it contains elements that I could not have envisioned at the beginning. That's the excitement of the search, of the quest—to use a favorite word of mine, the "hunt." It's the process of doing it that's so exciting to me. I'm always disappointed when I do get the finished product. It's like having a child grow up and you have to abandon him.

From Louis Untermeyer's house I talked on the phone with Arthur Miller about his plays. I had seen something of his I liked, and he said, "I'm glad you liked it, Jim. You know, you should have seen it before it was written."

You have great grandiose hopes for your work, but it turns into something else. In the end, if it's good at all, it's good in a different way from what you had conceived that it would be. Frankly, even the subject matter changes sometimes.

GIVENS: Do you have to go out and look for things to write about?

DICKEY: No. At least that is not one of my problems. I fill notebook after notebook with stuff I want to write about. Sometimes when I'm flying and go over some huge city like Chicago or New York and see all those houses, thousands of houses down there, I think, "In every one of them there is a story." That's the basic raw material of poetry, of the novel, the drama, of movies. It's the basic set of human existence, and there's plenty of that.

GIVENS: What do you think is the relationship between art and morality?

DICKEY: That's the question priests and philosophers have argued themselves into cold graves about. D. H. Lawrence said, "Art is moral; it's intrinsically moral." It's hard to figure out what he meant when he used a word with as much clang as that one has. I think ultimately art is moral in some way, but certainly not in any narrow sense. It's anti-moral in the narrow sense of promoting certain codes of behavior, but moral in the sense of changing somebody's inner life to make him experience more as a human being and give him some sort of personal value, insight, and interpretation. Art is moral in that sense.

GIVENS: What effect, if any, has fame had on your writing?

DICKEY: Not any on my writing. . . . This is one thing, one piece of advice I could give young writers. There's only one thing that will carry you through the disappointment of the writing life, and that's the sheer and simple love for the doing of it. You've just got to like it! You know what painters like, people like Michelangelo? Paint! That's what they like. It's that simple. Why do they like paint? Nobody knows but the painters. The point is that they just do! What do writers like? Especially poets? Words. It's that simple. . . .

Poetry is capable of any kind of attitude. It can be satirical, it can deal with sublimity, it can deal with triviality, anything that the mind can think of. If you write poetry, you must throw the net wide and get your sensibility into the world and let it operate and see what it gives you. It's a great way to live, but sometimes it may lead to excesses of one sort or another, but that's all right, too. We've got too many calm people.

24
RIVER CITY INTERVIEW WITH JAMES DICKEY

WILLIAM PAGE / 1984

PAGE: This question may be related to what you once said about Wallace Stevens. Do you think that originality has sometimes subordinated communication?

DICKEY: That's the center of a lot of thorns—that question. Originality can be construed in so many different ways. It's almost impossible to make a blanket statement on it. I think a search for some sort of linguistic originality sometimes yields remarkable results, as in the case of Gerard Manley Hopkins's example, and in the case of John Berryman also, to take a more modern instance. But it also can result in a sense of a great deal of strain in the writer—that is, the trying-for-it effect.

PAGE: Are you thinking of Berryman's *Bradstreet* or *The Dream Songs*?

DICKEY: All of it, from *Bradstreet* on. This is not what I'm after myself. I like mannerism when it works. But what I want most to try to get in my own work is some kind of deep, simple clarity—mysterious clarity.

PAGE: You said in *Sorties,* I believe, something about the novel you're finishing up being based somehow on your son Chris.

DICKEY: Yes, I think one of the main characters who never does appear is sort of based on him.

PAGE: The pilot who's killed?

DICKEY: Yes, or disappears. He's kind of a spellbinder, a charismatic kid who can get other people to do what he wants them

---

Reprinted with permission from *Memphis State Review,* 5 (Fall 1984), 30–39.

to do, and operates according to some mysterious mystique of his own that the other kids are trying to latch on to. It's really a study in the nature of power, the exertion of power by personal influence.

PAGE: Do you have a title for that novel?

DICKEY: It's called *Alnilam*.

PAGE: Do you agree that what you are doing in *Puella* seems to use a style that you predicted maybe a dozen or so years ago when you were working away from the sustained narrative?

DICKEY: Yes, I want to break the ironclad boundaries of the anecdote poem. It's easy to write poems. Everybody says, "My God, why doesn't Dickey write more poems like 'The Performance' or 'Walking on Water' or 'The Life Guard.'" Those are all right for their time. In fact, they will stand as however they are able to stand. But to repeat that sort of approach to poetry *ad infinitum* and perhaps *ad nauseum* is to reduce it to a formula. And that's the exact thing I won't do! I want to move out and do something that is different—quite different—from any of those poems that were conceived around an imaginative reconstruction of an incident. I want to get away from that to see what other thing might be possible.

PAGE: Often you have said that you thought a great deal about how you framed your poems and the first novel before you got down to the actual writing.

DICKEY: It's obvious that you have to start somewhere. And I start with a poem or with anything I write somewhere, but there is such a transformational process that goes on after you start that that's where the discoveries lie really. Discoveries sometimes lie at the beginning or at the first flash of intuition or inspiration or whatever you want to call it. But for me and my own particular practice the discoveries are made along the way so that as in vector analysis one variable will change the direction of the whole thing. You could say I started out with this idea which would have worked out all right, but during the attempt at working it out, this other thing occurred to me which is so much better. So I'll abandon the first and try to pursue this.

PAGE: Do you ever start out with an idea that you think perhaps is ineffective from the beginning and blunder along?

DICKEY: No, although I do plenty of blundering, I don't start out with anything that I don't think could come to some sort of profitable conclusion under some circumstances. In other words, as Mr. Auden said somewhere, "I don't like the idea of writing a poem because I am supposed to write some poem!"

PAGE: Do you still revise as extensively as you used to?

DICKEY: Indeed I do, yes, endlessly. Things change. Things can change with the flicker of an eyelash or with a comma or with a semicolon or with the way a line ends; it can change everything. Sometimes for the worse, sometimes for the better.

PAGE: Do you tend to write it out in longhand?

DICKEY: No, I like the look of type myself. I like to type. Typing is a much more physical activity, more sort of an athletic feat. I enjoy working with a typewriter.

PAGE: Which one of your poetic works thus far do you regard as most significant?

DICKEY: I have no idea. That I really can't say. It will have to be said *for* me. I tend to like the longer things. I think the best thing I've done is probably the "May Day Sermon." Again, that is just a matter of personal prejudice. Again, I wrote it all—the long ones and the short ones. It's like being asked which one of your children you prefer. You know which one you really do prefer, but it's not really a good idea to say so.

PAGE: You wouldn't care then to say anything about why you think the "May Day Sermon" is liked?

DICKEY: Because I like a poem that has length to build—to build in the same sense that some sort of shattering experience could be depicted in a novel or a short story or on film. I like to give the space to build up to involve the reader, even if it's yourself, and to swallow him up. To get him into the thing which you can't do nearly to that extent in a shorter piece, say, like the haiku, which is a very great form. I like the sense of enormous involvement. I want the poem to grab the reader by the throat and shake him, so that he thinks when he gets out of the poem at the end he's got the full Aristotelian thing of pity and terror. It's hard to get catharsis from a haiku.

PAGE: Would you mention a few names of current poets you like?

DICKEY: Yes, I'm very high on some of the new women poets. The best one is a girl named Betty Adcock, who is super good. And there's Mary Oliver who is very good. Margaret Atwood is very fine indeed. There are many. Jane Cooper continues to write well.

PAGE: You've spoken with great candor about sex, politics, religion, and so forth. How do you find the courage to do this?

DICKEY: I don't think it takes any courage. Anybody asks you what you think, I don't think it is a matter of great fortitude to tell him. Again, you get misinterpreted a lot, but this makes you patriotic. This is one of the good things about the country. You can say what you think.

PAGE: Don't you think relatively speaking that it is rather rare though for writers to do that?

DICKEY: Yes, I think so. I think when people are interviewed they usually say what they think they ought to say or what people want them to say. Life is too short for that.

PAGE: You don't think maybe that's out of a certain fear that they have?

DICKEY: Yes, writers are very hag-ridden with fear—all kinds of fears—fear of other writers, fears of bad reviews, fear this and fear that. I haven't the time for that.

PAGE: But you do have courage.

DICKEY: It is nice to hear somebody else say so, but I don't really think, "Goodness, I am going to say this. Is this going to be courageous of me to say it?" We just bypass all that.

PAGE: What is your response to people who complain that your writing and your life-style is too macho?

DICKEY: That's a silly word, and it has become one of the bigger and less serviceable cliches in our time or maybe too serviceable and less expressive. I don't know exactly what to answer to that—macho. I like physical things and I like being a man. All my life I've enjoyed the fact that I'm large and used to be able to run fast and move quickly and do things in the field of athletics that were physically rewarding to me. But it really doesn't go any further than that. I love to hit a good shot at tennis even today and get out there and move the body around. It feels good. I have a sense of performing rightly something that's proper for me to be doing.

PAGE: Although there's this legend widely held about James Dickey's being a sort of a wild man, aren't you actually a deeply stoical person?

DICKEY: I don't know about how stoical. I suppose one must come to that in the end, but wild, no; I don't think so. I've had a few episodes that I suppose might be construed as wild. I'd like to think so anyway. But I don't maintain that as a life-style. My grandmother was from Germany. My household upbringing—someone instilled in me a great love of order and procedure. I couldn't do as much traveling as I do if I didn't go to as great and meticulous care to pack a suitcase right. I enjoy doing things right. The big word around our household was *tuchtig*. Do it right.

PAGE: Although you are widely celebrated and admired, you have spoken of having numerous enemies. Do you have any theory of why that is?

DICKEY: I don't know. Sometimes it's because people are not on the same track as I am, nor should they be if that isn't the way for them to go. Some of it is envy, I suppose. One hesitates to say that about one's own case, but if it is true—you spoke earlier of honesty—if you are going to be honest, you better be honest about that, too.

PAGE: What direction do you see your work going in the future?

DICKEY: My work—well, the poetry will go one way and the prose will go maybe in another way, but the informing word—not exactly principle—but the informing spirit of everything I do is some kind of personal imaginative touch on the words no matter what the subject or no matter what the approach linguistically might be. If it doesn't have that I don't go on with it.

I go somewhere else where I may find that—some other mental direction where I might conceivably find it.

PAGE: Do you still feel that a collection of poems is worth a hundred novels?

DICKEY: If they are good poems they are worth a hundred novels, even a hundred good novels. Yes, because poetry—the Greeks knew this, everybody has known it, primitive people know it—is the highest use of language, language itself which is the thing that has made, for better or for worse, everything possible for the human race. It was the great gift—the development of a very great resource that was possible to mankind. Language itself is the miracle and the poetic use of language—I mean true poetry; I don't mean poetical, but the poetic use of language when it really does work, when it has a full consignment of magic and mystery about it—is the miracle within the miracle.

PAGE: What do you think of the Zen idea that the poet's concerns should be with the thingness of the object without concern for the poet's personality?

DICKEY: The thing itself. I don't know. I like the Zen people and some of the oriental cultures—what little I have known. I don't know. I think it's somewhat illusionary to think that you can deal with the subject, say an egg or rock or a breaking wave or something, as though your perception of it were not a part of us. It is part of it no matter what.

PAGE: What do you mean by that term "country surrealism"?

DICKEY: I don't know whether I made that up or somebody else made it up. I like it. Maybe I did make it up. "Country surrealism." Well, you know what surrealism is generally speaking although this is a drastic over-simplification: A juxtaposition of unlikely things, entities, or objects, and so on. Such as Lautréamont's famous conjunction of the umbrella and the sewing machine on the operating table. This is a pretty good example of the surrealistic approach. But what I would think about, as far as country surrealism is concerned, would be an employment of this sort of disorderment in having to do with country scenes, objects, and themes, and people. Also, maybe in some modified form of dialect. Country surrealism has not yet come to flower. But we are going to try to make that happen if we can.

PAGE: Jim, you had said that "Genius is the discovery of an idiom."

DICKEY: It is. And exploration and exploitation of it.

PAGE: Can you say anything about how a writer inclines himself toward this discovery?

DICKEY: Constant experimentation.

PAGE: Most poetry written for children seems to have an adult's idea of a child's state of mind. Now, you have that collection of children's—

DICKEY: I have one out and another one is coming out.[61]

PAGE: It seems to have a kind of realism that scarcely any such work has. Is that intentional on your part?

DICKEY: I'll tell you what, about writing for children. I don't know the field all that well. It seems to me that the main thing that you should encourage children in is that exercising of their own imagination and fantasy life. That dies out as one gets older when, Mr. Wordsworth says, "Shades of the prison-house begin to close / Upon the growing boy." Isn't that good? Before the shades of the prison house are fully closed we should give the child some imagination. His innocence is like the first day of creation and to him it is. We should give that full license and full play, and that's the end of that catechism.

PAGE: What do you see as the main value of *Jericho*?

DICKEY: Oh, I don't know—the main value of *Jericho*? It seems to me maybe most books of that sort—coffee-table books—are essentially throwaway items, and Hubert Shuptrine and I tried to create one that was not a throwaway item. What we wanted to do was produce the ultimate coffee-table book which would be so interesting that it would never get put back on the coffee table. People would read it and look at it. The value of it is negative, to get people to look at the South from maybe a little different angle than would have been possible without the book.

PAGE: Are you looking for a more objective language and now feeling it's less important to associate the poet with his poetry?

River City Interview 231

DICKEY: It's hard to say. Objective language, subjective language. I don't know. I notice you had a book of mine called *Night Hurdling* which had an address I made to a SAMLA group.[62] I took off from a text by an American poet, Winfield Townley Scott, another one of these sad cases of a serious American poet killing himself. He was neglected but was quite good. In one of his notebooks he says there are two approaches to language. One of them is a poetic language conceived of as a sort of magic gesture exemplified by the line of Hart Crane "the seal's wide spindrift gaze toward paradise." This is the magic language approach, and the other one is the reality approach exemplified by the line of Edwin Arlington Robinson which was "And he was all alone there when he died." It was about a real man in a real situation. The seal in Hart Crane's line is a literary seal. I'm not trying to load the dice in favor of the Robinson approach, but most of my work up until *Puella* was written with the reality approach, the situation, the anecdote approach. *Puella* is an attempt to break with that to see what the magic language side of things might offer. I'm still stumbling around with that.

PAGE: You thought about that a long time before it was actually written, because you talked about that idea.

Dickey: I think there is sort of a touchstone, to use one of Matthew Arnold's ringing phrases, as to the kind of person you are, capable of being determined by the kind of poetry that you aspire to, whether it's one sort or the other. In other words, what would be your idea of the best line of poetry you know or some line of poetry that's among the best. I would ask you that or I would ask the other person that. And what he said would determine what the poetry's essential orientation inevitably is.

PAGE: Do you think that the admiration that your parents bestowed upon your dead brother contributed to your drive?

DICKEY: No, I don't really think so because I never did hear very much about him. My father almost never mentioned him, but my mother would mention him only when someone else brought the subject up. No, no, she was not a person who dwelt on that at all. I know she was deeply affected and moved by Gene's death. But it was not something she would ever inflict on anybody else; that is, her feelings about it. She would never bring that out to anybody else. She was a deeply feeling, quiet sort of retiring person who stayed alone in her thoughts most of the time, but humorous and sweet as she could be, and helpful. She was almost the ideal mother because she stayed out of the way. You asked her something, she would tell you what she thought, but she sure wouldn't impose it on you. It's hard for me to believe that she is gone. The last twenty-five years of my life I saw almost nothing of her. I never went home, hardly. My brother and sister were around and they saw a lot of her, but not me. I was the original wandering boy.

PAGE: I've heard you talk about Hopkins and Thomas a good deal. Would you see them as influences on your work?

DICKEY: Not technically at all, although I like them. . . .

PAGE: Has this mythic and mystic attitude that is so pervasive in your writings always been a major part of your adult life?

DICKEY: I suppose. I remember something Ted Roethke once said: "It's my greatest ambition to be a rich mystic." I never met one, but he must be one of the holy men of the earth.

PAGE: Do you think in the long haul that Southern writers, especially poets, are more in touch with the natural universe, the God-made elements of the world?

DICKEY: I imagine so, because we have more contact with the wilderness down here than in a lot of other parts of the country. The South with its agrarian tradition—you know, farming is closely allied with hunting. Every farmer—I don't know how many farmers you know; I don't know all that many of them myself—but every farmer that I have ever known is an avid hunter and fisherman. It's all part of the same cycle. It's essentially a primitive cycle. Farming is primitive despite the sophisticated applications. It's essentially that of planting and raising and reaping. There's a time to reap and a time to sow. The time is the same now as it was in the days of Moses, and much before him. It's part of the same kind of pattern. You go out and kill food and eat it.

PAGE: Do you think the writer has to have a lot of failure in order to gain success?

DICKEY: Oh, I don't know. I can't formularize at all. Most of them do have a lot of failures. Whatever writing is done, whatever writing survives—has continuing vitality—is very largely a matter of luck in any case. Luck and perseverance, or talent, genius, whatever. Literary standards change quickly. No one's reputation is secure. Look at the attack Tolstoy made on Shakespeare. A very great writer—Tolstoy—maybe greater than Shakespeare. How do you make those kinds of distinctions?

PAGE: Your brief acting venture in *Deliverance* was admired. Why don't you choose to act again?

DICKEY: Well, that is just not my thing. My wife is an actress and very good, too. She's very much wrapped up in the stage and everything that has to do with it. Unlike so many writers—American writers especially—the stage has never had that much fascination for me. I don't believe I've seen over twenty plays, actual plays being played, in my life. Movies, I like them, but plays—it doesn't seem to get to me as it does to other people. I don't know why.

PAGE: Did you find the study of prosody helpful to you as a poet?

DICKEY: Sure. I like anything that has to do with numbers. Not that I am all that great as a mathematician because I distinctly am not, but I like the idea that one can take hard stresses and light stresses and manipulate them to produce certain effects. Poe was a very great theoretician of his approach, although his own practices are maybe not to everybody's taste. He understood the function, the spellbinding effect that rhythm can have, and the fact that this is very closely allied to mathematics is a subject that fascinates me, as it fascinated Poe, as it fascinated Mallarmé, as it fascinated Valéry, who was probably the best modern theoretician of poetry who is also a good poet himself.

PAGE: Okay, here's the last question and maybe one that's totally unanswerable. How does one, as you once said, "rigorously guide abandon"?

DICKEY: The best example I can think of, and it just occurred to me immediately, is somebody surfboarding down one of those big waves in Waikiki or somewhere like that, where they get up there and the wave is going all out, you know, and the guy certainly must feel a marvelous sense of release when he's tobogganing down that thing on that fragile board and so on. And yet he's able to have a sense of release and freedom because he's so skillful in manipulating the board. You know, if he just flopped into the wave, the wave would overwhelm him, and then even if he survived it he wouldn't have the same sense of exhilaration that his own skill has given him.

PAGE: Thanks, that's a perfect example. And that's my last question.

DICKEY: And that's my last answer.

25
James Dickey: Limitations and Infinities

Hank Nuwer / 1985

NUWER: Is your vision of the world the same as or different from what it was twenty years ago?

DICKEY: I don't know. History changes and we change with it. I really don't know my vision of the world then any more than I do now. I'm more confirmed now in what I thought then, I think, about the basic sanctity of the inner life and the necessity for having a good one.

NUWER: Do you enjoy the good life here in Columbia, South Carolina?

DICKEY: Yes, it's good. In many ways, it's good. Any writer's life has a good deal of frustration. I wouldn't be doing anything else.

NUWER: Have your midlife years and experiences made you a better poet?

DICKEY: By far. I was raised in two sorts of milieus: athletics and war. Those were especially formative, especially warfare, but I give athletics plenty of credit, as well. Or discredit—or, at least influence. I have two grown children, and a newborn, and a grandchild. My wife, Maxine, of nearly thirty years died years ago; I've been through the long, slow part of sorrow, instead of the fast and sudden part. You learn both limitations and the unlimited things—limitations and infinities.

NUWER: Do all the experinces that you've amassed go into the creation of your poetry?

Reprinted with permission from *Rendezvous*, 21 (Fall 1985), 43–54.

DICKEY: Sure. That would be true of any poet or any writer or any human being. Everything that happens, even from second to second, adds to your experiences. Some of it you don't understand yourself; it's subconscious or unconscious.

NUWER: Do you think one has to be ruthless to succeed?

DICKEY: Yes—especially on yourself. You've got to have the personal quality that will preclude fooling yourself about what you're doing—maintaining something that you've written is good simply because *you* wrote it. This is a common failing among writers, especially among student writers, but not limited to them.

. . .

NUWER: Have you sent something out that you regretted when it reached print?

DICKEY: Well, sure. But I don't believe in being cautious. I believe in saying what you believe at the time. I don't mind if I contradict myself at all—neither did Whitman. . . . The main thing is to bring out something forthright. All my books are being reissued now, and I just brought out a book of criticism of mine.[63] I repudiated about half the opinions that were earlier expressed. You change your opinions. Any critic that nails himself into a position and feels that he has to hold on to it, whether he still believes it or not, is stultifying himself. You must allow for change. I don't have the same opinion of *any* writer, much less myself, from year to year. Sometimes you like one, and then you like somebody else. That is necessary, I think. You must keep it fluid. You must allow for the momentary, spontaneous reaction to anything, even in something that you've read many times and are familiar with. You mustn't say, "Well, in 1968, I said *this* about this guy; so if I say anything about him again I gotta say something to approximate this." I don't believe in that. You might think the guy was good then, and you don't think he's so good now. You should be free to say it! You should keep your sensibilities subject to change.

NUWER: Will you revise your early poems—the way W. H. Auden did, let's say?

DICKEY: No. You must protect the integrity of the person you were at the time. I know some people who revised their work, and their best work was what they did when they were young and didn't know so much about poetry and were not so cautious. They should have let it stand. Unfortunately, Auden was one of these people. Although he was good in some later things, the early Auden was by far the best. When you go back as a middle-aged or old man and dissect the young man, it's a form of betrayal. Aside from a few typographical errors, I don't change anything.

NUWER: Like Hemingway, your personal life is the source of much intrigue for *non*readers of your work.

DICKEY: This is a mistake. If I have made a mistake, it is encouraging and allowing too much of that. My life is not at all that spectacular, nothing like his. I didn't go around killing elephants and lions and that sort of thing. I like to handle guns, and I like to hunt, but my success has not been spectacular. And the more the ecological balance goes against the wild things, the less inclined I feel to hunt.

NUWER: Does a writer lose something if he's not been in a war?

DICKEY: Hemingway thought so, said it was the one truly indispensable thing. Most writers, all writers, needed that if they were going to be great. I can say with the rest of the veterans—the people of my generation—*I* wouldn't have missed it. *But,* I wouldn't want to do it again.

NUWER: Athletics?

DICKEY: I like sports very much: all of them. I've done most—although not the ones where you have to fasten things to your feet—skating, ice hockey, skiing. Southerners are usually not very good at those. I was in collision sports like football. Football and track were the two best for me.

NUWER: Was there any identification with you with the narrator in the Vince Lombardi poem?[64] "I never played for you. You'd have thrown / Me off the team on my best day— / No guts, maybe."

DICKEY: I think so. I was afraid of being passed over. Any athlete has that. You don't know what another person's, a coach's, opinion is going to be. You have to have a special kind of guts to play for somebody like Lombardi. As I said somewhere in that poem, "love-hate is stronger / Than either love or hate." He's the kind of coach who inspired that feeling; and it's true, too, of human affairs, I think.

NUWER: Do you agree with Lombardi that winning is everything?

DICKEY: It's hard. Too many unpleasant people like General Patton and Hitler have had that extremist kind of attitude. In this country where competition is fierce, the guy who believes that and can bring it about is going to be the top guy. Everybody else is going to be an also-ran to him.

NUWER: Is there such a thing as a good loser?

DICKEY: Was it Leo Durocher who said those guys finish last?

NUWER: Was there a time when the media version of James Dickey took over your life?

DICKEY: I don't know. You can't really say *what* determines *when* it takes over. It's more an irritation than anything else. I'm a writer; I begin and end there.

NUWER: In *John Barleycorn,* Jack London wrote that he was "inspired" by drink. Have you lost any creative edge by easing up on your drinking?

DICKEY: No. I don't know how Jack approached writing; it's possible that his drinking destroyed it. American writers seem to have a vested interest in alcohol, but I don't. I enjoyed it, but it's time to leave it behind. You get dependent on it. Everybody now is taking uppers and downers—all these basketball players and weight lifters and javelin throwers. What's the drug—?

NUWER: Steroids?

DICKEY: Steroids. All those things weren't around to be frowned upon when I was doing these kinds of activities.

NUWER: You never got into drugs?

DICKEY: I couldn't smoke a Chesterfield, much less marijuana. I've seen a lot of it, but I—I remember what André Gide said to Jean Cocteau. Cocteau was, early on, big on the narcotics back at the turn of the century. Cocteau was trying to get the straitlaced Gide to join in some of these revelations, but

Limitations and Infinities 239

Gide said, "No, I wouldn't be interested in that. Lucidity is my drug."

NUWER: Anything else you feel like saying right now?

DICKEY: I *like* to write; I'm a compulsive writer. My trouble is keeping away from it—far more than drink or sex or anything else. It's got a permanent interest for me; it does not fluctuate.

. . .

NUWER: Are you the kind of person who writes anywhere, anytime?

DICKEY: I learned to write on a troop train; if you can write on a troop train, you can write anywhere. I like to have a sense of life going on around me. I don't like to be in a box. I like to see people at least part of every day. Solitude is all right, but I'm not that much addicted to it.

NUWER: You're not what Henry David Thoreau claimed to be?

DICKEY: No, but I admire him greatly. He's one of the very good people in American literature. He had a profound relationship to the world, the natural world, that I like. I always admire anybody of whom it would be true, as it was true of him, that you could chloroform him and put him in the wilderness anywhere around Concord, and when he awakened, he would be able to tell from the state of the vegetation and wildlife, within three days, what day of the year it was. That's something I admire; nobody could do that now.

NUWER: Vladimir Nabokov did know his butterflies—

DICKEY: I like *Lolita;* I think it's by far the best thing of his I ever read. Nabokov strikes me as rather clever and supercilious, but *that* is a real story, a love story, really. The protagonist really does love that awful little girl. She doesn't care anything about him, but he really does love her. It's not just a sexual thing. He loves her, which is quite different.

NUWER: Have you read Nabokov's *Pale Fire*?

DICKEY: I have. Think of it: a whole novel written in footnotes. It's all footnotes and *awful* poems.

NUWER: About you—do you think you've achieved the goals that you've set?

DICKEY: I don't think art has anything to do with winning out over somebody else. It's one field where athletic criteria don't apply in the slightest. . . .

NUWER: Do you see things in your mind in movie frames when you write?

DICKEY: No, but making movies is another thing that's helped any sort of writing I do. I did the screenplay for *Deliverance,* and I did another television movie, my particular and personal version of Jack London's story of atavism, *Call of the Wild.* I enjoy it. My imagination is very visual anyway, and visualizing scenes and sequences in film is extremely advantageous for the poetry I've been writing.

NUWER: It hasn't had an adverse effect?

DICKEY: Not at all. Everything goes together. I think if you're essentially a creative person, anything you do adds to your creative effort. *Anything!* I draw on my advertising experience all the time. You learn the right things for you no matter where you are or what you're doing.

NUWER: Even in your teaching? There's no sapping of creative juices?

DICKEY: Not in the slightest; it has exactly the opposite effect. Those kids love poetry, and it's gratifying to be in a milieu in which what you love is what the people you're dealing with also love. There's no need to persuade anybody of anything or coerce somebody into something, as is true of the business world: none of that sort of friction! Everybody wins. And *you* learn a great deal. I agree very much with Bernard Shaw, who said, "If you want to learn a subject, teach it." Teaching forces you to come to terms with your own conception of things, and you get your own ideas straight. When you get up in front of a class, you can't do a soft shoe dance or string tricks—although if I could do them, I would.

. . .

NUWER: Do you have any problem with students being intimidated by you?

DICKEY: I get them over that fast with my downhome manner—which is totally authentic.

NUWER: In your classes do you recommend any particular poets?

DICKEY: Oh, yes. We read an awful lot of them. I like a lot of bad poetry. I get tired of sublimity, even my own. Especially my own!

NUWER: You look like you have a ball out of everything you do—that you *really* do enjoy yourself.

DICKEY: Why live if you don't? You're the same way. I like that. I'm a natural-born gambler. I want to try something new: to see if it works or if I can work something out that I haven't done before. So that's what I'm doing with the new book,[65] and will do with the work beyond that.

NUWER: Speaking of experiences before—was it terrifying when you were blinded?

DICKEY: In a way, it was. I got a very good intuition of what it feels like not to *be* blind, but to *go* blind. The plaster for the life-mask the guy was making broke, and I sustained some eye damage. But it all turned out all right.[66]

NUWER: What was your attitude toward the sculptor, William Dunlap?

DICKEY: Very fraternal. He's a nice fellow. That, too, is an experience that got exaggerated. It really wasn't all that bad. But there were some moments of uncertainty. Actually, the stuff burned the cornea, so for a while, I had eyes, following hours of temporary blindness, like a newborn. I had been wearing glasses, but for several years after I didn't have to wear any. I do wear them now, but for a while I didn't have to.

NUWER: Do you wear glasses to shoot a bow?

DICKEY: No.

NUWER: Have you ever considered buying a word processor?

DICKEY: I don't care for those. It makes the words too intimidating. I'd like to think I have a certain mastery over myself instead of them coming at me from a machine. I've never worked one; I might not have that opinion now if I was to. I think I don't want to feel what I write is intimidated.

NUWER: Do you work first drafts in pen or pencil?

DICKEY: I work catch-as-catch-can. I work with typewriters, pen, pencils, knees, elbows, eyelashes, toenails, eyebrows—anything I can get hold of.

NUWER: Your book *Puella* is dedicated to your second wife, Deborah, in "the new life." Did "new life" lead to revitalization in your poetry?

DICKEY: In a way. There was a change in technical approach because I felt at the time I didn't want to repeat myself. . . . The business of a creative person is to work out there on the edge of things, to risk being wrong, to take a chance, to gamble.

NUWER: Don't you consider whether something you write is also commercial?

DICKEY: No. You, as a writer, can't second-guess what people are going to respond to. That's death. That's the death of creativity. . . .

NUWER: This may be because of faulty reading, but I don't think a *typical* James Dickey poem exists.

DICKEY: I think that is true; I believe you're the only person I've met who's read a lot of poetry who is of that opinion. A lot of times I can read something of mine in an anthology, and I don't remember exactly that I've written it.

NUWER: Do you have any particular educational theories that you've formed over the years?

DICKEY: Yes, I do. I try to go with each student, to the heart of what concerns him most deeply in his own life, his own past, his own experience, his own temperament and his own psychology, to try to find some way to objectify that and get it down in words by some sort of formal means.

NUWER: I understand that you are an advocate of students' learning fundmentals about their language before they try to write creatively.

DICKEY: I think it is necessary to do. You take a field like music. There are some extraordinary musicians who don't read music, but they do what is *written* on the music whether they read it or not. Some students kick a little about fundamentals. They think they are a little too mundane for poets to fool with. They don't understand that it is structure that makes the very flights that they want to attempt. You're not able to do it without a knowledge—either implicit or instinctive, but more or less intrinsic—of your efforts. You have to gain that knowledge whether you have it by rote or learning it in school or by some other means—you still have to have it.

NUWER: Is it difficult for you to assess another person's writing, particularly a young person's?

DICKEY: It is difficult. It requires a certain amount of tact which I'm not always able to evince. You do have to be careful. I don't want to hurt anybody's feelings. So much of the individual ego is involved in the writing of poetry. A certain type of person feels that if you say his work is no good, it's tantamount to saying he's no good, or she's no good. You work to avoid that confrontation, or what someone might consider a brutal putdown.

NUWER: Did you ever have a thin shell?

DICKEY: No, not really. I wanted to learn. Just like if a fellow knew how to do a guitar piece, I would want to see how he did it. If he could do it and I couldn't do it, I would want to find out from him. I've always been an avid learner all my life. I like that attitude in other people.

NUWER: Are there any poets you learn from today?

DICKEY: You learn from everybody. It comes from a process of osmosis. I read a lot—all writers do. It's our medium: poetry, prose, plays, screenplays, even advertising. You're using words to produce an effect of some sort, and you like to see how other people do it. You just like words generally. You like to listen to words—yours or someone else's. You just like being in the medium. You read a lot, and what influences that come to you are due to the process of absorption. You don't do that consciously, or at least I don't.

NUWER: The South of the high-tech Eighties certainly differs from the tragic South that produced the likes of Robert Penn Warren, William Faulkner, Harry Crews, and yourself. Do you think the South has lost its tragic sense?

DICKEY: I think the tragedy is changing. We've been living off the Civil War and its aftermath for a mighty long time now. If there is tragedy in the South now, it's in the conversion from a rural, farming economy to an industrialized one. The South is industrializing very heavily, and it might be argued—as it was eloquently argued by Warren and some others in the twenties and thirties—that this is wrong for our part of the country, that we should stay on the land and we should not industrialize. We should try to keep the old ways, particularly the family together—and the cousins and the bloodlines and so on. We should try to keep a way of life that has some very good things about it. Slavery was a part of it a hundred, hundred-fifty years ago, but that was part of the Southern ethos. The fact that slavery was a part of the way of life in the antebellum South does not mean that everything about the South is thereby eviscerated, or is made evil and wrong. It's like other things in human history and human motivation. The South has some very good things about it and some unfortunate things. . . .

NUWER: You have a sense of fascination for the Appalachian region, don't you?

DICKEY: Yes. My father and his family come from there, and I have lots of relatives back up in there. I love those people. They are a unique people, and their culture's unique. But those places, too, will go and become like Gatlinburg, Tennessee, and Helen, Georgia, which is like a reconverted Alpine Village, of all things. When you see these things you know that the end is in sight for Appalachia, too.

NUWER: You think that's all doomed?

DICKEY: Yes.

NUWER: Many of your poems depend upon a strong narrative thrust. Do you see yourself allied with Southern storytellers?

DICKEY: No. I like narrative; I like stories. But in the latest poems that I've written I've tried to bypass that or transcend that element. In my last book, I've tried deliberately to avoid versified anecdotes, although I don't entirely avoid it. It's too easy, fatally easy, for me to make that kind of poem and turn out a lifetime of versified anecdotes like "Cherrylog Road" and so on, which I like, but I want to get off that track. That's enough of that. Try to do something else, I said.

NUWER: You never stay still. You don't have any affinity for any particular movement.

DICKEY: No, I don't. I would avoid that any way I could. I don't like that sort of literary cliquism. No. I'm essentially a loner.

NUWER: Old bullfighters used to shave the horns of their bulls to give themselves an edge. Are there tricks that old poets have to get them by?

DICKEY: I don't know. I don't talk about what other people do that much. If somebody's good I like to read him. If he's not good or if I don't think he's good, I don't read him.

NUWER: In your poem "Gamecock," you seem to have some borrowings from Dylan Thomas—

DICKEY: I don't think it has anything at all to do with Dylan Thomas. If it has any affinities at all it's with the writer Randall Jarrell, whom I greatly admire. I like Thomas's work, but . . . I would not have any affinity stylistically with him at all. If I found anything at all of him in my work, I would ruthlessly scrub it out. . . .

NUWER: Do you have any poets that you feel are blood brothers or blood sisters?

DICKEY: Yes, I think so. I think Laurence Lieberman is working in the same vein that I am. Dave Smith is very good. I have high hopes for Betty Adcock of Raleigh, who's had a book . . . that's good. There's a woman out of Provincetown named Mary Oliver whom I think everybody ought to read. She's outstandingly good and doing some of the same things as I. We're all of us different from the role emphasis on personality and personal conflicts and agony and that sort of thing. People are worn out listening to somebody else's weeping and sackcloth-and-ashes attitudes, breastbeating, and gnashing of teeth, frustration, and tearing of hair and personal grievances. That wears out fast. People like Theodore Roethke, Dave Smith, and, I hope, myself are trying to do something different from that in throwing experiences open to the possibilities in a reader's own life, instead of limiting experiences in a poem to *my* life, and *my* ancestry, and *my* upbringing, and *my* suicidal drive. . . . No poet should be so egotistical as to ask the reader to fasten onto his own personality and his own confessions, that sort of thing. Experience is capable of far larger things than that.

NUWER: Any plans to retire to the high country of South Carolina?

DICKEY: It's my particular job as I see it to drive the thing on through to the end, to write as well as I can to the last breath. I want to write the ultimate poem; we all want to do that.

26
LIVING BEYOND RECALL: AN INTERVIEW WITH JAMES DICKEY
GORDON VAN NESS /1987

VAN NESS: In *Sorties* you state: "Things matter to me; big things and little things. I feel for them in some manner, and so I remember them. My whole poetic work, pretty much, has been made of such memories." You've written a number of what might be called family poems, and I'm wondering if you have any vivid impressions about your early years in Atlanta at 166 West Wesley.

DICKEY: Those years were the Depression years, but I don't remember really that there was any special pinch on us financially. Maybe because my mother's income was from patent medicine and depression years are very good for patent medicine because people can't afford to pay doctors. We never really suffered, but we were not rich. My father liked to go out into the country a lot. He hunted with a shotgun, and he would bring back rabbits and squirrels which we ate.

    The contrast between my mother and father is so very, very apparent. My mother was a semi-invalid, and she had hardly any existence at all outside of her immediate family. Things having to do with her children constituted her entire world. My father was a frustrated country man. All of his relatives came from up around Mineral Bluff, Georgia, which is up near the Tennessee line. His real heart was in country people and country things and country ways, which my mother looked down on as being extremely low class and sorry. But my father loved sorry people, especially if they were country people, and his main interest in life was in cock fighting.

Reprinted with permission from the *James Dickey Newsletter,* 3 (Spring 1987), 17–26.

VAN NESS: You had a gamecock over in the Pacific.

DICKEY: Yes, I had a pretty good one, too, named Max, that got killed. That was the only rapport between me and my father. He gave me all the instructions as to how to get Max up to his fighting best.

VAN NESS: In the letters you wrote home from the Pacific, you often mentioned Peg Roney.

DICKEY: Peg Roney was a girl whose father, I believe, was head of the French or language department at Rollins College in Winter Park, Florida, which is a kind of rich kids' school—was then and still is. She was rather elusive for me. I like that. She was an interesting, sort of witty, rather pretty girl in an unusual way. Although she was blond, she had a slightly oriental cast to her eyes. But she never really cared much about me, which was too bad. She married a Navy pilot. She wrote me some nice letters overseas, but not really warm or passionate letters. I got word that she had married just before I went into Okinawa.

VAN NESS: Your comment, "More and more I see myself as the poet of survival," has often been quoted. Could you elaborate on this? What, finally, did the war, and in particular the final months when the fighting was so intense, mean in terms of your attitudes and even your poetic development?

DICKEY: The war did not really come completely to bear on me significantly, other than my personal participation in it, until the years after the real war was over and this sort of Proustian memory thing takes over and makes of it not what it was but what it was to you. That's when the poems began to be written about various aspects of it. I think if it's possible that I live long enough I'll write a sequel to *Alnilam* called *Crux* about that. I sort of shrink from the prospect of researching so much. I don't care that much about that aspect of writing certain kinds of novels. In other words, there's just going to be a point that I'll have to decide whether I want to spend what will amount to the rest of my life back in the Pacific air war, living that again so I can write about it.

VAN NESS: Do you need to purge it from you in some sense?

DICKEY: It won't be purged. I never believed in that at all. I think if you dwell on something enough to write about it, it makes it that much more present to you. Purging it is the last thing it does. . . . If what you remember constitutes a sickness, it makes you twice as sick to dwell on it, to write about it.

VAN NESS: When you wrote home from the Pacific, did you assume a persona of any sort in order to protect your parents from the danger you were in? Were you, in other words, undergoing profound changes in your personality and outlook but not reflecting them in your letters home?

DICKEY: Perhaps. I must have been, but I don't think I had recognized it except maybe semiconsciously.

VAN NESS: In what ways did Roy Campbell and Ernest Dowson influence how you viewed poetry?

DICKEY: What an unlikely pair of bedfellows! Ernest Dowson appealed to me the same way he appeals to any young person. He's got that certain melancholia. On my, yes! Ernest Dowson. I can't hear his name without the whole thing coming back to me.

VAN NESS: "Wine and woman and song."

DICKEY: Yes, right! It's funny that minor 1890s versifier could have been such a phrase-maker such as everybody and his brother could have picked up on. "Gone with the wind" comes from Ernest Dowson. "Wine and woman and song" and "days of wine and roses" come from him. "Faithful . . . in my fashion" comes from him.

VAN NESS: Campbell?

DICKEY: I liked his energy and his satirical bite.

VAN NESS: And you named your plane after him—"The Flaming Terrapin."

DICKEY: Yes. As clumsy as he is, he had a lot of masculine vigor that I liked. I think anybody's taste could be judged by the good-bad poets that he liked or the bad-good poets. He was mine.

VAN NESS: In *Self-Interviews* you cite Shelley's "The Cloud" as perhaps your earliest memory of poetry, that it was "a very pretty piece of something-or-other about clouds." One of the lines in that poem is "I change, but I cannot die."

DICKEY: Yes, that ain't bad.

VAN NESS: Do you think this unconsciously may have attracted you?

DICKEY: Possibly. Shelley figures in *Alnilam*. There's a passage in there where the Alnilam conspirators quote, as part of a ritual that they have, a thing of Shelley's. In a way Shelley is like Joel Cahill. He's impractical and fantastic and charismatic and uncompromising. Extremely. Shelley can write about the air, too, about anything that's disembodied.

VAN NESS: You read a great deal of Hemingway and Wolfe during the war.

DICKEY: Oh yes! They were my serious writers that I read. Also Faulkner and James T. Farrell.

VAN NESS: *Studs Lonigan?*

DICKEY: Yes, that especially, but also some of the short stories because in that sort of plodding way of his, he seemed to be more desperately honest in a human rather than a literary way.

VAN NESS: You were writing poems then, sonnets for example, but also blank verse like "Rain in Darkness,"[67] based on Robert Bridges's "London Snow."

DICKEY: Yes, I remember writing that. Robert Bridges is a strange one for me to have been influenced by even to the extent of trying to write an imitation of him. But I think what interested me in Bridges is that he was such a fanatic about prosody itself, about the mechanics of it. That's what appealed to me. I had an idea then, and to a certain extent still do, probably stemming from those years, that the poem can be engineered, can be put together like a machine. This was Valéry's idea. He has got much more claim to the validity of it than I have, but to have somebody like him roughly of the same opinion is very heartening.

VAN NESS: How was Gwen Leege influential to you?

Living Beyond Recall 251

DICKEY: Yes, she was a high spot. She was a sort of Grace Kelly of mine.

VAN NESS: You were engaged to her?

DICKEY: Well, in a way. I never did give her a ring or anything. That was the closest I'd ever really gotten to marrying anybody. She was just a class act. She was a Bryn Mawr girl. Her father had been a biologist. Her mother was German-born and had been a nurse for the German side in World War I. She was rich and she was interested in some of the same things I was. She knew literature pretty well, especially poetry, and she was multilingual, which was an interesting thing about her. But she was a rich man's woman. She could never have survived the scruffy life I lived as a student. She did not influence my *Weltanschauung*. She was not that deep a person, but she was very decorative and pretty. I think she was the prettiest girl I ever had anything to do with; I mean as the world considers those standards. Ah, God knows. I liked Gwen a lot. She got what she wanted. She was not made for the nitty gritty of life, of getting in there and shoving with the rest of 'em like Maxine. Maxine liked the struggle and the getting there. She would get in there and do what needed to be done.

VAN NESS: In a letter home dated 29 June 1944, when you were in flight school, you stated: "I have foolproof instruments that do all my thinking for me." Does the mechanical, habitual, reflex act—the unconscious "procedure" or "performance"—allow the pilot or poet to "enter" into an experience? You seem to have just taken quite naturally to the flight controls.

DICKEY: Yes, I was good. I like things like intercept problems. I still do a lot of that just as an exercise because I like it and I use it in *Alnilam*. All that comes together in the novel, the instrumentation, and the problem-solving and the stars.

VAN NESS: Does that sort of mechanical approach enable you to get into an experience?

DICKEY: Or maybe out of it in the sense that you have a certain detachment, too. Either into it all the way or above it or outside it looking in at it in some way.

VAN NESS: What specific memories of the Pacific are especially vivid to you?

DICKEY: You get to thinking about the memories, and the episodes throng back. There were a lot of things. I remember that once we got up into combat everything was geared to the next mission. You come down from one and the main thing is the mail and then the briefing. They say, "This is what you're going to do, this is where you're going to go, this is the target." We just worked it out.

VAN NESS: Do you remember having to find a B-24 that was lost?

DICKEY: I sure do. Bradley and I went out—up off the west coast of Mindoro—and found him. He didn't have the slightest idea where he was. The damned thing was going to run out of gas.

VAN NESS: How about the battlefield when you went into Okinawa and pitched camp? There was a battle just previous to your arrival.

DICKEY: It was just absolute chaos, absolutely. There was a place up in back of our area which was all coral caves and where the Marines and infantry had just gone and scoured through those with flame throwers. There were Japanese guys sitting up there in what must have been a machine-gun emplacement just incinerated. Just black.

VAN NESS: In another letter home you wrote: "I look forward to every mission. It has a horrible fascination. It makes everything else seem trivial."

DICKEY: Yes! Did I say that then? That's exactly right.

VAN NESS: Did your fascination derive from your being balanced so near death? Was this a dance with the void?

DICKEY: Yes. Yes, it was. Yes, definitely.

VAN NESS: In *Self-Interviews* you write: "The difference between the natives' outlook and the outlook of so-called 'civilized' people was very instructive to me." Could you tell how?

DICKEY: I read a lot of anthropology in those days. I figured that might have some of the answers for me.

VAN NESS: To what?

DICKEY: Well, to a *Weltanschauung*. I felt that the kind of situation where I was raised and the kind of situation from which I came was not the only outlook that one could have. I read a lot of anthropologists, especially the field workers such as Bronislaw Malinowski and A. R. Radcliffe-Brown and W. H. R. Rivers who were among the first to psychoanalyze primitive peoples to find out what their views of things were. Reading from the books and field reports of these anthropologists was where I got a great deal of the stuff about animals.

VAN NESS: Did the separate stanza which serves as a summation or coda contribute in your first volume to calling up something deep within the reader?

DICKEY: Perhaps so. I don't know if I would ever submit that to the reasoning process myself so much as to make that kind of judgment. I think there is something satisfied in the psyche when you can bring off a kind of tour-de-force feat like that and have the thing come around to the same words again but slightly altered.

VAN NESS: From the poet's point of view?

DICKEY: Yes. I think there's something about that kind of complex ordering that people approve of and respond to when they see or when they experience it.

VAN NESS: Why do you think they respond to it?

DICKEY: That's very, very deep in the mind, I think, and also in the nerves and blood.

VAN NESS: In your comments on "The String" you note the passing on of technique through the generations of whatever one is privileged to pass on. What are you as a poet attempting to pass on?

DICKEY: Apart from personal technique, I think a poet is trying, whether he would say this or not, to validate the individual viewpoint. I think that is more important as things get more computerized and plasticized. The vision and the true reaction of people to things, the true and if possible imaginative individual reaction to things, are threatened more and more. The poet has never been more valuable than he is now because he is the one who stands at the gate saying, "Thou shalt not pass." This is something that is different from Eliot's notions, but it is exactly mine. I'm not all that great an admirer of Wallace Stevens. Most of the time I feel he's somebody who's been foisted on me, but this is exactly what I think about the individual voice. He had a very subtle mind. Even though he was an insurance executive, he was an European-type, a Valéry-type mentality. He seems almost an anomaly as an American. Stevens says: "The thing that is incessantly overlooked: the artist, the presence of the determining personality. Without that reality no amount of other things matters much." Eliot says that art is autotelic, that it does not matter who wrote this, that, or the other poem. All that matters is the poem. I think that it does matter who wrote it, and so does Stevens. The presence of the determining personality. Yes! That is what makes a Yeats poem not a Dylan Thomas poem.

VAN NESS: In "The Heaven of Animals" you comment on creating something like Eliot's "still point." Do you attempt to create a magical moment for the reader, a moment where time stops, where he can break through—?

DICKEY: Yes, to some unchanging meaning, but I go against my own real preoccupations there because the changingness of any meaning is a part of the value of the poem. The good thing about poetry is that the poem will change its meaning as the person changes. This is why poems which attempt to set forth eternal verities are foredoomed because that cancels out the fluid, the protean.

VAN NESS: And why the *Zodiac* poet fails?

DICKEY: Yes. That's more or less right.

VAN NESS: Talking about "Drowning With Others," you declare: "It seems to me that the essential human act is for you to try to keep somebody else up, even though you're all going to die." Are you trying in some way to keep mankind "up"? Do you see your poems as "vessels"?

DICKEY: I'd like to, but I surely wouldn't insist on their being seen that way. I think it was Frost who said that the poem is a "momentary stay against confusion." Maybe something like that.

Living Beyond Recall

VAN NESS: In *Self-Interviews* you state: "Illusion is a very great part of human experience; it enables you to bear up under the circumstances that you have to face." What does illusion do?

DICKEY: Illusion is maybe not too far from delusion. I think for me the best play of Eugene O'Neill, whom I don't really care much about, is *The Iceman Cometh,* which is set in a bar where the people have their various fantasies about themselves by means of which they live. And this guy Hickey comes up and destroys each one's illusions, and he destroys them and, in the end, is destroyed by his own illusions.

VAN NESS: But doesn't the poet create the illusion as a source of possibility? Isn't he in a sense a magician?

DICKEY: Yes, he does, and he is. So much of an attempt has been made over the ages from even before Plato to equate poetry and truth, like Keats's famous statement, "Beauty is truth, truth beauty." I never believed that. I never believed that truth is important. What the poet—I just take myself as an example, but I'm sure this is true of others, too—is doing is that he has a subject, even an object, that he is writing about. He is not trying to say that what he says is *the* truth; he is trying to say that what he says or the way he looks at this is an interesting way to look at it. Let others take from it what they will.

VAN NESS: And do with it what they want? You have no hope of what they do with it resulting in anything particular?

DICKEY: No, I don't. I'd like to think it will have something to do with people's experiencing more and being more than they would be without it, but there is no guarantee that will happen.

VAN NESS: In many of your poems—"Springer Mountain," "The Performance," "Approaching Prayer," and others—the speaker engages in an action to reach a heightened awareness. How much, do you think, is that ritual, that act, necessary?

DICKEY: To different people it would be desirable, I suppose. What poets are after more than other people is consequence, or consequentiality. Something mattering, something being important. It may be something that other people wouldn't think is important, but to the poet it is important and he thinks it is for these reasons.

VAN NESS: And the act is a way to—

DICKEY: To establish a kind of consequentiality to the subject.

. . .

VAN NESS: You declare in *Self-Interviews*: "You shouldn't expect a consistent philosophical attitude from a poet. . . . Because really a poet like me is writing about experiences and ideas based on them. . . . The larger consistency that the body of a poet's work should have should come from the totality of the poet's personality, including all its contradictions." Are you a study in contrasts?

DICKEY: Sure, you bet. Nobody more. This is the reason that absolutists like Yvor Winters, who is my great example of this attitude, are not the great spirits. They are people who are trying desperately to set up fences and lay down foundations, but poetry won't be caught that way. You can't ossify it.

VAN NESS: So the poet should be as many different things as he can?

DICKEY: Yes, he should. Keats is very good on this. He says that what confounds the philosopher delights the chameleon poet. He liked the changes and the different perspectives.

VAN NESS: Despite the success of *Deliverance* you have always maintained that the novel was—like archery and guitar playing—a peripheral attempt, a diversion from the "central motion" of poetry. If this is so, what is it you're trying to accomplish with your new novel that you didn't already do with *Deliverance*?

DICKEY: To see if I can do it. Like wolves that have tasted blood, they want to see if they can do it again and do it a different way, to take a different subject and a different technique. You just want to see what you can do. You've had some success with working in this form before. It seems almost immoral to let it lapse there. . . . You're fascinated with the possibilities of what you might be able to do. You don't want to pass those by.

VAN NESS: All right, so you have *Deliverance* and *Alnilam* as the bookends, as it were, even maybe as the alpha and omega. Do you want your poetry viewed as the middle?

DICKEY: Well, no. Wordsworth was a great system builder at making edifices out of his own works. *The Prelude* and *The Excursion* were supposed to form such and such a part of the corpus of this enormous, mighty mega-poem that he was writing. No, I let the chips fall where they may. I'm not a system builder.

VAN NESS: Is there a consistent philosophical attitude in your work toward man and his world?

DICKEY: If I could formulate it, I wouldn't because that might knock out some other possibilities that were directly counter to it.

VAN NESS: As a result of your recent illness[68] in which, as you have written, you "lay in the hospital consorting with the brothers, Sleep and Death," do you feel, even more, that you are a poet of survival?

DICKEY: Yes, now more than ever!

27

ALNILAM: JAMES DICKEY'S NOVEL EXPLORES FATHER AND SON RELATIONSHIPS

WILLIAM W. STARR /1987

James Dickey's second novel, *Alnilam,* is definitely not another *Deliverance,* which created a storm of acclaim and readership when it appeared seventeen years ago.

But that's just fine with Dickey, author of two dozen literary works and holder of a host of prizes to go with them.

... The University of South Carolina poet-in-residence and a Columbian for nearly two decades said, "This is no *Deliverance 2* or *Son of Deliverance.* I'm not going to do that kind of thing. People will just have to take it for what it is."

And what *Alnilam* is—once the reader gets by a title that catches in the mouth—is a massive, ambitious, seriously focused novel that at times soars with the majesty and power of Dickey's imaginative writing. It deals with "big" issues: the nature and sources of power, leadership, faith, and the relationship between fathers and sons.

"I'm sixty-four now, and I figure I don't have infinite time left to me, so I wanted to get these things out and deal with them in the novel," Dickey explained in an interview at his Lake Katherine home almost eleven months after a scary experience with brain surgery.

He had suffered severe headaches and vision problems for several months last year before doctors diagnosed a massive blood clot and ordered brain surgery. The June 30 operation followed within days of his becoming the first inductee in the new South

---

Reprinted with permission from *The State* [Columbia, S.C.] (17 May 1987), F-1, F-10.

Carolina Academy of Authors. Today, Dickey says his recovery is complete.

"I was going blind in my left eye," Dickey recalled, perhaps with a touch of irony. The principal character in *Alnilam*—Frank Cahill—is a man who goes blind early in the novel.

"Cahill is an inarticulate, redneck carpenter, who acts only for himself," Dickey said. And yet it is Cahill, and his determination to understand the son he never knew, who ultimately opens the doors for the exploration of large-scale, powerfully articulated themes in *Alnilam*.

Dickey's story is set in World War II. Cahill—who has become blind as a result of diabetes—and his ferocious dog, Zack, head for the small town of Peckover, N.C. That's the location of an Army Air Corps base where his son, Joel, apparently has died in a flight training accident.

Why Cahill is in Peckover is not clear—especially to him. For while Joel had listed him as next of kin, Cahill has never actually seen his son, having separated from the boy's mother at the time of Joel's birth.

Once at the base, Cahill talks with the officers and cadets who knew Joel. From them, he pieces together the story of his son's brilliant but oddly enigmatic and charismatic personality, and the mysterious and ultimately disturbing meaning of *Alnilam*.

The son's spellbinding, perhaps fanatical hold over his fellow cadets—even after his presumed death—is both puzzling and challenging to Cahill.

The father struggles to grasp the impact of Joel's continuing authority and relationship to his peers and those who commanded him. Readers who confront that same mystery may unravel the key to *Alnilam* as well, Dickey said.

"The nature of power, one man's power over another, is a very mysterious thing, and it has always fascinated me.

"It doesn't take a whole lot to exercise power over people. The leadership concept is varied, but there are certain similarities in all forms. One of those is that leaders possess a great deal of charisma, and the other is an enigmatic quality."

The question for readers is why these young cadets act the way they do, even to the extent of forming a secret society (named Alnilam, after the central star in the belt of the constellation Orion) that could undermine the chain of command.

And why would they do that with no more apparent reason than their relationship with the charismatic, enigmatic Joel?

"The answer, of course, is that's exactly why they behave the way they do. And that's the core of *Alnilam*. If readers can get that, they have the central point of the novel," said Dickey, who flew night fighter missions in the Pacific during World War II.

Many readers who come to *Alnilam* may not be prepared for what they find. The sprawling novel—nearly seven-hundred pages, more than twice as long as *Deliverance*—lacks that earlier work's sustained intensity. *Alnilam* is a "bigger" novel in every sense, however, in its heightened vision and profound thematic concepts.

It also features an audacious, dramatic typographical layout that may at once confuse, startle, and illuminate. Dickey calls it "my great experiment."

In *Alnilam*, Dickey seeks to combine the inner vision of the blind man with the visible world of those around him—a James Joyce-like attempt to embrace the seen and the felt simultaneously. To convey that, a number of pages are split in parallel columns, the bold words on the left side embodying Cahill's sensations and the right side depicting what is actually happening in the sighted world.

"It's a double point of observation, internal and external vision," Dickey said.

Some early readers of the novel have found it initially confusing but adapted to it. Others, including a reviewer in *Publisher's Weekly*,[69] describe it as "merely awkward."

Regardless of the reaction to such techniques, the novel is getting a big publicity push from Doubleday. The huge New York-based publishing house is issuing *Alnilam* in a substantial first printing of 100,000 copies later this month, and reportedly is spending six figures for promotion.

There's plenty of talk, but no details, about movie rights.

And since Dickey is a national literary figure, he's in demand for interviews by major publications in advance of the book's official release date.

Dickey, who has seldom shied from publicity, seems to relish the experience and is eager to talk about the novel.

He said he isn't concerned that some readers will find *Alnilam* a little tougher going than *Deliverance*.

"A writer has to go with his imagination," he said. "You're not really an artist if you try to give the people what they want. Because most of the time they don't know what they want until they get it."

Sometimes that applies to the author as well, for Dickey has worked at the idea of *Alnilam* off and on for thirty-seven years, trying to get it in the shape he wanted.

"I wrote it at intermittent times going back to 1950. I started when I was teaching at Rice Institute (now Rice University) in Texas. I remember I went out on the grassy part of campus and opened a brand new notebooklike ledger because I once heard Thomas Wolfe wrote in those. I had bought one figuring what worked for him might work for me," Dickey told a Doubleday interviewer.

"I was writing a lot of poetry at that time, not very good poetry, so I put the novel aside. I took it up again when I lived in the south of France in 1954, but the story wasn't clear in my mind. I only knew it had to do with a man who lost his son in a training accident in the early days of World War II. But after I wrote about his journey to this small town where the air base was I didn't know what would happen. But I kept my notes, and eventually the story began to develop and I finished it in early 1986."

In its final form—incomplete portions were published twice in *Esquire*[70] magazine, the first in 1976—Dickey's novel examines the shape of relationships between fathers and sons, but with a twist.

Usually it is the son who comes to an understanding of himself through an exploration of the father's life. In *Alnilam,* the father discovers the truth about his son.

"But also I like to hint in a couple of places that the son is trying in his own way to bring his father to him. So the novel may be seen in some ways as a reciprocal search under the strangest of circumstances," Dickey said.

"Also, it's hinted that the son has been trying to figure out ways to come in contact with the father he has never seen, because, after all, the son might not be dead. He's been in a crash, but his body has never been found."

Early readers of the novel seem in agreement that *Alnilam* contains some of Dickey's finest prose ever.

Always a poet first, Dickey evokes his poetic foundations strongly throughout the novel, particularly in his writing about the blind man's world and the grandeur and heart-pounding excitement of flight.

"I have tried to give strong emphasis to the mystique of flying," he said. "I try to give the reader the physical sensation of flying on the human body. Being on a jet is like being in a hotel lobby twenty-thousand feet up. But in one of those small trainers you truly get a sense of being precariously sustained in another element, the air, that you're not supposed to be in, and yet one in which you have some kind of control over."

Dickey's editors at Doubleday—he's had seven during the creation of *Alnilam*—have been unstinting in their expressions of support and praise for the novel. And Dickey is grateful for their counsel in the editing process.

But he also made it clear that the direction and style is his and his alone—and it has always been that way.

He cited an incident in the late 1960s when he had completed the manuscript of *Deliverance,* and confronted the editor-in-chief at his publishing house, then Houghton Mifflin.

"He read the cliff-climbing episode in the novel and told me he thought it was entirely too long, that it shouldn't be more than one page. I said um-hum not very enthusiastically. And he said of course maybe I'd like to talk to another editor about it, although it's rare for a first-time novelist not to accept the advice of an editor-in-chief.

"Anyway, I went to see the other editor, who was younger, and he read it and told me the cliff-climbing scene couldn't possibly be cut, in fact it ought to be even longer. I told him 'Now you're talking!' and that's the way we left it."

Dickey said he is prepared for the public's and critics' verdicts on *Alnilam,* but he seems comfortable with his accomplishment. It is a work that extends his imaginative novelistic craft into new dimensions, and he's eager to get out and talk with readers about their reactions.

"I'm not going to tell people exactly what it means. I don't write deliberately to provoke mystery, but I do try to invest my stories and poems with many layers of meanings. Each reader can find his own, make his own interpretation. That's what's really important about a novel or a poem: what you can take from it."

28

JAMES DICKEY TALKS ABOUT STORY BEHIND *ALNILAM*

Bob Gingher /1987

GINGHER: *Alnilam* is about the quest for a lost son.

DICKEY: Well, in a way it turns into that but you do have to remember that Frank Cahill, the protagonist, didn't start out with any notion of questings or anything. He's a guy with an enormous amount of willpower, and he wants to dominate every situation he's in and everybody that he meets. He wants to take blindness as something that doesn't take away from his ability to do this but adds to it. As he keeps saying in there, they have to come to me. But it's odd for him, and he has this dog about half-trained, and he's ready to take on the world, and he's sort of using this as a test. It's a pretext for him to get out among people and see how he does. And he goes up there to the Air Force base and hits around deeper and deeper into his son's identity and what affects him and the people that he has affected and so on. So it becomes a quest and he becomes determined to find out everything he can. Some people lie to him, some people are not honest with him, but what he discovers is not anything that he would ever have been able to imagine in a million years.

GINGHER: And the parallel text works with blindness, light and dark—

DICKEY: Yes, that bothers some people, but it shouldn't. I mean, it was part of my intention when I wrote those sections that way so that everyone would find his own best way of doing it, you know.

Reprinted with permission from *Greensboro* [N.C.] *News & Record* (19 July 1987), E-5.

GINGHER: Isn't there a sense in which *Alnilam* is about power over the environment and over others?

DICKEY: Yes, yes, it's about power. Sure, Frank Cahill's kind of power and his son Joel's quite different sort of power. It's also about cults, you know, and leadership, where the boy is one of these mysterious creatures who has his own mystiques. And I think most people meet somebody like that along in life, somewhere or other, who seems to have a whole different slant on existence than you or I.

GINGHER: *Alnilam* is like that.

DICKEY: Yes, well it's kind of like—someone, some reviewer or critic, said that Joel is like Hitler come back as Christ because there is the possibility of his resurrection or reappearing. The boys think he's going to show up most when they need him. But it's kind of, in a way, analogous to Jesus and Peter. Jesus is sort of a mystic and seer, but it's Peter who organizes the Church out of Jesus's examples. The same way with Shears. Shears is the organization man. And he doesn't want Joel to come back, because he's got the organization himself now. It's also like Dostoyevski's Grand Inquisitor's scene in *The Brothers Karamozov* where Jesus comes back and appears to the Grand Inquisitor. And the Inquisitor says, "Leave. Don't let anybody know you're here because everything we've organized in your name would collapse with your simple message of love one another. We've got this enormous organization we've built up on Christianity, and we can't—you would obliterate your own Church if you returned."

GINGHER: *Alnilam* has been compared to *Moby-Dick*. Our reviewer felt it was a mistake to compare *Alnilam* with *Moby-Dick,* as another reviewer has done. It's not really that helpful. Although the book is, in a way, a kind of anatomy, like *Moby-Dick* is.

DICKEY: I'd like to think I was in that class.

GINGHER: A reader wonders about the air, the Lucretius and Hume quotations, and wonders how much—it's the old dangerous question—how much came from idea into fiction.

DICKEY: No, I came on those quotations later, and they seemed to fit so perfectly that I just used them. Lucretius is good. I love him. Those Hume things I just had because they are part of my personality. I love to read dull books. And I majored in philosophy in Vanderbilt, and I was just dredging through David Hume's "Essay Concerning Human Understanding," and I came on those and I said, By God, this is it—one of them fits Joel, the thing about falling from the sky with that taste of snow, and the other one about what beings surround me, for the blind man.

GINGHER: The idea of transmutation and the four elements and what happens in the black farm—all these things do seem to work together.

DICKEY: Yes, I don't want to insist on the symbolical nature of it all. That should be more or less implicit than too much insisted on.

GINGHER: Cahill is the protagonist, the hero of the book, but as our reviewer of *Alnilam* mentioned to me: "He's a weight lifter, an interesting guy, but I'm not sure I'd want to have him over for dinner."

DICKEY: No, you hate him. You start hating him. I want you to start hating him. He's so sullen and truculent with everybody. But then you're drawn into his plight as he's drawn into his son's identity. And you end up with a lot of sympathy for him. You're never crazy about him, but you do sympathize with him, and he's a brave, uncompromising guy, and as it comes out not totally without humor either. You think he's without it to begin with, but he has some rather funny things.

GINGHER: Is it a war novel in a way?

DICKEY: I suppose it is. It's about wartime. Although the only scenes from actual combat are the recollection of the bombardier and the navigator.

GINGHER: Now how much of these are your own reminiscences?

DICKEY: It's hard to explain explicitly. I was not in heavies. I knew a lot of pilots and crews who were in them. I was in night fighters, and if I write a sequel to this, which they're urging me to do and I want to do, it'll be called *Crux,* which is the name of the most famous of the southern constellations below the equator, the Southern Cross, and it will be, broadly speaking, about the fight, as I see it now, the struggle between the titular heads of the military out there and the Alnilam group, so that the Alnilam group takes over the whole Pacific night air war, and people are getting their orders from there instead of from the United States government. So it will be a clash between the authority and the rebellious faction based on this mystical guy, saviour kind of.

GINGHER: The whole Oliver North thing is sad. In one way it's a conflict between the idea of a hero with an era of celebrities.

DICKEY: Oliver North and his secret group is only a minor part. We just threw Oliver North to the public so that the real things can go on *unimpeded*. But it really is frightening like that, isn't it? Oliver North with his secret CIA within the CIA. He takes orders from himself rather than from the high-up. It's very similar, frighteningly similar.

GINGHER: It's a book about the reality of things unseen—the navigator's wings—the control with precision.

DICKEY: Or what Joel calls *precision mysticism*. The navigator's story about the Rabaul raid is very good, I think. He can't get any fixes. He's up there looking in the astrodome and there ain't anything there. He's relieved because it isn't going to be his fault if they get killed. But then the clouds start to tatter and he gets a glimpse of a star. And he has to go back to work and do his job, you know, and he gets right back into his discipline. As Whitehall, the navigator, says, it's a fundamental mystery, but it works. Joel was concerned with what was behind it, what underlay all this, but for Whitehall it's enough that it just works. As he tells Cahill right at the end, it's great to know that if you've got the key in your hand to unlock these particular secrets of the stars and mathematics that these celestial bodies *have* to tell you where you are if you know how to ask them. They *have* to tell you. That there is a place in the universe that the universe cannot deny you.

GINGHER: Who's the most likeable character in this novel?

DICKEY: Whitehall. Don't you think so? He's the most responsible man.

GINGHER: Here's a silly question, but let me throw it out anyway. Did you finish the same novel you started?

Dickey Talks About *Alnilam*

DICKEY: No, you can't know that. No, but it's much *better* than the one I started. It got to be better. It *became* better. The more I thought about the people and the more I was able to bring to it—I went through a whole correspondence course in celestial navigation, not to have that material for the novel but because the *subject* interests me. And I wanted to do that before I left the earthly scene to know what went on, how you do it. And it *does* work. It's remarkable, if you can triangulate on selected stars or planets or use the sun at noon or the sun and the moon together—those are the kinds of combinations you can make. And it's the *real* sun and the *real* moon and the *real* planets and the *real* stars. You know its not something in a movie; it actually works. But anyway, when I had that particular discipline, I had the knowledge I needed to write the navigator's story.

GINGHER: It's a very knowledgeable account of the discipline, and you have the sense you've just come from the scene.

DICKEY: When I saw that the novel was going to center on the mystique of flight, I read a lot of things written about flying. . . . But contemporary flying, especially combat flying, is so bogged down in technology and procedure. . . . What I was interested in was the *feeling* of flight, the sensation of it. So I tried to find writers who were as interested as I was in that aspect of it. . . . The best I found was a British guy, who I think was in the RAF, who was killed flying. But I think he was only twenty-three or twenty-four years old when he was killed. And he only published two stories. His name was Rollo Wooley, and I don't think anybody knows anything about him except John Lehmann, who was his publisher. There were some things of his in a magazine. One of them was the story about a student pilot at about the same stage of things as these cadets are. He's fascinated with the flight when he goes on solo. He gets mesmerized by it, and he doesn't want to come down. He goes to his death rather than come in and land. The other story is called "The Search," which is about some pilots who are sent to look for the wreckage of a plane which has gone down. Wooley does some interesting things with time. They're up there, these pilots, searching for the plane, and this one guy comes to doubt that there ever was a plane that went down. And they're up there looking for something that may never have happened.

It's very good. The first Wooley story is called "The Pupil." But those came the closest to what I wanted, but none of them had it exactly, so I just had to invent it.

GINGHER: Did you read that diary of the RAF pilot who was killed in action or Roald Dahl's *Going Solo*?[71]

DICKEY: No, I missed that, but I read Richard Hillary's *Falling through Space*[72] which is very good about the Blitz. There's a lot of good writing on flying, but none of it had exactly this sensation I wanted. What I wanted to do with the book more than anything else was to restore to the human being the sense of *bodily* flight. I mean, men have only been able to do this for less than a hundred years, to get way up there in the element that they *breathe,* you know, to sustain life, to get up in it. It's different with those fragile little trainers where your body really does feel the contact of the sustaining medium. . . . In those little planes it's primitive, and it has more to do with the body. The experience is a sort of compound of exhilaration and fear and, above all, of transgression, of being where you are really not supposed to be.

NOTES

1. Unlocated; in a headnote to the *Per/Se* interview, Francis Roberts states that he conducted the Voice of America interview with Dickey while Dickey was at San Fernando Valley State College in 1964–1965.

2. *Falling*, composed of previously uncollected poems, appears as the final section of *Poems 1957–1967*.

3. "Confession Is Not Enough," *New York Times Book Review* (9 July 1961), p. 14. Part of this review is collected as "Allen Ginsberg" in *The Suspect in Poetry* and *Babel to Byzantium*.

4. Guthrie, *Bound for Glory* (New York: Dutton, 1943); Ives, *The Wayfaring Stranger* (New York: Whittelsey House, 1948).

5. "Orientations," *American Scholar,* 34 (Autumn 1965), 646, 648, 650, 656, 658. The sections of the review treating John Berryman, J. V. Cunningham, Louis Simpson, William Meredith, and Robert Duncan are collected in *Babel to Byzantium*.

6. Randall Jarrell died on 14 October 1965.

7. "The Language of Poetry," *New York Times Book Review* (7 November 1965), p. 6.

8. "Barnstorming for Poetry," *New York Times Book Review* (3 January 1965), pp. 1, 22–23. Collected in *Babel to Byzantium*.

9. 32 (Spring 1965), 206–209.

10. Unlocated.

11. Andrei Sinyavski and Yuli Daniel. "An Open Letter," *Partisan Review,* 33 (Spring 1966), 225–226.

12. Henry Taylor, *The Horse Show at Midnight: Poems* (Baton Rouge: Louisiana State University Press, 1966).

13. *The New Yorker Book of Poems* (New York: Viking Press, 1969). Includes 15 poems by Dickey.

14. At the Library of Congress.

15. 104 (May 1964), 63–72.

16. Boston: Houghton Mifflin, 1927.

17. 41 (14 August 1965), 28–29.

18. Unproduced.

19. *Celebration,* produced 1966. Although he worked on the script, Dickey's name does not appear in the film's credits.

20. "Edwin Arlington Robinson: The Many Truths," *Selected Poems of Edwin Arlington Robinson,* ed. Morton Dauwen Zabel (New York: Macmillan, 1963). Introduction collected as "Edwin Arlington Robinson" in *Babel to Byzantium.*

21. "The Shark at the Window," *Sewanee Review,* 59 (April–June 1951), 290–291.

22. *The Poetry of W. H. Auden* (New York: Oxford University Press, 1963).

23. Unpublished.

24. The first reference to the novel that became *Alnilam.* In *Sorties,* published in December 1971, Dickey uses the working title *Death's Baby Machine.*

25. Title of the spiritual autobiography by Nikos Kazantzakis.

26. *Quarterly Review of Literature,* 13 (Winter–Spring 1964), 38–40.

27. *Poetry,* 90 (May 1957), 97–102.

28. Unlocated.

29. 38 (16 June 1962), 32.

30. "Myth, Ritual, and Nonsense," *Kenyon Review,* 11 (Summer 1949), 455–475.

31. *Quarterly Review of Literature,* 9 (Winter 1958), 272–273.

32. Eileen K. Glancy, *James Dickey: The Critic as Poet: An Annotated Bibliography with an Introductory Essay* (Troy, N.Y.: Whitsun, 1971).

33. William Packard, "Craft Interview with James Dickey," *New York Quarterly,* No. 10 (Spring 1972), 16–35. Collected as "In New York" in *Night Hurdling.*

34. Ezra Pound died on 1 November 1972.

35. Some of this correspondence is reprinted in Lee Bartlett and Hugh Witemeyer, "Ezra Pound and James Dickey: A Correspondence and a Kinship," *Paideuma,* 11 (Fall 1982), 290–312.

36. "Exchanges," *Harvard Bulletin,* 72 (6 July 1970), 36–39. Collected in *Exchanges* and *The Strength of Fields.*

37. In November 1973 the Drake, North Dakota, school board burned Kurt Vonnegut's *Slaughterhouse-Five* and banned, for allegedly obscene language, classroom use of *Deliverance* and certain short stories by William Faulkner, John Steinbeck, and Ernest Hemingway.

38. *Call of the Wild,* with a screenplay by Dickey, was produced by Charles Fries in 1976.

39. John Unterecker, *Voyager: A Life of Hart Crane* (New York: Farrar, Straus & Giroux, 1969).

40. At the time of this interview, two volumes of Lawrance Thompson's Frost biography had been published: *Robert Frost: The Early Years, 1874–1915* (New York, Chicago, & San Francisco: Holt, Rinehart & Winston, 1966) and *Robert Frost: The Years of Triumph, 1915–1938* (New York, Chicago, & San Francisco: Holt, Rinehart & Winston, 1970).

41. *Advertisements for Myself* (New York: Putnam's 1959).

42. "[The Collapse of James Dickey] *Buckdancer's Choice,*" *The Sixties,* No. 9 (Spring 1967), 70–79.

43. Lawrance Thompson and R. H. Winnick, *Robert Frost: The Later Years, 1938–1963* (New York: Holt, Rinehart & Winston, 1976). Thompson died of a brain tumor while working on the final volume of the Frost biography. Winnick completed the volume.

44. *Literature and Western Man* (London: Heinemann, 1960).

45. "A Speech on Robert Frost: A Cultural Episode," *Partisan Review,* 26 (Summer 1959), 445–452.

46. "Robert Frost's 'Home Burial,'" *The Third Book of Criticism* (New York: Farrar, Straus & Giroux, 1969).

47. "The Difficulties of Being Major: The Poetry of Robert Lowell and James Dickey," *Atlantic Monthly,* 220 (October 1967), 116–121.

48. 42 (11 February 1967), 38–40.

49. "'The Best People I Have Ever Known, and Also the Worst, Were Poets': A Talk with James Dickey," *Mademoiselle,* 75 (August 1972), 282–283, 417–420.

50. "The Strength of Fields," which Dickey read during President Carter's inaugural celebration at the Kennedy Center.

51. Robert Penn Warren, "A Poem About the Ambition of Poetry," *New York Times Book Review* (14 November 1976), p. 8.

52. "Star-Beasts of Intellect and Madness," *Washington Post* (21 November 1976), p. E-1.

53. Dickey delivered the University of Idaho's fifth annual Pound Lecture in the Humanities on 26 April 1979. "The Water-Bug's Mittens: Ezra Pound: What We Can Use," separately published by the University of Idaho in 1979 and by Bruccoli Clark in 1980, was subsequently collected in *Night Hurdling*.

54. "The Enemy from Eden" had originally appeared as "Blowjob on a Rattlesnake," *Esquire,* 82 (October 1974), 177–178, 368.

55. "Guilt as Blackmail."

56. "Robert Penn Warren's Courage," *Saturday Review,* No. 7 (August 1980), 56–57. Collected as "The Weathered Hand and Silent Space" in *Night Hurdling*.

57. "Why I Live Where I Live," *Esquire,* 95 (April 1981), 62–64. Collected as "The Starry Place Between the Antlers" in *The Starry Place Between the Antlers* and *Night Hurdling*.

58. The book was published in 1988 as *Wayfarer: A Voice from the Southern Mountains*.

59. Unlocated.

60. "The 'More Life' School and James Dickey," *Saturday Review,* 53 (28 March 1970), 25–26, 38.

61. *Tucky the Hunter* (1978) and *Bronwen, the Traw, and the Shape-Shifter* (1986).

62. "The G. I. Can of Beets, the Fox in the Wave, and the Hammers Over Open Ground."

63. *Night Hurdling*.

64. "For the Death of Lombardi."

65. *Puella*.

66. A photo in a life-mask appeared on the cover of *Esquire,* 85 (February 1976).

67. Unpublished.

68. Dickey had had brain surgery.

69. 231 (17 April 1987), 65.

70. "Cahill Is Blind," *Esquire,* 85 (February 1976), 67–69, 139–144, 146; "The Captains," *Esquire,* 107 (April 1987), 176–178, 181–182, 185–186.

71. London: Cape, 1986.

72. London: Reynal & Hitchcock, 1942; reissued, New York: Macmillan, 1980.

INDEX

The Academics, 26
Achilles, 47, 183, 217
"Acquainted with the Night" (Frost), 114, 142
Adcock, Betty, 227, 245
Advertisements for Myself (Mailer), 123n.41
The African Queen (movie), 82–83
"After Apple-Picking" (Frost), 135, 142
Agee, James, 82–83, 120
Ali, Muhammad, 174
Allnutt, Charlie, 82
"All Revelation" (Frost), 139
All the King's Men (Warren), 81–82
Alnilam, 200, 259, 266
American Poetry Review, 177
American Scholar, 19n.5
"The American Writers Against the War in Vietnam" (Bly et al.), 32
Anaximander, 45
Apollinaire, Guillaume, 44, 218
Aristotle, 81, 227
Armour Fertilizer, 202
Armstrong, Neil, 68
Arnold, Matthew, 195, 231
Ashman, Richard A., 74
Atlantic Monthly, 146
Atlas, Charles, 74
Atwood, Margaret, 176, 227
Auden, W. H., 64, 85, 141, 155, 177, 191, 195, 221, 226, 236–237

Barker, George, 20
Bartlett, Lee, 86n.35
Bear, Fred, 111
The Beats, 26, 28–29, 35
Beatty, Ned, 106
Beckett, Samuel, 179
Beethoven, Ludwig van, 221
Bellitt, Ben, 176
Belloc, Hilaire, 128
Berger, Vic, 99
Berryman, John, 16, 18, 19n.5, 87–88, 118–119, 224
Berry, Wendell, 172, 176
"'The Best People I Have Ever Known, and Also the Worst, Were Poets': A Talk with James Dickey," 149n.49
Betjeman, John, 161
The Bible, 16, 148, 154, 199
Billy the Kid, 174
"Birches" (Frost), 134, 139
Bishop, Elizabeth, 35
Blanchot, Maurice, 26
The Blue Knight (TV mini-series), 107
Bly, Robert, 13, 15, 26–27, 32–33, 123–124, 176–177
Bogan, Louise, 175
Book of Obadiah, 80
Boorman, John, 53–54, 106–107, 129
Borges, Jorge Luis, 218
Bound for Glory (Guthrie), 17n.4
Brando, Marlon, 209
Braselton, Al, 71
Breton, André, 26, 87
Bridges, Robert, 250
Brinkley, David, 67
Brooks, Cleanth, 176
The Brothers Karamozov (Dostoyevski), 264
Bruccoli Clark (publisher), 185n.53
Bryn Mawr College, 251
Burnshaw, Stanley, 178
Burns, Robert, 114

Cadou, René Guy, 20
Cage, John, 16
Caldwell, Erskine, 85, 164
California State University, 172
Calley, John, 53
The Call of the Wild (London), 108, 240
Campbell, Roy, 248
Cantos (Pound), 86
Cape, Jonathan. *See* Jonathan Cape (publisher)
Capp, Al, 123
Carson, Johnny, 84
Carter, Jimmy, 151, 162n.50, 211
Cavett, Dick, 84
Celebration (movie), 53n.19
Central Intelligence Agency (CIA), 266
Charles Scribner's Sons (publisher), 57

Index

Chattooga River, 77, 107, 132
Chekhov, Anton, 215
"The City in the Sea" (Poe), 182
Classics of the Bar, 214
Clay, Cassius. *See* Muhammad Ali
Clemson University, 37–38, 168
"The Cloud" (Shelley), 249
Coca-Cola, 201–202, 204
Cocteau, Jean, 14, 238
Coke Time (TV show), 201
Coldstream Guards, 150–151
Coleridge, Samuel Taylor, 23, 44
"[The Collapse of James Dickey] Buckdancer's Choice" (Bly), 123n.42
Collected Poems (Kunitz), 177
Conrad, Joseph, 214
Conway, Jim, 56
Coolidge, Calvin, 204
Cooper, Jane, 172, 176, 227
Coosawattee River, 77
Coriolanus (Shakespeare), 81
Corso, Gregory, 16
Cortez, Hernando, 218
Council of Archery, 76
Cozzens, James Gould, 197
"Craft Interview with James Dickey" (Packard), 85n.33
Crane, Hart, 118–119, 145, 182–183, 198, 231
Crane, Stephen, 25, 175
Crazy Jane (Yeats), 156
Creeley, Robert, 16
Crews, Harry, 243
Crux, 200
Cummings, E. E., 180
Cunningham, J. V., 19n.5

Dahl, Roald, 268
Dali, Salvador, 26
Daniel, Yuli, 33n.11
Darrow, Clarence, 214
Darwin, Charles, 202
Davidson, Donald, 22, 82
Davison, Peter, 146
Davis, Rev. Gary, 107
Death in the Afternoon (Hemingway), 97
"The Death of the Hired Man" (Frost), 136
Dell Books, 54
Delta Air Lines, 202
DeMott, Benjamin, 212
"Design" (Frost), 135
Desnos, Robert, 26
Dickey, Bronwen (daughter), 187, 235
Dickey, Christopher (son), 63, 124, 235
Dickey, Deborah (wife), 187, 242

Dickey, Eugene (brother), 231
Dickey, Eugene (father), 101–103, 214–215, 231, 247–248

DICKEY, JAMES
Characters
Armstrong, Donald, 216
Ballinger, Drew, 73, 78, 90, 97
Bullard, Sheriff, 107, 129
Cahill, Frank, 259–260, 263–266
Cahill, Joel, 250, 259, 263–266
Gates, Charlie, 61
Gentry, Ed, 52, 56, 71–76, 78, 122, 126–128, 216
Marsman, Hendrik, 90, 150, 179–180
Medlock, Lewis, 56, 71–77, 124
Shears, Cadet Colonel Malcolm, 264
Trippe, Bobby, 73, 75
Whitehall, Captain Lennox, 266
Zack (dog), 259, 263
Works
"Allen Ginsberg," 15n.3
Alnilam, 67n.24, 148, 162, 188, 198–200, 208, 225, 248, 250–251, 257, 258–268
"Apollo," 90
"Approaching Prayer," 144, 255
Babel to Byzantium, 15n.3, 19n.5, 24n.8, 59n.20, 85, 134–135, 157, 191
"Barnstorming for Poetry," 24n.8, 157
"The Bee," 32
"A Beginning Poet, Aged Sixty-Five," 79n.31
"Blood," 84
"Blowjob on a Rattlesnake," 194n.54
Bronwen, the Traw, and the Shape-Shifter, 230n.61
Buckdancer's Choice, 14, 17, 24, 30–32, 42, 51, 59, 68
"Buckdancer's Choice," 32
"By Canoe Through the Fir Forest," 77n.29
"Cahill Is Blind," 261n.70
The Call of the Wild (screenplay), 108n.38, 245
"The Captains," 261n.70
"Cave Master" (unpublished), 46
"Cherrylog Road," 244
A Closer Walk (unused title), 68
"Confession Is Not Enough," 15n.3
Crux (unpublished novel), 200, 248, 265
Death's Baby Machine (unused title), 67n.24
Deliverance (novel), 50–55, 59–60, 66, 68, 71–81, 86, 92–93, 100, 103n.37,

104, 112, 122, 124–128, 147–148, 151, 163, 170, 189, 198, 214, 216, 256–258, 260, 262
Deliverance (movie), 53–56, 88, 90–91, 93, 99, 105, 108, 125, 128–129, 147, 163–164, 189, 212, 233, 240
The Deliverer (unused title), 80–81
"Diabetes," 92
"The Dream Flood," 79
"Drinking from a Helmet," 42
"The Driver," 79
Drowning With Others, 14, 57
"Drowning With Others," 254
"Drums Where I Live," 130
"The Enemy from Eden," 194
Exchanges, 90n.36
"Exchanges," 90n.36
"The Eye-Beaters," 90
The Eye-Beaters, Blood, Victory, Madness, Buckhead and Mercy, 55, 60, 91
Falling, 14n.2, 23
"Falling," 148–149
The Field of Dogs (unused title), 67n.24, 68
"The Fiend," 17–18, 25
"The Firebombing," 42, 117, 123, 150, 171
"The First Morning of Cancer," 74n.27
"A Folk Singer of the Thirties," 16–17, 74
"For the Death of Lombardi," 237n.64
"For the Linden Moth," 74n.26
"Gamecock," 245
"The G. I. Can of Beets, the Fox in the Wave, and the Hammers Over Open Ground," 231n.62
"Guilt as Blackmail," 194n.55
"The Heaven of Animals," 254
Helmets, 14, 16, 58
The Indian Maiden (unpublished), 66n.23, 68
Into the Stone, 57
"The Invasion of Okinawa" (unpublished), 168
Jericho, 230
"The Language of Poetry," 23n.7
"The Lifeguard," 74, 225
"Looking for the Buckhead Boys," 60
"Madness," 89
"Mathematics," 184
"May Day Sermon to the Women of Gilmer County, Georgia, by a Woman Preacher Leaving the Baptist Church," 169, 171, 173, 226

"The Movement of Fish," 79
Night Hurdling, 85n.33, 185n.53, 193–195, 196n.56, 203n.57, 212, 231, 236n.63
"On the Coosawatee," 77
"Orientations," 19n.5
"Peace-Raids" (unpublished), 200
"The Performance," 225, 255
Poems 1957–1967, 14n.2
Puella, 187, 210, 225, 231, 241n.65, 242
"Rain in Darkness" (unpublished), 250
"Reincarnation (II)," 171
"Robert Penn Warren's Courage," 196n.56
Self-Interviews, 61, 74, 78–79, 82, 84, 180, 249, 252, 255–256
"The Shark at the Window," 63n.21, 113
"The Shark's Parlor," 37–40
"Slave Quarters," 13, 46
"Sleeping Out at Easter," 74, 170
Slowly Toward Hercules (unused title), 68
Sorties, 67n.24, 80, 175, 224, 247
"Springer Mountain," 151, 255
The Starry Place Between the Antlers, 203n.57
"The Starry Place Between the Antlers," 203
The Strength of Fields, 90n.36, 211
"The Strength of Fields," 162n.50
"The String," 253
The Suspect in Poetry, 15n.3, 19, 59
"To Landrum Guy," 79
Tucky the Hunter, 230n.61
"Turning Away," 91–92
Two Poems of the Air, 58
"Walking on Water," 225
"The Water-Bug's Mittens: Ezra Pound: What We Can Use," 185n.53
Wayfarer: A Voice from the Southern Mountains, 212n.58
"The Weathered Hand and Silent Space," 196n.56
"Why I Live Where I Live," 203n.57
The Wilderness of Heaven (unused title), 212n.58
"Winter Trout," 79
The Zodiac, 90, 150, 169, 177–178, 254

Dickey, Kevin (son), 63, 190, 235
Dickey, Maibelle Swift (mother), 17, 41, 231–232, 247

Index

Dickey, Maibelle Swift (sister), 232
Dickey, Maxine (wife), 63, 65, 121, 235, 251
Dickey, Tom (brother), 62, 113, 232
Dickinson, Emily, 42
"The Difficulties of Being Major: The Poetry of Robert Lowell and James Dickey" (Davison), 146n.47
"Directive" (Frost), 139, 141
Donne, John, 45, 69
Dostoyevski, Fyodor, 215, 264
Doubleday (publisher), 55, 60–62, 151, 260–262
Dowson, Ernest, 249
The Dream Songs (Berryman), 224
Dryden, John, 64, 211
Ducasse, Isidore. *See* Lautréamont
"Duellin' Banjos," 100, 164, 212
Duncan, Robert, 16, 19n.5
Dunlap, William, 241
Durocher, Leo, 238
Dutton, E. P. *See* E. P. Dutton (publisher)

Eastern Airlines, 149
Eddie Fisher Show (TV), 201–202
"Edwin Arlington Robinson," 59n.20
"Edwin Arlington Robinson: The Many Truths," 59n.20
Eliot, T. S., 20–21, 31, 43, 69, 114, 138, 140, 158–159, 195, 254
Eluard, Paul, 26, 43
Emerson, Ralph Waldo, 137
E. P. Dutton (publisher), 17n.4
Esquire, 194, 203, 241n.66, 261
"Essay Concerning Human Understanding" (Hume), 265
"Essay on Criticism" (Pope), 219
Euclid, 44–45
The Excursion (Wordsworth), 257
"Ezra Pound and James Dickey: A Correspondence and a Kinship," 86n.35

Falling through Space (Hillary), 268
Farrar, Straus & Giroux (publisher), 118n.39, 138n.46
Farrell, James T., 250
Faulkner, William, 37, 85, 103n.37, 104, 114, 164, 243, 250
"The Fear" (Frost), 136
Ferlinghetti, Lawrence, 28, 177
"The Fiend," 13
Finnegans Wake (Joyce), 86
"Fire and Ice" (Frost), 138, 140
Fisher, Eddie, 202
Fitzgerald, F. Scott, 124, 189, 191

Florida State University, 106
418th Night Fighter Squadron, 62, 216
Frénaud, André, 20
Fries, Charles, 108n.38
Frost, Robert, 18, 48, 59, 114, 118–119, 123, 133–142, 191, 195, 254

Garcia Lorca, Federico, 158–159
Gardner, John, 149
Gazzara, Ben, 53
G. I. Bill, 168
Gide, André, 238–239
"The Gift Outright" (Frost), 134
Ginsberg, Allen, 16, 28, 35, 87
Glancy, Eileen K., 79n.32
Goethe, Johann Wolfgang von, 156
Going Solo (Dahl), 268
Golding, William, 78
Gonne, Maud, 157
Gotfryd, Alex, 55
G. P. Putnam's Sons (publisher), 123n.41
Greek tragedy, 81
Grieg, Nordahl, 114
Grumman Aircraft, 53
Guggenheim Fellowship, 57, 162, 202, 205, 211
Guthrie, Woody, 17n.4

Hale, Bill, 53
Hamlet (Shakespeare), 21, 219
"The Hand Writes of the Writing of God" (Borges), 218
Hardy, Thomas, 155
Harlequin Romances, 190
Harper, Marion, 201
Harper's, 32
Harper's Bazaar, 35, 145
Harvard Bulletin, 90n.36
Harvard University, 90
"Heart of Darkness" (Conrad), 214
Hector, 183
Heinemann, William. *See* William Heinemann (publisher)
Hell in the Pacific (movie), 53
Hemingway, Ernest, 43–44, 49, 65, 97–98, 103n.37, 104, 124, 172, 189, 191, 237, 250
Hera, 183
Heraclitus, 45, 79, 155
Hersey, John, 118, 199
Hesse, Hermann, 79
Heston, Charlton, 56
Hickey *(The Iceman Cometh)*, 255
Hillary, Richard, 268
Hill, Geoffrey, 43, 177
Hitler, Adolf, 34, 103, 238, 264

Holden, William, 107
Hollins College, 59
Holt, Rinehart & Winston (publisher), 118n.40, 135n.43
Homage to Mistress Bradstreet and Other Poems (Berryman), 224
"Home Burial" (Frost), 136, 138
Homer, 182–183
Hopkins, Gerard Manley, 20, 45, 209, 211, 224, 232
The Horse Show at Midnight: Poems (Taylor), 34n.12
Houghton Mifflin (publisher), 44n.16, 52, 62, 151, 262
Hubbard, Kin, 157
Hughes, Ted, 43, 92, 177
"Hugh Selwyn Mauberley," 86, 184
Hume, David, 264–265
Humphrey, Hubert, 64
Hunter, William, 64
Huxley, Thomas Henry, 16
Hyman, Stanley Edgar, 79n.30

The Iceman Cometh (O'Neill), 255
"Il Penseroso" (Milton), 21
Ingersoll, Robert, 214–215
"In New York," 85n.33
Ives, Burl, 17n.4

"James Dickey in Orbit" (Taylor), 34
James Dickey: The Critic as Poet: An Annotated Bibliography with an Introductory Essay (Glancy), 79n.32
James, Henry, 150
James, William, 93, 155, 157
Jarrell, Randall, 18, 19n.6, 49, 59, 87–88, 118, 138, 176, 191, 217, 245
Jefferson, Thomas, 164
Jiménez, Juan Ramón, 47
"Jimmy Crack Corn" (song), 17
John Barleycorn (London), 238
Johnson, Claudia (Lady Bird), 161
Johnson, Lionel, 185
Johnson, Lyndon B., 59
Johnson, Samuel, 86, 188–189
Jonathan Cape (publisher), 268n.71
Jones, James, 123
Jonson, Ben, 182
Joyce, James, 86, 148, 260
Jung, Carl Gustav, 45, 75
The Jungle (Sinclair), 116
"Just a Closer Walk with Thee" (hymn), 68

Kafka, Franz, 215
Kazantzakis, Nikos, 69n.25, 85
Keats, John, 82, 114, 171, 217, 255–56

Kees, Weldon, 87
Kelly, Grace, 251
Kennedy, Edward, 145
Kennedy, John F., 53
Kenyon Review, 35, 50, 79n.30
Kerouac, Jack, 28–29
King, Lewis, 71
King, Martin Luther, 59
Knebel, Fletcher, 130
Knoepfle, John, 26
Knott, Bill, 26
Kunitz, Stanley, 177

Lautréamont, 184, 229
Lawrence, D. H., 208, 222
Lawrence, T. E., 88, 158
Lay's Potato Chips, 202
Leege, Gwen, 250–251
Leger, Alexis [Saint-John Perse], 43
Lehmann, John, 267
Levertov, Denise, 91
Library of Congress, 36n.14, 59, 134, 161
Lieberman, Laurence, 245
Life, 166
Lindsay, Vachel, 191
Literature and Western Man (Priestley), 137n.44
Logan, John, 15
Lolita (Nabokov), 239
Lombardi, Vince, 237–238
London, Jack, 108, 238, 240
"London Snow" (Bridges), 250
Lord of the Flies (Golding), 78
Louisiana State University, 62
Louisiana State University Press, 34n.12
Lowell, Robert, 19, 30–31, 34–35, 59, 115, 146, 149, 172
Lowes, John Livingston, 44n.16
Lowry, Malcolm, 82, 114
Lucretius, 264
"Luke Havergal" (Robinson), 59
Lytle, Andrew, 85

Macalester College, 64
Macmillan (publisher), 59n.20, 268n.72
McCann-Erickson, 201
McKuen, Rod, 55
McLuhan, Marshall, 108
Mademoiselle, 149n.49
Mailer, Norman, 51, 114–115, 123, 155, 194
Malinowski, Bronislaw, 253
Mallarmé, Stéphane, 159, 233
Marvell, Andrew, 21
"Mathematics" (Lautréamont), 184

Index

Mauriac, Claude, 64
Mauriac, François, 64
Melville, Herman, 69–70, 112–113, 205
Ménard, René, 45
"Mending Wall" (Frost), 134, 139
Meredith, George, 92
Meredith, William, 19n.5
Merrill, James, 85
Merwin, W. S., 85
Michelangelo, 223
Milky Way, 208
Millay, Edna St. Vincent, 191
Miller, Arthur, 222
Milton, John, 21, 76, 86, 217
Mims, Puryear, 168
Moby-Dick (Melville), 112–114, 199, 264
Modern Love (Meredith), 92
Montale, Eugenio, 43, 146
"The 'More Life' School and James Dickey" (DeMott), 212n.60
Morris, Wright, 126
Moses, 232
"The Most of It" (Frost), 136
Mozart, Wolfgang Amadeus, 44, 221
"Mr. Flood's Party" (Robinson), 59
Muir, Edwin, 43, 85
Mumford, Lewis, 70
"Myth, Ritual, and Nonsense" (Hyman), 79n.30

Nabokov, Vladimir, 239
National Book Award, 41, 51, 123
A Nation of Immigrants (Kennedy), 53
"Neither Out Far nor In Deep" (Frost), 138
Nemerov, Howard, 176
New Orleans Poetry Journal, 74n.28
Newsweek, 115
New Yorker, 35, 46n.17, 77n.29, 149n.48
The New Yorker Book of Poems, 35n.13
New York Quarterly, 85n.33
New York Times, 15, 23–24, 178
New York Times Book Review, 15n.3, 23n.7, 24n.8, 178n.51
Nietzsche, Friedrich, 24
"Nimera," 34
Nobel Prize, 43, 47, 148
North of Boston (Frost), 141
North, Oliver, 266

O'Connor, Flannery, 148, 164
"October" (Frost), 138
"Ode: Intimations of Immortality from Recollections of Early Childhood" (Wordsworth), 21
Odysseus, 47, 88, 183

The Odyssey (Homer), 184
Old Testament, 148
Oliver, Mary, 227, 245
"On an Archaic Torso, Apollo" (Rilke), 220
O'Neill, Eugene, 255
"One Step Backward Taken" (Frost), 138
"An Open Letter," 33n.11
Orion, 200, 208, 259
Orwell, George, 116
Osiris, 78
Oxford University Press, 64n.22

Packard, William, 85n.33
Paideuma, 86n.35
Pale Fire (Nabokov), 239
Paradise Lost (Milton), 76, 86
Paris Soir, 14
Partisan Review, 25n.9, 33n.11, 137n.45
Patton, George, 238
Peacock, Thomas Love, 92
Pennsylvania State University, 217
Pepsi Cola, 202, 204
Perse, Saint-John. *See* Leger, Alexis
Phi Beta Kappa poem, 90
Picasso, Pablo, 14, 65, 141
Pindar, 34
Pizarro, Francisco, 218
Plath, Sylvia, 92, 120
Plato, 81, 255
Playboy, 124, 128
Poe, Edgar Allan, 14, 182, 233
"A Poem About the Ambition of Poetry" (Warren), 178n.51
Poetry, 42n.15, 74n.27
The Poetry of W. H. Auden (Spears), 64n.22
"Poets of Today" (series), 57
Point-Blank (movie), 53
Pope, Alexander, 64, 219
Pound, Ezra, 21, 43, 69, 86n.34, 87, 115, 138, 141, 175, 181–182, 184–185
Pound Lecture in the Humanities, 185n.53
The Prelude (Wordsworth), 257
Priestley, J. B., 136–137
Priestley, Tom, 136
Proust, Marcel, 44, 159, 248
"Provide, Provide" (Frost), 135, 141
Publishers Weekly, 260
Pulitzer Prize, 57, 123
"The Pupil" (Wooley), 268
Putnam's Sons, G. P. *See* G. P. Putnam's Sons
Pythagoras, 45

Index

Quarterly Review of Literature, 74n.26, 79n.31, 80
Quasimodo, Salvatore, 43

Rabbit, Run (Updike), 105
Radcliffe-Brown, A. R., 253
Random, John Crowe, 19
Read, 38
Read, Herbert, 188
Reed College, 23, 28, 58, 177, 184
Report to Greco (Kazantzakis), 69n.25
Reverdy, Pierre, 20
Rexroth, Kenneth, 177, 208
Reynal & Hitchcock (publisher), 268n.72
Reynolds, Burt, 99
Reynolds, Debbie, 202
Rice University, 38, 63–64, 173, 205, 261
Riesman, David, 104
Rilke, Rainer Maria, 158–160, 220
Rimbaud, Arthur, 183
The Rime of the Ancient Mariner (Coleridge), 23
Rivers, W. H. R., 253
The Road to Xanadu (Lowes), 44n.16
"Robert Frost's 'Home Burial'" (Jarrell), 138n.36
Robert Frost: The Early Years, 1874–1915 (Thompson), 118n.40, 135
Robert Frost: The Later Years, 1938–1963 (Thompson & Winnick), 135n.43
Robert Frost: The Years of Triumph, 1915–1938 (Thompson), 118n.40, 135
Robin Hood, 99
Robinson, Edwin Arlington, 59, 150, 231
Rockefeller, Fellowship, 162, 205
Roethke, Theodore, 19–20, 30–31, 35, 42, 82, 172, 217, 232, 245
Rollins College, 248
Roney, Peg, 248
Roth, Philip, 51, 104
Rusk, Dean, 33

Saint-Exupéry, Antoine de, 199
Saint Peter, 264
San Fernando Valley State College, 22–23, 59
Santayana, George, 24, 115
Sarah Lawrence College, 172, 176
Saturday Review, 196n.56, 212n.60
Schirra, Walter, 90
Schwartz, Delmore, 19, 217
Scott, Winfield Townley, 231
Scribner's Sons, Charles. *See* Charles Scribner's Sons (publisher)
"The Search" (Wooley), 267

Seferis, George, 43
Selected Poems of Edwin Arlington Robinson (ed. Zabel), 59n.20
Service, Robert, 14, 182
Seven Days in May (Knebel), 130
Sewanee Review, 35, 63n.21, 64
Shakespeare, William, 16, 21, 81, 182, 211, 219, 233
Shapiro, Karl, 19
Shaw, George Bernard, 240
Shelley, Percy Bysshe, 81, 249–250
"The Shooting of Dan McGrew" (Service), 14, 182
Shuptrine, Hubert, 230
Siddhartha (Hesse), 79
Siefert, Carl, 150
Silkin, Jon, 43
Simpson, Louis, 16, 19n.5, 57, 172, 176
Sinclair, Upton, 116
Sinyavski, Andrei, 33n.11
The Sixties, 15, 34, 123n.42
Slaughterhouse-Five (Vonnegut), 103n.37
Smith, Dave, 245
Smith, Oliver, 68
Snow, C. P., 120
Snyder, Gary, 176
Socrates, 45
Solzhenitsyn, Aleksandr, 115
South Atlantic Modern Language Association (SAMLA), 157, 231
South Carolina Academy of Authors, 258–259
Southern Cross, 200, 265
Spears, Monroe, 64
"A Speech on Robert Frost: A Cultural Episode" (Trilling), 137n.45
Sports Illustrated, 31n.10
Stafford, William, 16, 18, 26, 172, 176
Stalmaster, Lynn, 106
Stanford, Ann, 91, 172
"Star-Beasts of Intellect and Madness" (Burnshaw), 178n.52
Stark, Willie, 81
Steinbeck, John, 58, 103n.37, 104
Stevens, Wallace, 138, 140, 224, 254
Stickney, Trumbull, 90
"Stopping by Woods on a Snowy Evening" (Frost), 139
Stud Hustler, 103
Studs Lonigan (Farrell), 250
Styron, William, 51, 123
Supervielle, Jules, 20, 43
Swedenborg, Emanuel, 45
Swenson, May, 57
Swinburne, Algernon Charles, 133, 170

Index

Tate, Allen, 19, 70, 85, 149, 191
Taylor, Eleanor, 176–177
Taylor, Henry, 34n.12
Tennyson, Alfred, 43, 133, 171
Thalberg, Irving, 217
The Third Book of Criticism (Jarrell), 138n.46
Thomas, Dylan, 20, 29, 31, 43, 82, 87, 119, 143, 232, 245, 254
Thompson, Lawrance, 118n.40, 135n.43, 195
Thoreau, Henry David, 239
Today Show (TV), 84
"To Earthward" (Frost), 135
"To His Coy Mistress" (Marvell), 21
Tolstoy, Leo, 65, 233
Trilling, Lionel, 137
Truman, Harry, 167
Twain, Mark, 164
Tzara, Tristan, 26

Ulysses, 183
Ulysses (Joyce), 148
Understanding Poetry (Brooks & Warren), 176
Ungaretti, Giuseppe, 43
United States Information Agency (USIA), 53
University of Arkansas, 143
University of Chicago, 104
University of Idaho, 185n.53
University of Illinois, 177
University of Iowa, 143–144
University of Kentucky, 172
University of South Carolina, 60, 102, 197, 203, 210, 258
University of Virginia, 63, 84
The Unnamable (Beckett), 179
Unterecker, John, 118n.39
Untermeyer, Louis, 222
Updike, John, 52, 105

Valéry, Paul, 119, 158–159, 169, 233, 250, 254
Van Buren, Martin, 87
Vanderbilt University, 38, 63–64, 82, 90, 167–168
Van Duyn, Mona, 91, 176
Van Gennep, Arnold, 79
Victoria and Albert Museum, 188
Viking (publisher), 35n.13
Virginia Quarterly Review, 151

Voice of America, 14n.1
Voight, Jon, 90, 99, 106
Vonnegut, Kurt, 103n.37, 104
Voyager: A Life of Hart Crane (Unterecker), 118n.39

Wagoner, David, 184
The War Lover (Hersey), 118, 199
Warner Brothers, 53–54, 106, 163
Warren, Robert Penn, 22, 81–82, 85, 149, 176–177, 178n.51, 191, 196, 243–244
Washington Post, 178n.52
Washington University, St. Louis, 86
Watkins, Vernon, 85
The Wayfaring Stranger (Ives), 17n.4
Wayne, John, 39
Weaver, Raymond, 70
Wellesley, Dorothy, 154
Welty, Eudora, 164
Wesleyan College (Macon, Ga.), 194
Wesleyan University Press, 60
Wevill, David, 92
Whitman, Walt, 25, 42, 46, 155, 171, 217, 236
Whitsun (publisher), 79n.32
Whittelsey House (publisher), 17n.4
Wilbur, Richard, 31, 80
William Heinemann (publisher), 137n.44
Williams, John, 99
Williams, William Carlos, 171–172
Winnick, R. H., 135n.43
Winters, Yvor, 136, 256
Winton, Calhoun, 203
Witemeyer, Hugh, 86n.35
Wisconsin State University (Oshkosh), 32–33
Wolfe, Thomas, 37, 120, 124, 250
Wooley, Rollo, 267–268
Wordsworth, William, 21, 215, 230, 257
Wright, James, 13, 16, 26–27, 87–88, 172, 176
Wyeth, Andrew, 170
Wyeth, Jamie, 170

Yaddo, 16
Yeats, William Butler, 43, 45, 140, 154–160, 190, 254
Yevtushenko, Yevgeny, 116

Zabel, Morton Dauwen, 59n.20

OHIO UNIVERSITY LIBRARY

Please return this book as soon as you have finished with it. In order to avoid a fine it must be returned by the latest date stamped below.